THE T206

THE PLAYERS & THEIR STORIES

COLLECTION

THE T206
THE PLAYERS & THEIR STORIES
COLLECTION

TOM ZAPPALA & ELLEN ZAPPALA

with LOU BLASI

FOREWORD AND CONTRIBUTIONS BY JOE ORLANDO

100TH ANNIVERSARY
COMMEMORATIVE EDITION

PETER E. RANDALL PUBLISHER
Portsmouth, New Hampshire
2010

ISBN10: 1-931807-94-9

ISBN13: 978-1-931807-94-4

Library of Congress Control Number: 2009944215

Produced by Peter E. Randall Publisher

Box 4726

Portsmouth, NH 03802

www.perpublisher.com

Book design:

Grace Peirce

Photography credit:

© Images Anthony Dube/White Point Imaging 2009

www.whitepointimaging.com

Vintage baseball equipment provided by Brett Lowman of Play OK Antiques.

www.playokantiques.com

Additional copies available from:

www.t206players.com

Printed in China

To Bert, Gen,

Sonny and Toni

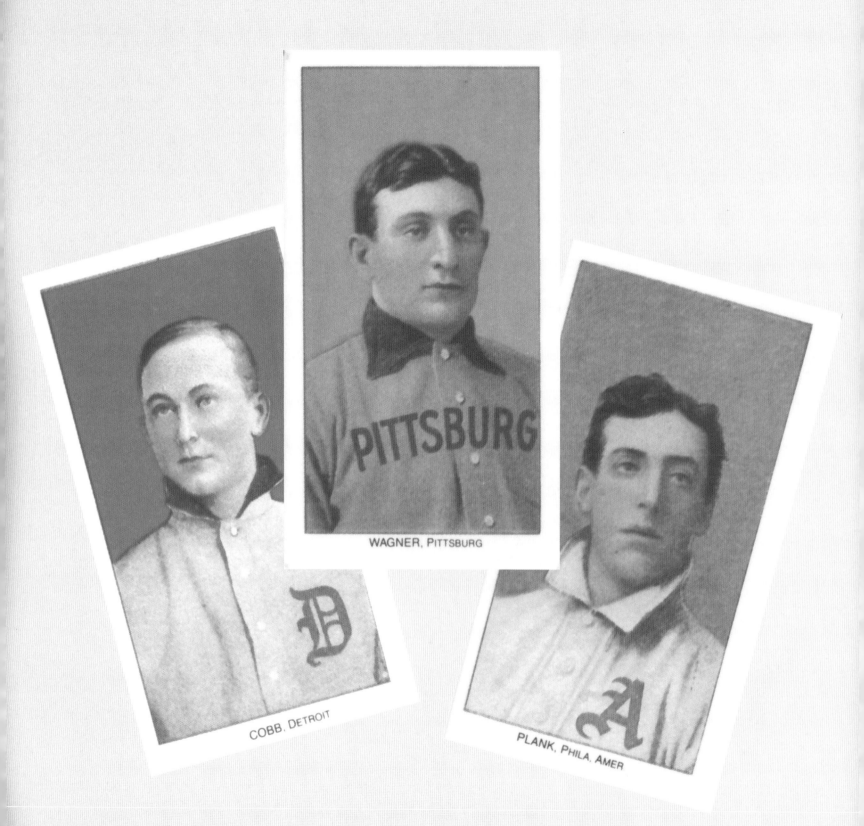

WAGNER, PITTSBURG

COBB, DETROIT

PLANK, PHILA. AMER

CONTENTS

FOREWORD

THE 1909 TO 1911 T206 BASEBALL CARD set has long been considered one of the most, if not *the* most, important issues in the entire hobby. The visual appeal of the cards, the immense size of the set, and the incredible player selection make this treasure a collector favorite. Along with the 1933 Goudey and 1952 Topps sets, the classic T206 set is one of "The Big Three" in the world of baseball cards.

You can easily make the argument that "The Monster," as it is commonly referred to, is truly the pinnacle of all trading cards sets. It is much larger than the 1933 Goudey set, requiring more than twice the amount of cards to complete. It is also, arguably, more visually appealing than the 1952 Topps set due to the superb artwork used in the design.

Furthermore, the 524-card T206 set is home to the most valuable trading card in the world, the card that has become the symbol of the hobby itself. Of course, I am referring to the Mona Lisa of trading cards . . . the T206 Honus Wagner. The Wagner card shares the limelight with 75 other cards featuring members of baseball's Hall of Fame, but it is worth more than the other 523 cards combined, assuming they are in the same condition. At the time of this writing (2009), the highest price ever paid for any trading card was \$2.8 million, a Wagner example that was graded NM-MT 8 by Professional Sports Authenticator, the leading third-party authentication and grading service.

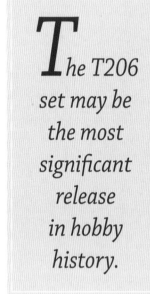

The T206 set may be the most significant release in hobby history.

The Wagner card is so desirable that even low-grade copies that receive only a Poor 1 on a scale of 1 to 10 (the lowest possible grade on the PSA grading scale) have fetched \$400,000 at auction. The card, like the set itself, has taken on a life of its own and become an iconic collectible. While Wagner was

WAGNER, PITTSBURG

a true legend of the game and one of the greatest shortstops in baseball history, the card depicting this Hall of Fame member has certainly surpassed the man himself in terms of fame.

Yes, the T206 set may be the most significant release in hobby history. Yes, Honus Wagner was one of the most significant players ever to put on a uniform. Yes, after being pulled from production early on by the manufacturer, only 50 or so examples of this card are known to exist, making it one of the true rarities in the trading card world. All of these facts may be true, but the reason why the T206 Wagner has reached such lofty heights in value is the story behind the man and the card.

The most prevalent misconception about this great card is that it is the rarest of the rare, resulting in its staggering value. What may come as a surprise to most casual collectors or even non-collectors is the fact that the T206 Wagner is not nearly as scarce as some other notable trading card rarities. The number of surviving copies is only part of the story.

There is more than one theory behind the rarity of the card, including a simple contract dispute theory. Many people believe Honus Wagner wanted his card pulled from production because Wagner, though an avid user of tobacco himself, did not want to promote tobacco to children since the cards were packaged with various brands of cigarettes. Knowing what we now know about the dangers of tobacco, especially as it relates to cigarettes, this stance taken by Wagner over 100 years ago becomes all the more interesting.

As with most other great collectibles, such as autographs, game-used equipment, and original photographs, the stories behind the items make them interesting and desirable. Every collectible, in its own way, is a conversation piece. How were these cards distributed? What makes this game-used bat special? Why did Babe Ruth sign this particular document? Every collectible has a story.

This is also true of every figure the collectible relates to, and that is what makes this particular book different from so many of the published hobby guides released over the years. If Honus Wagner were a relatively unknown player, would his T206 card carry the value it has today? No. If a Mickey Mantle game-used bat

ENGLE, N.Y. AMER.

was instead used by Mickey Vernon, would it be worth anywhere near the same amount? No. Would a baseball signed by Jackie Robinson and one signed by Jackie Jensen be valued the same? No. I think you get the point.

Above all, it is the story behind the person that drives the majority of the value. Otherwise, it may be *just* a card or *just* a bat or *just* a ball. More often than not, it is the sports figure's name that makes the collectible special. This book takes a look at each individual pictured on the cards, from superstars of the day like Ty Cobb and Cy Young to lesser-known major and minor leaguers like Clyde Engle and Bill Cranston. Each player has a story and each player contributed to the game . . . and all of them are part of the "monstrosity" known as the T206 set.

Today, we see virtually everything and know almost everything about current players, both on and off the field. In some cases, I would argue that we are presented with too much information, but this is the culture we live in today. With the immense sports coverage on television and the multitude of Internet sites devoted to sports, it seems as if the modern athlete cannot move a muscle without being caught on camera.

COBB, DETROIT

CRANSTON, MEMPHIS

We do not have that luxury when it comes to learning about baseball players who were active during the early part of the 20th Century. We often have to rely on period photographs and statistical information, at least whatever statistics can be found, in order to paint the picture of a time long past, to tell the story of the players who made history before history was documented on film after every pitch, every swing, and every catch.

That is what this book is all about, the story behind each man found in this legendary set, men who put on a uniform during a time when the equipment was a bit crude and the game wasn't plagued by performance-enhancing-drug controversies. The game of baseball, no matter the era, is a terrific sport. Somehow, it is complicated yet simple at the same time. Its combatants must use almost equal combinations of brain and brawn in order to defeat their foes, perhaps more so than in any other sport.

Like the game of chess, every move has an impact on the outcome. For the astute fan, there are many games within the game that go unnoticed by the casual spectator, but it is all part of what makes baseball so interesting. The subtle communication between defenders as they position themselves before each hitter, the tension between a base runner trying to steal a base and the catcher trying to stop him, and managers trying to outthink each other on every play are all part of the complicated dance known as baseball. Complexity defines the sport, and that term may best describe the iconic T206 set.

So, let the journey begin as we revisit history through these tiny time capsules we call baseball cards.

DONLIN, N.Y. NAT'L

ISBELL, CHICAGO AMER.

BERNHARD, NASHVILLE

Author's Note

IN RESEARCHING THE PLAYERS OF THE T206 collection, we have determined that there are several inconsistencies that have been included in the player lists that have circulated throughout the years. As many people know, there are many "error" cards that exist in the collection, like the famous "Magie" misspelling or the fact that "Sleepy Bill" Burns has his glove on the wrong hand.

We have concerned ourselves only with actual player profile errors. Every effort has been made to ensure the accuracy of each player narrative and player statistics. If you have other information on a particular player and can substantiate your research, we will consider it for a future printing. Submit it to: www.t206players.com.

Some of the following facts are already known by a segment of the collector and baseball historian population. We have corrected the following inconsistencies so that this book accurately portrays the players of the collection.

◆ In all cases we have used the accurate spelling of the player's name, even if it was spelled differently on the T206 card.

◆ The minor leaguer listed as Harry Lentz (Little Rock) is really Harry Sentz. As far as we can determine there was no player with the last name of Lentz. The 1909 Little Rock roster lists Harry Sentz, but no Lentz.

◆ The player listed as Otto Krueger (Columbus) is really Art Kruger (Arthur Theodore Kruger). Otto Krueger never played for Columbus. This seems to be a natural error as Kruger is sometimes misspelled as Krueger. Also, Otto's given name is Arthur William Krueger. Essentially, *two* Art Krugers/Kruegers played during the same era. Otto Krueger played in the major leagues from 1899 to 1905, and in the minors until 1912. Art Kruger played in the majors from 1907 to 1915, but also played some minor league ball during those years. The 1909 Columbus Senators' roster lists Art Kruger as a player.

◆ Wiley Taylor (Buffalo) is really Luther "Dummy" Taylor. Wiley Taylor never played for Buffalo although he did play in the majors from 1911 to 1914 and the minors from 1910 to 1917 and in 1923. Dummy Taylor played in the majors from 1900 to 1908 and in the minors through 1915. He played for Buffalo in 1909, 1910, and part of 1911, as listed on the Buffalo Bisons' team roster for those years. Some T206 player lists correctly include Dummy Taylor, while others include Wiley Taylor.

◆ Minor leaguer Foley White never played for Houston as his T206 card says. He played from 1905 to 1914 for several teams, including the Texas League's Waco Navigators during the 1909 and 1910 seasons. The player listed on the 1909 Houston team roster is Carl White, an outfielder who played in the minors in 1904, 1909, and 1910. This T206 player's identity is an ongoing controversy among collectors and historians. In the opinion of noted T206 historian Scot Reader, the player shown is Foley White and the error is the Houston team identification. The player shown on the T206 card has a catcher's mitt, and Foley White was a catcher while Carl White played in the outfield. Also, Foley White played for Waco in 1909 and 1910 with a team uniform that was very similar to the uniform on the T206 card. In addition, he played 80 games in 1909, but Carl White played only 20, making it unlikely that he would have a card.

◆ Since we are discussing the historical aspect of the player and not the card itself, we have used reproduction images in the first six chapters in order to remain consistent. All of the cards used in Chapter 7 by resident expert Joe Orlando, are authentic.

BATES, BOSTON NAT'L

McGRAW, NEW YORK NAT'L

SNODGRASS, N.Y. NAT'L

ACKNOWLEDGMENTS

THE SEED FOR THIS BOOK WAS PLANTED when I was staring at a Lena Blackburne card and wondering about what kind of major league career he had. After doing a little research I discovered that although he did not have a distinguished career he still made a major contribution to the game. I then became intrigued (my wife, Ellen, would call it obsessed) with gathering information on all of the other players in the T206 collection.

I had the idea of compiling all the information in book form, and Ellen and I decided to work on the project together. In reality, if it were not for her many years of experience in publishing, this project never would have gotten off the ground. She painstakingly edited my work, researched every player along with me, and steered the ship. We hope that you are happy with the result.

We would like to thank our friend Joe Orlando, president of Professional Sports Authenticator (PSA) and editor of *Sports Market Report*, for his contributions in making this book not only an historical reference tool but also an educational primer on the card-grading process. His expertise in everything T206 was invaluable.

The same holds true for our colleague Lou Blasi, a baseball historian, writer, radio personality, and senior baseball analyst for Insiderbaseball.com. A big thank you to him for his tremendous efforts in researching a number of the players from the collection and for his help in making this book a well-written, cohesive narrative.

Thank you to Deidre Randall, Grace Peirce, Margaret Cook, and the wonderful staff at Peter E. Randall Publisher for their guidance, creativity, and support, as well as for producing a beautiful publication.

We would be remiss if we did not mention a member of the Boston Red Sox Hall of Fame and a great shortstop, Rico Petrocelli. Rico, thanks for taking the time out of your busy schedule to give us feedback and ideas on how to make this project a success.

A special thanks goes to Tom Kayser, president of the Texas AA League. An innocent phone call to him at the very outset of this project helped us immensely. Tom was kind enough to point us in the right direction on how to research the Texas Leaguers of the collection. Tom, many thanks from Jack Bastian, Tony Thebo and the rest of the gang.

Lastly, thank you to the players who make up the T206 collection. Some were great players and others were not so good. However, they all contributed to making the game of baseball the greatest game in the world.

MORIARTY, Detroit

MURPHY, Phila. Amer.

DOYLE, N. Y. Nat'l

INTRODUCTION

ON OPENING DAY IN 1910, PRESIDENT
William Howard Taft declared that baseball would
officially become our "National Pastime." During this same
time period, the T206 collection, the most scrutinized baseball
card series in history, was released. The players in this storied
collection were the men who laid the foundation for the game as
we know it today.

I became intrigued with the T206 collection about 20 years
ago when I bought a Ted Easterly card in a small shop in
Cooperstown. I had the card mounted in a frame and it looked
great on the desk in my office. As time went on, collecting T206
cards became easier because of the Internet.

As my collection grew over the years, I began to wonder about
the careers of the players on those cards. Of course we all know
about Cobb, Speaker (my favorite, since I grew up in the Boston
area), Wagner, Mathewson, and most of the Hall of Famers. But
what about players like Blackburne, Herzog, Isbell, McGann, and
yes, Easterly? Were they any good? What were their careers like?

That is what this book is all about. You
now have information on all of the
T206 players right at your fingertips.
Chapter 7 is written by our good
friend Joe Orlando, editor of *Sports
Market Report* and president
of PSA Professional Sports
Authenticator. He discusses the
values and grading system that
have made the T206 collection
the most desirable in

the world, and explains
why some T206 cards
are more valuable
than others. The Ray
Demmitt St. Louis card
is worth a great deal of
money. So are the Bill
O'Hara card and the
Sherry Magie (Magee)
error card. And of
course we cannot forget
about Plank, Cobb, and
yes, Wagner—the crème
de la crème.

This book gives you
information on the
background and playing
days of every player in
the collection. Some
were farmers, some
came from big cities, and others from small towns. They all had
one common thread. They played the game of baseball.

A number of these players never made it to the big leagues, but
their backgrounds are interesting. Some are pictured in their
minor league uniforms because they stayed in the game after their
major league playing days were over.

In any event, I hope you enjoy this book and learn a little bit
about all of those players sitting in your top loaders, graded
cardholders, or scrapbooks.

For the record, the Ray Demmitt card is worth a lot, but
Ray Demmitt was only a marginal ballplayer. Now Ginger
Beaumont—there was a ballplayer!

Enjoy!

> *I* became
> intrigued
> with the T206
> collection about
> 20 years ago
> when I bought
> a Ted Easterly
> card.

EASTERLY, CLEVELAND

DEMMITT, ST LOUIS AMERICAN

MAGIE, PHILA. NAT'L

~1~

THE HALL OF FAMERS

Cornerstones of the Game

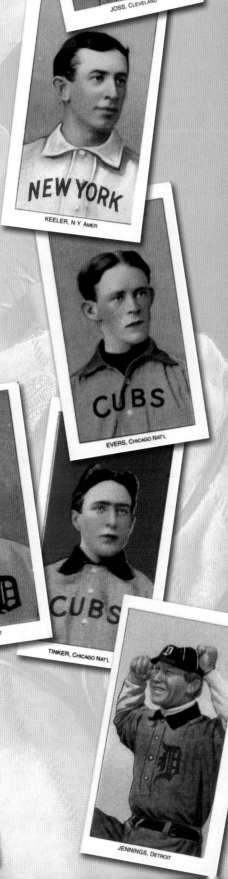

JOSS, CLEVELAND

NEW YORK

KEELER, N Y AMER

T HE PLAYERS PORTRAYED in the next few pages are really the first stars (and in some cases superstars) in the history of American sports. Yes, there was a handful that existed prior to this group. Great athletes like John L. Sullivan, Jim Jeffries, and Cap Anson dotted the sports landscape of America prior to this group, but these players were the first true stars. Some became household names, and some were not as well known. They all, however, were great at what they did, and became the cornerstones of baseball.

Meet the Hall of Famers.

CUBS

EVERS, CHICAGO NAT'L

BRESNAHAN, ST. LOUIS NAT'L.

CRAWFORD, DETROIT

NEW YORK

CHESBRO, N.Y. AMER.

COBB, DETROIT

DUFFY, CHICAGO AMER.

CUBS

TINKER, CHICAGO NAT'L

JENNINGS, DETROIT

Home Run Baker

Frank "Home Run" Baker got his nickname by taking both Rube Marquard and Christy Mathewson deep in the 1911 World Series. He was considered the best pre–World War I third baseman of his time. He played on three A's World Series championship teams and two American League pennant teams with the Yanks. Baker led the league in home runs four consecutive years (1911–1914), was the RBI champ in 1912 and 1913, and batted over .300 on six different occasions. He was part of Connie Mack's $100,000 infield along with Stuffy McInnis and Eddie Collins. Baker later became a minor league manager and discovered the great Jimmy Foxx. He was elected to the Hall of Fame in 1951.

Teams:
Philadelphia Athletics AL (1908–1914)
New York Yankees AL (1916–1919, 1921–1922)

Born:
March 13, 1886
Trappe, MD
Died:
June 28, 1963
Trappe, MD

▷ Batted: LH
▷ Threw: RH
▷ Position: 3B
▷ Career BA: .307

John Franklin Baker

Jake Beckley

Jake "Eagle Eye" Beckley was a solid, hard-nosed first baseman. He batted over .300 fourteen times over a career that spanned 20 years. His best year was 1894, when he batted .343 with 183 hits and 7 homers. After his major league years, he dabbled in the minors for five seasons, mostly for the Kansas City Blues of the American Association, which he also managed in 1909. After his playing days, Jake umpired in the Federal League for one season in 1913. Beckley then retired to private life in Kansas City, where he operated a grain business. He died from a heart ailment at the relatively young age of 50. He was elected to the Hall of Fame in 1971.

Born:
August 4, 1867
Hannibal, MO
Died:
June 25, 1919
Kansas City, MO

▷ Batted: LH
▷ Threw: LH
▷ Position: 1B
▷ Career BA: .308

Teams:
Pittsburgh Alleghenys NL (1888–1889)
Pittsburgh Burghers, Players' League (1890)
Pittsburgh Alleghenys/Pirates NL (1891–1896)
New York Giants NL (1896–1897)
Cincinnati Reds NL (1897–1903)
St. Louis Cardinals NL (1904–1907)

Jacob Peter Beckley

Chief Bender

BENDER, PHILA. AMER.

Described as one of the kindest, most honorable men ever to play the game, Hall of Famer Charles "Chief" Bender overcame discrimination to become one of the best pitchers of his time. A member of the Ojibwa tribe, he handled racial taunts with dignity and grace. Bender won 6 games in five World Series, and pitched 3 complete games in one of them. He won 20 or more games twice, pitched a no-hitter in 1910, and led the American League in winning percentage three times. Bender made an appearance for the White Sox in 1925, then managed in the minors, was head coach for the U.S. Naval Academy, and scouted for the A's until 1954. He was elected to the Hall of Fame in 1953.

BENDER, PHILA. AMER.

BENDER, PHILA. AMER.

Born:
May 5, 1884
Crow Wing County, MN
Died:
May 22, 1954
Philadelphia, PA

▷ Batted: RH
▷ Threw: RH
▷ Position: P
▷ MLB Pitching Record: 212–127
▷ ERA: 2.46

Teams:
Philadelphia Athletics AL (1903–1914)
Baltimore Terrapins FL (1915)
Philadelphia Phillies NL (1916–1917)
Chicago White Sox AL (1925)

Charles Albert Bender

Roger Bresnahan

BRESNAHAN, ST. LOUIS NAT'L.

BRESNAHAN, ST. LOUIS NAT'L.

Roger Bresnahan, nicknamed the "Duke of Tralee," was the first catcher ever elected to Cooperstown. The batterymate of the great Christy Mathewson, Bresnahan is credited with improving catching equipment by introducing shin guards worn over his stockings. A very good defensive catcher, solid hitter, and base stealer (212), Bresnahan was considered by many to be the best catcher of that era. He batted a lofty .350 in 1903, and caught 4 shutouts in the 1905 World Series. Bresnahan was a player/manager for the Cards as well as the Cubs, compiling a 328–432 managerial record. He bought the Toledo Iron Men in 1916 and managed them until 1925. He then coached for the Giants and the Tigers before retiring in 1931. Bresnahan was elected to the Hall of Fame in 1945.

Teams:
Washington Senators NL (1897)
Chicago Orphans/Cubs NL (1900, 1913–1914; player/manager: 1915)
Baltimore Orioles AL (1901–1902)
New York Giants NL (1902–1908)
St. Louis Cardinals NL (player/manager: 1909–1912)

Born:
June 11, 1879
Toledo, OH
Died:
December 4, 1944
Toledo, OH

▷ Batted: RH
▷ Threw: RH
▷ Position: C
▷ Career BA: .279
▷ Managerial Record: 328–432

Roger Philip Bresnahan

"Three Finger" Mordecai Brown

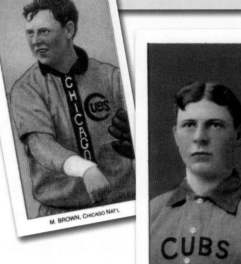

M. BROWN, Chicago Nat'l

M. BROWN, Chicago Nat'l

M. BROWN, Chicago Nat'l

"Three Finger" Mordecai Brown got his nickname because he lost parts of two fingers in a farm-machinery accident as a child. The injury was a blessing in disguise, allowing him to develop pitches with unusual spins. Brown's curveball was nasty as was his changeup due to the way he gripped the ball. Brown won 20 or more games 6 years in a row (1906–1911) and led the league in 1906 with his 1.04 ERA. He was part of the Cubs' 1907 and 1908 World Series championships. A great competitor, Brown had 55 career shutouts. His matchups against the great Christy Mathewson are legendary. After retiring, Brown pitched and managed in the minors until 1920, and later pitched in exhibitions. His 239–130 record and 1,375 K's were outstanding achievements. He was elected to the Hall of Fame in 1949.

Teams:
St. Louis Cardinals NL (1903)
Chicago Cubs NL (1904–1912, 1916)
Cincinnati Reds NL (1913)
St. Louis Terriers FL (player/manager: 1914)
Brooklyn Tip-Tops FL (1914)
Chicago Whales FL (1915)

Mordecai Peter Centennial Brown

Born:
October 19, 1876
Nyesville, IN
Died:
February 14, 1948
Terre Haute, IN

▷ Batted: Switch
▷ Threw: RH
▷ Position: P
▷ MLB Pitching Record: 239–130
▷ ERA: 2.06
▷ Managerial Record: 50–63

Frank Chance

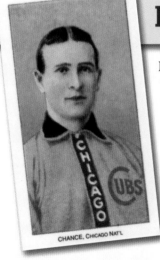

CHANCE, Chicago Nat'l

Frank Chance was an excellent ballplayer and manager. Immortalized in "Baseball's Sad Lexicon," also known as "Tinker to Evers to Chance," a 1910 poem by Franklin Pierce Adams, he earned the nickname "The Peerless Leader" by leading the Cubs to four National League pennants and two World Series titles in 5 years. Their record of 116 victories in 1906 still remains unsurpassed. Chance batted over .300 on four occasions, and led the National League in stolen bases twice. He was also the first player ever to be ejected from a World Series Game. His 946–648 record as manager is outstanding. Chance managed in the minors, and came back to manage the Sox in 1923. He became ill after that season, and died the next year at age 48. He was elected to the Hall of Fame in 1946.

Teams:
Chicago Orphans/Cubs NL
(1898–1904; player/manager: 1905–1912)
New York Yankees AL (player/manager: 1913–1914)
Boston Red Sox AL (manager: 1923)

Born:
September 9, 1876
Fresno, CA
Died:
September 15, 1924
Los Angeles, CA

▷ Batted: RH
▷ Threw: RH
▷ Position: 1B
▷ Career BA: .296
▷ Managerial Record: 946–648

CHANCE, Chicago Nat'l

CHANCE, Chicago Nat'l

Frank Leroy Chance

Jack Chesbro

CHESBRO, N.Y. AMER.

Teams:
Pittsburgh Pirates NL (1899–1902)
New York Highlanders AL (1903–1909)
Boston Red Sox AL (1909)

Born:
June 5, 1874
North Adams, MA
Died:
November 6, 1931
Conway, MA

▷ Batted: RH
▷ Threw: RH
▷ Position: P
▷ MLB Pitching Record: 198–132
▷ Career ERA: 2.68

"Happy Jack" Chesbro was a master of the spitball. A fierce competitor, his 41 wins in 1904 along with his 1.82 ERA will probably never be duplicated. That season is considered by many to be the single-greatest season for a pitcher in MLB baseball history. (Some Cy Young fans may take exception.) He won 20 or more games on five different occasions, and won 19 in 1905. Chesbro pitched on two National League pennant-winning teams in 1901 and 1902, and led the American League in wins in 1902 and 1904. He also led the league with 6 shutouts in 1901 and 8 in 1902. The Veteran's Committee elected Jack Chesbro to the Hall of Fame in 1946.

John Dwight Chesbro

Fred Clarke

Born:
October 3, 1872
Winterset, IA
Died:
August 14, 1960
Winfield, KS

▷ Batted: LH
▷ Threw: RH
▷ Position: OF
▷ Career BA: .312
▷ Managerial Record: 1,602–1,181

Teams:
Louisville Colonels NL (1894–1896; player/manager: 1897–1899)
Pittsburgh Pirates NL (player/manager: 1900–1911, 1913–1915; manager: 1912)

F. CLARKE, PITTSBURG

CLARKE, PITTSBURG

A great player and manager over his long career, Fred Clarke played alongside Honus Wagner and Vic Willis. He batted over .300 on 11 different occasions, and in 1897 batted an outstanding .390. In 1903 Clarke led the league in doubles (32), triples (13), slugging percentage (.532), and on-base plus slugging percentage (.946). He wound up seventh on the all-time triples list, and scored 100-plus runs five times. As manager, he won 1,602 games, led the Pirates to four National League pennants, and won the World Series in 1909. Clarke retired in 1915, but came back as the Pirates' vice president and assistant manager in 1925 and 1926. Clarke was elected to the Hall of Fame in 1945. He died at age 87 from pneumonia.

Fred Clifford Clarke

Ty Cobb

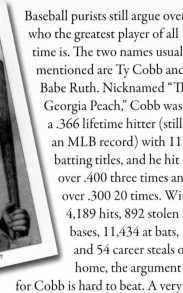

Baseball purists still argue over who the greatest player of all time is. The two names usually mentioned are Ty Cobb and Babe Ruth. Nicknamed "The Georgia Peach," Cobb was a .366 lifetime hitter (still an MLB record) with 11 batting titles, and he hit over .400 three times and over .300 20 times. With 4,189 hits, 892 stolen bases, 11,434 at bats, and 54 career steals of home, the argument for Cobb is hard to beat. A very complex man, Cobb was not well liked by his peers. He was surly, sometimes played dirty (legend has it that he sharpened his spikes), and was considered a racist by many. However, Cobb also was extremely generous and philanthropic, helping many people behind the scenes. Above all, he was a truly great player. Besides holding just about every major batting record at one time or another, and being considered the greatest player of all time, Cobb was also an extremely successful businessman. He was one of the early shareholders in Coca-Cola and went on to own three bottling plants and become a company spokesman. He also made very good investments in both real estate and the stock market. Cobb's net worth of $11 million at the time would be approximately $86 million in today's dollars. He was elected to the Hall of Fame's inaugural class in 1936.

Tyrus Raymond Cobb

Teams:
Detroit Tigers AL (1905–1920; player/manager: 1921–1926)
Philadelphia Athletics AL (1927–1928)

Born:
December 18, 1886
Narrows, GA
Died:
July 17, 1961
Atlanta, GA

▷ Batted: LH
▷ Threw: RH
▷ Position: OF
▷ Career BA: .366
▷ Managerial Record: 479–444

Eddie Collins

COLLINS, PHILA AMER

Teams:
Philadelphia Athletics AL
(1906–1914, 1927–1930)
Chicago White Sox AL
(1915–1923; player/manager:
1924–1926)

Possibly the greatest second baseman of all time, Eddie Collins was a superstar in the true sense of the word. Outstanding both offensively and defensively, he holds the records for a second baseman in career games (2,650), assists (7,630), and total chances (14,591). With his 3,315 career hits and .333 batting average, he helped the A's to four pennants and three championships. Collins won two more pennants with the White Sox in 1917 and 1919. He was the first player in history to steal 80 bases in a season. After his playing days, he coached for the A's in 1931 and 1932. He then became general manager of the Boston Red Sox from 1933 to 1947, signing Ted Williams during his tenure. Eddie Collins was elected to the Hall of Fame in 1939.

Edward Trowbridge Collins

Born:
May 2, 1887
Millerton, NY
Died:
March 25, 1951
Boston, MA

▷ Batted: LH
▷ Threw: RH
▷ Position: 2B
▷ Career BA: .333
▷ Managerial Record: 174–160

Jimmy Collins

Born:
January 16, 1870
Buffalo, NY
Died:
March 6, 1943
Buffalo, NY

▷ Batted: RH
▷ Threw: RH
▷ Position: 3B
▷ Career BA: .294
▷ Managerial Record: 455–376

Jimmy Collins is considered one of the three or four greatest third basemen that ever played the game. A great star both offensively and defensively, he batted over .300 five times, hitting .346 and driving in 132 runs in 1897. Collins led the National League in home runs (15) in 1898, and still stands second in all-time putouts. In 1901 he became player/manager for Boston in the new American League, and he starred in the first World Series in 1903, leading his team to the championship. They came back to win the American League pennant in 1904. Collins played for several other pennant winners in both the AL and NL. As one of the most adept defenders of the bunt, he helped neutralize one of the era's primary offensive weapons, and he established the standards of play at third base. He later managed the Minneapolis Millers in the American Association and the Providence Grays in the Eastern League. Jimmy Collins was elected to the Hall of Fame in 1945.

COLLINS, MINNEAPOLIS

Teams:
Louisville Colonels NL (1895)
Boston Beaneaters NL (1895–1900)
Boston Americans AL (player/manager: 1901–1906, player: 1907)
Philadelphia Athletics AL (1907–1908)

James Joseph Collins

Sam Crawford

Considered one of the best pure hitters of all time, "Wahoo Sam" Crawford led both the AL and NL in many hitting categories during his illustrious career. He was the first player to lead the American League and National League in home runs. Crawford also banged out over 2,900 hits, and still holds the MLB record for triples (309). In 1901 he slammed 16 homers and batted .330. He batted over .300 11 times. Crawford played alongside Ty Cobb for 13 seasons, and they had a somewhat contentious relationship. Despite their occasional feuds, however, Cobb wrote several letters to the Hall of Fame endorsing Crawford's election, which occurred in 1957.

Teams:
Cincinnati Reds NL (1899–1902)
Detroit Tigers AL (1903–1917)

Samuel Earl Crawford

Born:
April 18, 1880
Wahoo, NE
Died:
June 15, 1968
Hollywood, CA

▷ Batted: LH
▷ Threw: LH
▷ Position: OF
▷ Career BA: .309

George Davis

Although he is a Hall of Famer, George Davis has never really gotten his due. A skilled hitter and superb base stealer, he batted .355 and stole 37 bases in 1893. Davis batted over .300 on nine different occasions, and ranks in the top 100 ballplayers with games played, at bats, runs, hits, doubles, triples, RBI, stolen bases, and singles. He helped lead the White Sox to a World Series win in 1906. At one time Davis was the second-highest-paid player behind Nap Lajoie. Very well liked and modest, he was player/manager of the Giants in 1895, 1900, and 1901. After his MLB days, Davis managed in the minors, and coached at Amherst College until 1918. He then moved on from baseball to work as a car salesman and even tried his hand at professional bowling. George Davis was elected to the Hall of Fame in 1998.

Teams:
Cleveland Spiders NL (1890–1892)
New York Giants NL (1893–1901, 1903; player/manager: 1895, 1900–1901)
Chicago White Sox AL (1902, 1904–1909)

George Stacey Davis

Born:
August 23, 1870
Cohoes, NY
Died:
October 17, 1940
Philadelphia, PA

▷ Batted: Switch
▷ Threw: RH
▷ Position: IF
▷ Career BA: .295
▷ Managerial Record: 107–139

"Sir" Hugh Duffy

One of the more highly celebrated players of his era, "Sir" Hugh Duffy holds the record for the highest single-season batting average in history, hitting .440 in 1894. In addition to his .440 batting average that season, Duffy hit 18 home runs and drove in 145 RBI, winning baseball's first Triple Crown. Duffy won the home run title again in 1897 with 11. A New England native, Duffy originally turned down more money from Boston to play for his idol, Cap Anson, with the White Stockings. Duffy hit over .300 nine times in his career. He managed in the minors for 11 seasons, mostly for the Providence Grays and the Portland Duffs in the New England League. Duffy capped off his career as a Red Sox coach in the 1930s, tutoring a player he described as "the best hitter I ever saw"; that hitter was Ted Williams. Hugh Duffy was inducted into the Hall of Fame in 1945.

DUFFY, CHICAGO AMER.

Teams:
Chicago White Stockings NL (1888–1889)
Chicago Pirates PL (1890)
Boston Reds AA/Beaneaters NL (1891–1900)
Milwaukee Brewers AL (player/manager: 1901)
Philadelphia Phillies NL (player/manager: 1904–1906)
Chicago White Sox AL (manager: 1910–1911)
Boston Red Sox AL (manager: 1921–1922)

Hugh Duffy

Born:
November 26, 1866
Cranston, RI
Died:
October 19, 1954
Boston, MA

▷ Batted: RH
▷ Threw: RH
▷ Position: OF
▷ Career BA: .324
▷ Managerial Record: 535–671

Johnny Evers

EVERS, CHICAGO NAT'L.

Johnny Evers was the last piece placed in the famed "Tinker to Evers to Chance" trio that is credited with defining the modern double play. All three future Hall of Famers were moved to their famous positions in 1902, but Evers was the backup at second base until starter Bobby Lowe broke his ankle. Nicknamed "The Crab" for his penchant for shuffling sideways to get in front of ground balls, Evers drove in the winning runs in both the 1907 and 1908 World Series and was the National League MVP in 1914. Surprisingly Evers and Tinker didn't speak to each other during their final few years as teammates, occasionally even coming to blows in the clubhouse. Johnny Evers was inducted into the Hall of Fame in 1946.

EVERS, CHICAGO NAT'L.

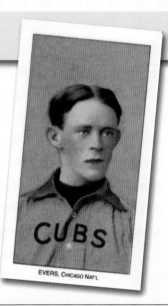

EVERS, CHICAGO NAT'L.

Teams:
Chicago Orphans/Cubs NL (1902–1913)
Boston Braves NL (1914–1917, 1929)
Philadelphia Phillies NL (1917)
Chicago White Sox AL (1922)

John Joseph Evers

Born:
July 21, 1881
Troy, NY
Died:
March 28, 1947
Albany, NY

▷ Batted: LH
▷ Threw: RH
▷ Position: 2B
▷ Career BA: .270

Elmer Flick

FLICK, CLEVELAND

The Hall of Famer that no one knows, Elmer Flick hit .300 or better in eight of his ten seasons with 450 or more at bats. He hit .297 in 1902 after being traded to Cleveland and .296 in 1903, having hit .333 or better the previous three seasons. Flick won the batting title in 1905, and won additional league titles in slugging percentage, runs, triples, RBI, and stolen bases. Flick and Nap Lajoie were batting rivals in Philadelphia, resulting in a pregame fight in 1900 in which Lajoie broke his hand and then missed five weeks, costing the Phillies a pennant chance. After the 1907 season the Detroit Tigers offered Ty Cobb to Cleveland straight up for Flick, but the Naps declined. Due to an undiagnosed stomach ailment, Flick collected just 88 major league at bats over the next three seasons. Elmer Flick was elected to the Hall of Fame in 1963.

Elmer Harrison Flick

Born:
January 11, 1876
Bedford, OH

Died:
January 9, 1971
Bedford, OH

▷ Batted: LH
▷ Threw: RH
▷ Position: OF
▷ Career BA: .313

Teams:
Philadelphia Phillies NL (1898–1901)
Philadelphia Athletics AL (1902)
Cleveland Bronchos/Naps AL (1902–1910)

Clark Griffith

GRIFFITH, CINCINNATI

GRIFFITH, CINCINNATI

Few can claim more influence over professional baseball's early years than Clark Griffith, "The Old Fox." As a manager and owner of the Senators, Griffith, along with Giants' manager John McGraw, legitimized relief pitching and pioneered strategic use of the bullpen. As a player, he won 20 or more games in seven seasons during his 20-year career. He was a professional trapper by the age of 10, and turned to vaudeville during the 1893 players' strike that he organized. In 1900 he helped engineer the first universal players' union strike, which became a critical factor in the birth of the American League. He was one of the best ball "doctors" of his time, and although he pioneered the screwball he later fought to ban the practice. He signed Cuban players as early as 1911, and in 1946, as a promotion, he recorded pitching speed for the first time using a U.S. Army device. He was elected to the Hall of Fame in 1946.

Teams:
St. Louis Browns AA (1891)
Boston Reds AA (1891)
Chicago Colts/Orphans NL (1893–1900)
Chicago White Sox AL (player/manager: 1901–1902)
New York Highlanders AL (player/manager: 1903–1907; manager: 1908)
Cincinnati Reds NL (player/manager: 1909; manager: 1910–1911)
Washington Senators AL (player/manager: 1912–1914; manager: 1914–1920; owner: 1920–1955)

Clark Calvin Griffith

Born:
November 20, 1869
Clear Creek, MO

Died:
October 27, 1955
Washington, D.C.

▷ Batted: RH
▷ Threw: RH
▷ Position: P
▷ MLB Pitching Record: 237-146
▷ ERA: 3.31
▷ Managerial Record: 1,491-1,367

Miller Huggins

Miller "Mighty Mite" Huggins was a nice little player with a good bat and outstanding baserunning abilities. The story, however, does not end there. He also managed the greatest team ever assembled, the 1927 New York Yankees. Coming from a managerial stint with St. Louis, he helped build the Yankees juggernaut with Babe Ruth, Lou Gehrig, and company. His Yankees won the 1923, 1927, and 1928 World Series along with the 1921, 1922, and 1926 AL pennants. Huggins died at age 50 in 1929 from a bacterial infection. Thousands of fans came to Yankee Stadium to view his casket and honor this beloved figure. Huggins was inducted into the Hall of Fame in 1964.

Teams:
Cincinnati Reds NL (1904–1909)
St. Louis Cardinals NL (1910–1912; player/manager: 1913–1916; manager: 1917)
New York Yankees AL (manager: 1918–1929)

Miller James Huggins

Born:
March 27, 1879
Cincinnati, OH
Died:
September 25, 1929
New York, NY

▷ Batted: Switch
▷ Threw: RH
▷ Position: 2B
▷ Career BA: .265
▷ Managerial Record: 1,413–1,134

Hughie Jennings

One of the most colorful player/managers in the history of the game, Hughie Jennings was known for his famous shouts from the coaching box, earning him the nickname "Ee-Yah." Although his accomplishments as a player are sometimes overlooked, he batted .335, .386, and .401 over three seasons and played on two National League pennant teams for the Superbas (1899, 1900). He also holds the MLB record for being hit by pitches (287). As a manager, he led the Tigers to three American League pennants (1907, 1908, 1909) and the Giants to the National League pennant in 1924, but his teams never won the big one. Medical issues forced him to retire in 1925. He was elected to the Hall of Fame in 1945.

Hugh Ambrose Jennings

Born:
April 2, 1869
Pittston, PA
Died:
February 1, 1928
Scranton, PA

▷ Batted: RH
▷ Threw: RH
▷ Position: SS/1B
▷ Career BA: .311
▷ Managerial Record: 1,131–972

Teams:
Louisville Colonels NL (1891–1893)
Baltimore Orioles NL (1893–1899)
Brooklyn Superbas NL (1899–1900, 1903)
Philadelphia Phillies NL (1901–1902)
Detroit Tigers AL (1907, 1909, 1912, 1918; manager: 1907–1920)
New York Giants NL (manager: 1924–1925)

Walter Johnson

Teams:
Washington Senators AL (1907–1927;
manager: 1929–1932)
Cleveland Indians AL (manager: 1933–1935)

Walter Perry Johnson

Born:
November 6, 1887
Humboldt, KS
Died:
December 10, 1946
Washington, D.C.

▷ Batted: RH
▷ Threw: RH
▷ Position: P
▷ MLB Pitching Record: 417–279
▷ ERA: 2.17
▷ Managerial Record: 529–432

When the topic of the greatest pitcher of all time comes up, Walter Johnson, "The Big Train," is usually at the forefront of the discussion. With an amazing 417 wins, he won 30 or more games twice and had twelve 20-win seasons. His record of 3,509 K's stood for more than a half century. In 1913 Johnson had an incredible 1.14 ERA. His gentle demeanor was legendary, and he was one of the most well respected and loved players ever to step onto a field. He was the American League MVP twice (1913, 1924) and in 1924 he pitched the Senators to the World Series championship. He managed for 7 years after his playing days, posting a 529–432 record. Truly a special player, "The Big Train" was elected to the Hall's inaugural class in 1936. Walter Johnson died of a brain tumor in 1946.

Addie Joss

Born:
April 12, 1880
Woodland, WI
Died:
April 14, 1911
Toledo, OH

▷ Batted: RH
▷ Threw: RH
▷ Position: P
▷ MLB Pitching Record: 160–97
▷ ERA: 1.89

Had Addie Joss not died at such an early age, he would probably be considered part of the top tier of greatest pitchers, along with Christy Mathewson, Walter Johnson, and Cy Young. His 1.89 career ERA is the second-best record in major league history. His walks to hits ratio (WHIP) is the greatest of all time. Joss had a great command of his fastball and changeup, and his pitching mechanics were very deceiving. His best season was 1908, when he went 24–11 with an unbelievable 1.16 ERA. His career was cut short when he contracted tubercular meningitis and died at 31. He was elected to the Hall of Fame in 1978.

Team:
Cleveland Bronchos/Naps AL (1902–1910)

Adrian Joss

Willie Keeler

"Wee Willie" Keeler was one of the greatest pure hitters of all time. With an amazing eye for the ball, he had the uncanny ability to place a bunt or hit just about anywhere he chose. His theory for his great hitting was to "Keep your eyes clear and hit 'em where they ain't." Keeler hit over .300 sixteen times, batted over .400 once, and had a 44-game hitting streak in 1897. While he was with the Orioles, he perfected the "Baltimore Chop," hitting the ball so hard into the ground that it bounced high enough for him to reach first base before the fielder's throw could get there. "Wee Willie" was elected to the Hall of Fame in 1939.

Born:
March 3, 1872
Brooklyn, NY
Died:
January 1, 1923
Brooklyn, NY

▷ Batted: LH
▷ Threw: LH
▷ Position: OF
▷ Career BA: .341

Teams:
New York Giants NL (1892–1893, 1910)
Brooklyn Grooms/Superbas NL (1893, 1899–1902)
Baltimore Orioles NL (1894–1898)
New York Highlanders AL (1903–1909)

William Henry Keeler

Joe Kelley

Teams:
Boston Beaneaters/Doves NL (1891; player/manager: 1908)
Pittsburgh Pirates NL (1892)
Baltimore Orioles NL (1892–1898)
Brooklyn Superbas NL (1899–1901)
Baltimore Orioles AL (1902)
Cincinnati Reds NL (player/manager: 1902–1905, player: 1906)

Joe Kelley was the star left fielder for the great Baltimore Orioles teams of the late 1800s. He hit .351 in seven seasons with the Orioles and stole 290 of his 443 career stolen bases by the Inner Harbor as well. He hit over .300 for 11 consecutive seasons starting in 1893, driving in 100 or more runs in 5 of those years. Kelley stole 30 or more bases six times in his career, including a league-leading 87 steals in 1896. A career .317 hitter, he posted a .402 career on-base percentage and a .451 career slugging percentage. His best season was 1894, when he hit .393 with 111 RBI and 165 runs scored, posting an amazing .502 on-base percentage. Kelley managed the Toronto Maple Leafs in the International League to a pennant win in 1907, and then managed the Boston Doves in 1908. He returned to Toronto as player/manager from 1909 to 1914, winning another pennant in 1912. Joe Kelley was inducted into the Hall of Fame in 1971.

Joseph James Kelley

Born:
December 9, 1871
Cambridge, MA
Died:
August 14, 1943
Baltimore, MD

▷ Batted: RH
▷ Threw: RH
▷ Position: OF
▷ Career BA: .317
▷ Managerial Record: 338–321

LAJOIE, CLEVELAND

LAJOIE, Cleveland

LAJOIE, CLEVELAND

Nap Lajoie

Teams:
Philadelphia Phillies NL (1896–1900)
Philadelphia Athletics AL (1901–1902, 1915–1916)
Cleveland Bronchos/Naps AL (1902–1914; player/
manager: 1905–1909)

Born:
September 5, 1874
Woonsocket, RI
Died:
February 7, 1959
Daytona Beach, FL

▷ Batted: RH
▷ Threw: RH
▷ Position: 2B
▷ Career BA: .338
▷ Managerial Record: 377–309

Nap Lajoie, also known as Larry, was a truly great player. He and his rival, Ty Cobb, spent most of baseball's early years vying for the title of the game's greatest player. A slick-fielding second baseman and tremendous hitter, Lajoie won three batting titles, had 3,242 hits, and won the American League Triple Crown in 1901. That year he also batted an astounding .426, and he batted over .300 more than 15 times during his great career. As a testament to his great play, when he played for Cleveland, they renamed the team the Naps. Nap Lajoie was respected and loved by fans. He was elected to the Hall of Fame in 1937.

Napoleon Lajoie

Rube Marquard

MARQUARD, N.Y. NAT'L

MARQUARD, N.Y. NAT'L

Although modern baseball historians consider Richard "Rube" Marquard a marginal Hall of Famer, no one disputes that he was a dominant pitcher. He won 20 or more games on three occasions, and played on five pennant-winning teams. There are, however, players who are not in the Hall of Fame who have records as good as or better than Marquard's. He did win 19 games in a row in 1912, which is a great feat. Rube also led the league with his 26 wins that year. His 1,593 career strikeouts ranked him third in MLB history among southpaws and remained a National League record until 1942. Marquard both played and managed in the minor leagues through the 1933 season, and retired at the age of 46. He also performed in vaudeville with Blossom Seeley, whom he married in 1913 (they divorced in 1920). Rube Marquard was inducted into the Hall of Fame in 1971.

MARQUARD, N.Y. NAT'L

Born:
October 9, 1886
Cleveland, OH
Died:
June 1, 1980
Baltimore, MD

▷ Batted: Switch
▷ Threw: Left
▷ Position: P
▷ MLB Pitching Record: 201–177
▷ ERA: 3.08

Richard William Marquard

Teams:
New York Giants NL (1908–1915)
Brooklyn Robins NL (1915–1920)
Cincinnati Reds NL (1921)
Boston Braves NL (1922–1925)

Christy Mathewson

Christy "Big Six" Mathewson was one of the dominant pitchers of this era, along with Walter Johnson and Cy Young, and when it comes to the greatest pitcher of all time, he certainly deserves consideration. He won an amazing 373 games over his 17-year career, and "owned" some of the greatest hitters of the day. His team won the World Series in 1905. Mathewson topped the 30-win column four times and the 20-win column nine times. He won the National League Pitcher's Triple Crown in 1905 and 1908, and was the ERA champion and the strikeout champion five times. After his playing days were over, he managed the Cincinnati Reds through 1918 and became president of the Boston Braves in 1923. During WWI he was accidentally gassed in a training maneuver; this eventually caused the tuberculosis that killed him in 1925. Christy Mathewson was one of the five charter members of the Hall of Fame inducted in 1936.

MATHEWSON, N.Y. NAT'L

MATHEWSON, N.Y. NAT'L

MATHEWSON, N.Y. NAT'L

Teams:
New York Giants NL (1900–1916)
Cincinnati Reds NL (player/manager: 1916; manager: 1917–1918)

Christopher Mathewson

Born:
August 12, 1880
Factoryville, PA

Died:
October 7, 1925
Saranac Lake, NY

▷ Batted: RH
▷ Threw: RH
▷ Position: P
▷ MLB Pitching Record: 373–188
▷ ERA: 2.13
▷ Managerial Record: 164–176

Iron Man McGinnity

MCGINNITY, NEWARK

Teams:
Baltimore Orioles NL (1899)
Brooklyn Superbas NL (1900)
Baltimore Orioles AL (1901–1902)
New York Giants NL (1902–1908)

"Iron Man" Joe McGinnity claimed his nickname came from his off-season work in a foundry, but he was an iron man on the mound as well. In 1903 he became famous for pitching both ends of doubleheaders three times in 1 month, winning all 6 games. That year he also won 31 games while pitching 434 innings, which is still a record to this day. McGinnity led the league in innings pitched four times from 1900 to 1905. Over his spectacular career, he led the National League in wins five times and led the league in games played by a pitcher six times. McGinnity didn't start his MLB career until age 28, but he pitched in the pros until he was 54 and won 246 MLB games and another 207 in the minors. On his T206 card he is shown in his uniform for the Newark Indians, where he was player/manager from 1909 to 1912 and his pitching record was 87–64. His durability was due to a mix of deliveries, including an underhand curve he called "Old Sal." McGinnity was elected to the Hall of Fame in 1946.

Joseph Jerome McGinnity

Born:
March 20, 1871
Cornwall Township, IL

Died:
November 14, 1929
Brooklyn, NY

▷ Batted: RH
▷ Threw: RH
▷ Position: P
▷ MLB Pitching Record: 246–142
▷ ERA: 2.66

John McGraw

McGRAW, N.Y. NAT'L.

McGRAW, N.Y. NAT'L.

McGRAW, N.Y. NAT'L.

McGRAW, NEW YORK NAT'L.

Teams:
Baltimore Orioles AA/NL (1891–1898; player/manager: 1899)
St. Louis Cardinals NL (1900)
Baltimore Orioles AL (player/manager: 1901–1902)
New York Giants NL (player/manager: 1902–1906; manager: 1907–1932)

John McGraw reigned supreme over the National League for 30 years beginning in 1902. In that span his Giants won 10 pennants, three World Series, and placed first or second in the league 21 times. As a player McGraw hit over .320 nine straight seasons and his career .466 on-base percentage trails only Babe Ruth and Ted Williams. The cantankerous McGraw became a celebrity of his day. He owned a pool hall with Arnold Rothstein, who provided the cash for fixing the 1919 World Series, and shared ownership of a racetrack and casino in Cuba with Charles Stoneham, who bought the Giants in 1919. McGraw helped Jacob Ruppert buy the Yankees, but later warred with the Bombers when Babe Ruth and the home run era threatened his favored "inside baseball" style of play. In 1933, although retired, McGraw was chosen as National League manager for the first All-Star Game. He was inducted into the Hall of Fame in 1937.

Born:
April 7, 1873
Truxton, NY
Died:
February 25, 1934
New Rochelle, NY

▷ Batted: LH
▷ Threw: RH
▷ Position: 3B
▷ Career BA: .334
▷ Managerial Record: 2,763–1,948

John Joseph McGraw

Eddie Plank

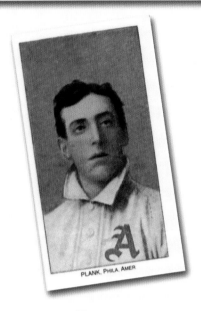

PLANK, PHILA. AMER

Teams:
Philadelphia Athletics AL (1901–1914)
St. Louis Terriers FL (1915)
St. Louis Browns AL (1916–1917)

"Gettysburg Eddie" Plank was famous for his quirks on the mound and his unusual crossfire delivery. He was known for talking to the ball about how many outs remained in the game, and his long pauses and fidgeting on the mound could frustrate players and irritate fans. Known as the slowest pitcher in the majors, Plank may have annoyed everyone on game day, but he won ballgames, 326 of them, making him third among lefties behind only Steve Carlton and Warren Spahn. His career 410 complete games and 69 shutouts are southpaw records that still stand today. Plank's career game was Game 5 of the 1913 World Series when he threw a 2-hitter against Christy Mathewson, defeating the Giants 3–1 to win the World Series. Eddie Plank was inducted into the Hall of Fame in 1946.

Born:
August 31, 1875
Gettysburg, PA
Died:
February 24, 1926
Gettysburg, PA

▷ Batted: LH
▷ Threw: LH
▷ Position: P
▷ MLB Pitching Record: 326–194
▷ ERA: 2.35

Edward Stewart Plank

Tris Speaker

A Texas native, Tris Speaker was born right-handed but learned to throw and bat lefty after breaking his right arm twice while being thrown from broncos. With his lifetime .345 batting average, Speaker is considered one of the purest hitters of all time. He was a legendary outfielder, and helped the Red Sox win two World Series championships. He was also American League MVP in 1912. Speaker is still the all-time leader in putouts and double plays for his position, and owns the top spot for career doubles. He and Ty Cobb, a close friend, were considered the best hitters of the time. Speaker was also a successful manager for Cleveland, leading the Indians to a World Series win in 1920. He was elected to the Hall of Fame in 1937.

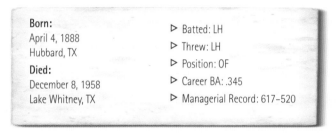

Born:
April 4, 1888
Hubbard, TX
Died:
December 8, 1958
Lake Whitney, TX

▷ Batted: LH
▷ Threw: LH
▷ Position: OF
▷ Career BA: .345
▷ Managerial Record: 617–520

Teams:
Boston Americans/Red Sox AL (1907–1915)
Cleveland Indians AL (1916–1918; player/manager: 1919–1926)
Washington Senators AL (1927)
Philadelphia Athletics AL (1928)

SPEAKER, BOSTON AMER.

Tristram E. Speaker

Joe Tinker

TINKER, Chicago Nat'l

TINKER, Chicago Nat'l

TINKER, Chicago Nat'l

TINKER, Chicago Nat'l

Born:
July 27, 1880
Muscotah, KS

Died:
July 27, 1948
Orlando, FL

▷ Batted: RH
▷ Threw: RH
▷ Position: SS
▷ Career BA: .262
▷ Managerial Record: 304–308

Joe Tinker is the Tinker of "Baseball's Sad Lexicon," more popularly known as "Tinker to Evers to Chance." He was the left side of the middle infield duo who not only popularized the double play, but also began the end of the dead-ball era, devising new and effective strategies against the era's main weapons: the bunt, the hit and run, and the stolen base. Despite their success on the field, Tinker and Johnny Evers actually did not speak for decades beginning with an on-field fight over cab fare in 1905. Tinker stole home twice in one game in 1910 and helped the Cubs to four World Series, eventually becoming their manager. Although he was a respectable hitter, Tinker was more well regarded for his aggressive yet elegant shortstop play. He was inducted into the Hall of Fame in 1946.

Teams:
Chicago Orphans/Cubs NL (1902–1912; player/manager: 1916)
Cincinnati Reds NL (player/manager: 1913)
Chicago Chi-Feds/Whales FL (player/manager: 1914–1915)

Joseph Bert Tinker

Rube Waddell

Honus Wagner

Teams:
Louisville Colonels NL (1897–1899)
Pittsburgh Pirates NL (1900–1916; player/manager: 1917)

Johannes Peter Wagner

Volumes could be written about the strange career of George "Rube" Waddell. One of the game's first power pitchers; he won the American League Pitching Triple Crown in 1905 and led the league in ERA that year with 1.48. He also led the National League in ERA in 1900 with 2.37. Waddell ranks among the top 20 pitchers of all time in several categories. On the other side of the coin, he was an alcoholic, suffered from delusions, and sometimes behaved erratically. His leaving the mound to chase fire trucks is a myth, but he did fight with teammates, managers, and fans, and sometimes disappeared for days. When all is said and done, however, he was a very gifted pitcher. Waddell died at age 37 from tuberculosis. He was elected to the Hall of Fame in 1946.

Known as "The Flying Dutchman," Honus Wagner is the focal point of the T206 collection. Putting the value of his card aside, he is considered by many to be the greatest shortstop of all time. He led the National League in batting eight times and hit over .300 an amazing 16 times. His best year was 1900, when he batted an incredible .381. Over his historic career, Wagner banged out 3,415 hits and knocked in 1,732 runs. Many books have been written about the great Wagner. Suffice it to say that the T206 set has become the most sought after collection because of one player, The Flying Dutchman. A member of the first class elected to the Hall of Fame in 1936, Wagner placed second in the voting (to Ty Cobb), tied with Babe Ruth.

Born:
October 13, 1876
Bradford, PA
Died:
April 1, 1914
San Antonio, TX

▷ Batted: RH
▷ Threw: LH
▷ Position: P
▷ MLB Pitching Record: 193–143
▷ ERA: 2.16

Teams:
Louisville Colonels NL (1897, 1899)
Pittsburgh Pirates NL (1900–1901)
Chicago Orphans NL (1901)
Philadelphia Athletics AL (1902–1907)
St. Louis Browns AL (1908–1910)

Born:
February 24, 1874
Chartiers, PA
Died:
December 6, 1955
Carnegie, PA

▷ Batted: RH
▷ Threw: RH
▷ Position: SS
▷ Career BA: .327
▷ Managerial Record: 1–4

George Edward Waddell

Bobby Wallace

WALLACE, ST. LOUIS AMER.

Teams:
Cleveland Spiders NL (1894–1898)
St. Louis Perfectos/Cardinals NL
(1899–1901, 1917–1918)
St. Louis Browns AL (1902–1916;
player/manager: 1911–1912)
Cincinnati Reds NL (manager: 1937)

Bobby Wallace was the first great defensive shortstop in baseball, and perhaps the first player to field his way into the Hall of Fame. He redefined infield play by refining the process of fielding and throwing a grounder, diminishing the role of the infield hit in the early game. In 1902, after the AL Browns lured him away from the NL Cardinals for a 5-year contract worth a staggering (for the times) $32,000, Wallace fielded 17 chances in a game— still the American League record today. He became the player/manager for the Browns for two seasons, going 57–134. After retiring, Wallace played and managed in the minors for 2 years, umpired in the American League for 2 years, then managed the Reds for 25 games, going 5–20. Bobby Wallace was inducted into the Hall of Fame in 1953.

Born:
November 4, 1873
Pittsburgh, PA
Died:
November 3, 1960
Torrance, CA

▷ Batted: RH
▷ Threw: RH
▷ Position: SS
▷ Career BA: .268
▷ Managerial Record: 62–154

Rhoderick John Wallace

Ed Walsh

"Big Ed" Walsh was the early gold standard for pitchers. The numbers from his 13 seasons with the White Sox are just stunning. In 1908 he pitched 464 innings (still an American League record) with an amazing 1.42 ERA and posted the first 40-win season in the majors. For four seasons, Walsh led the league in innings pitched, topping 400 twice and pitching 393 once. In 1907 and 1910 he led the league in ERA, and collected six sub-2.00 seasons overall. He struck out 200-plus batters five times and led the league in strikeouts twice. Walsh threw his only no-hitter against Boston in 1911. The innings took their toll on him, however, and after 4 years of less than 100 innings pitched, he was released in 1916. He tried a comeback with the Braves but only lasted 18 innings. Walsh is still baseball's all-time career leader in ERA at 1.82. He was elected to the Hall of Fame in 1946.

WALSH, CHICAGO AMER.

Teams:
Chicago White Sox AL (1904–1916; manager: 1924)
Boston Braves NL (1917)

Edward Augustine Walsh

Born:
May 14, 1881
Plains Township, PA
Died:
May 26, 1959
Pompano Beach, FL

▷ Batted: RH
▷ Threw: RH
▷ Position: P
▷ MLB Pitching Record: 195–126
▷ ERA: 1.82
▷ Managerial Record: 1–2

Zack Wheat

WHEAT, BROOKLYN

Born:
May 23, 1888
Hamilton, MO
Died:
March 11, 1972
Sedalia, MO

▷ Batted: LH
▷ Threw: RH
▷ Position: OF
▷ Career BA: .317

Teams:
Brooklyn Superbas/Dodgers/Robins NL (1909–1926)
Philadelphia Athletics NL (1927)

Zack "Buck" Wheat's iconic career was just beginning when the T206 set was distributed in 1909, but for the next 17 years he was the face of the Dodgers. His sweet and effortless swing from the left side produced a barrage of vicious line drives throughout his career. Wheat finished in the top five in batting in seven seasons from 1913 to 1925. Starting at the age of 32, when the live ball was introduced, he hit .320 or better for 6 straight years, including 2 years (1923, 1924) when he hit .375. During that span, he also quadrupled his career average of 3 home runs a year. Wheat was so adept at hitting a curveball that John McGraw once ordered his pitchers not to throw him one. The Veterans Committee inducted Zack Wheat into the Hall of Fame in 1959.

Zachariah Davis Wheat

Vic Willis

Nicknamed "The Delaware Peach," Vic Willis was a hard-working, durable pitcher who won 20 or more games eight times in his career. He also lost 20 or more games on three occasions. Known as a real workhorse, Willis pitched 388 complete games over his career, and still holds the record for complete games (45) in a single season. He posted a 22–11 record for the World Series championship Pirates in 1909. While with the Beaneaters, he won 25 games as a rookie in 1898 and 27 games in 1899 and 1902. Willis led the National League in shutouts in 1889 (5) and 1901 (6). He was the league leader in ERA (2.50) in 1899 and strikeouts in 1902 (225). He pitched a no-hitter in 1899. Vic Willis was inducted into the Hall of Fame in 1995.

Teams:
Boston Beaneaters NL (1898–1905)
Pittsburgh Pirates NL (1906–1909)
St. Louis Cardinals NL (1910)

Born:
April 12, 1876
Cecil County, MD
Died:
August 3, 1947
Elkton, MD

▷ Batted: RH
▷ Threw: RH
▷ Position: P
▷ MLB Pitching Record: 249–205
▷ ERA: 2.63

WILLIS, PITTSBURG

WILLIS, ST LOUIS NAT'L

Victor Gazaway Willis

WILLIS, ST LOUIS NAT'L

Cy Young

YOUNG, CLEVELAND

YOUNG, CLEVELAND

YOUNG, CLEVELAND

Cy Young was featured in the T206 collection at the end of his illustrious career. The MLB career leader in wins (511), most innings pitched (7,354), games started (815), and complete games (749), Denton "Cy" (short for "Cyclone") Young is considered one of the top-five pitchers of all time. He won 30 or more games 5 times and 20 or more games 10 times. Young also pitched 3 no-hitters, and in 1904 he pitched the first perfect game in modern baseball history. He was known for his control and durability rather than his overpowering fastball. In 1956 the Cy Young Award was created to honor the best pitcher in baseball. Since 1967, it has been given to the best pitcher in the American League and the National League. Cy Young was elected to the Hall of Fame in 1937.

Denton True Young

Born:
March 29, 1867
Gilmore, OH
Died:
November 4, 1955
Newcomerstown, OH

▷ Batted: RH
▷ Threw: RH
▷ Position: P
▷ MLB Pitching Record: 511–316
▷ ERA: 2.63

Teams:
Cleveland Spiders NL (1890–1898)
St. Louis Perfectos/Cardinals NL (1899–1900)
Boston Americans/Red Sox AL (1901–1908)
Cleveland Naps AL (1909–1911)
Boston Rustlers NL (1911)

2

OVERLOOKED BY COOPERSTOWN?

OVER THE YEARS, THE argument has persisted about who is worthy of Cooperstown and who is not. There are a number of players scattered over the annals of baseball who for one reason or another haven't made it into the Hall of Fame—yet.

In our estimation, the following ballplayers from the T206 collection should be considered for induction into the Hall of Fame. In some cases, the records and personal stats of these players equal or exceed those of existing Hall of Famers. In fact, at the time of this writing (2009), a few of these players are still being considered, and a few are "on the bubble."

Judge for yourself.

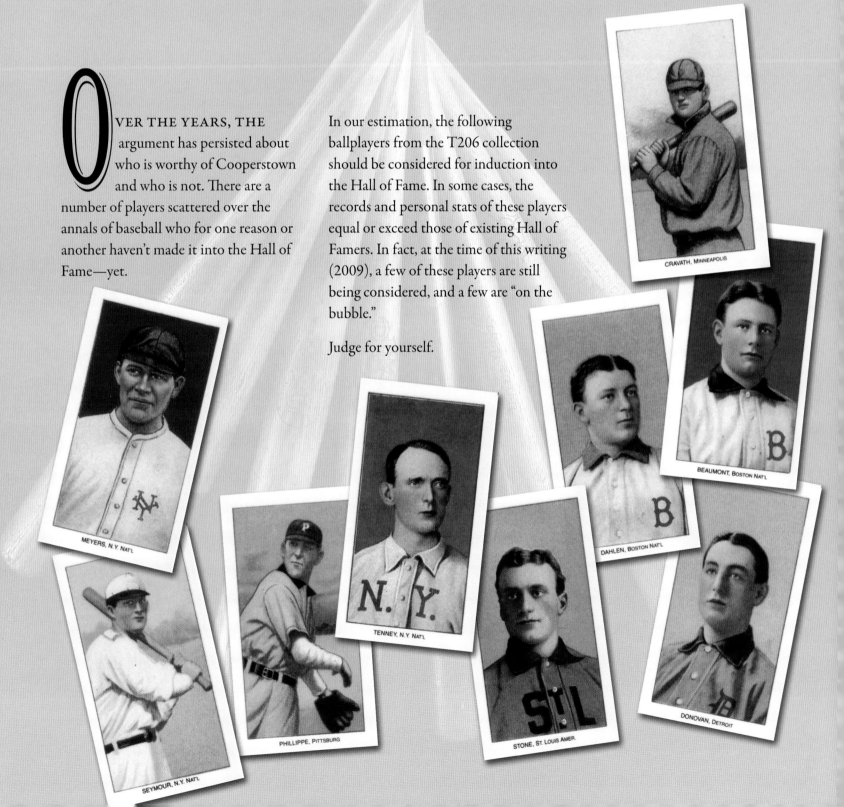

CRAVATH, MINNEAPOLIS

BEAUMONT, BOSTON NAT'L

DAHLEN, BOSTON NAT'L

MEYERS, N.Y. NAT'L

PHILLIPPE, PITTSBURG

TENNEY, N.Y. NAT'L

STONE, ST. LOUIS AMER.

DONOVAN, DETROIT

SEYMOUR, N.Y. NAT'L

Ginger Beaumont

BEAUMONT, BOSTON NAT'L.

As leadoff hitter for the Pirates, redheaded Clarence "Ginger" Beaumont had the distinction of being the first person to bat in the first World Series in 1903. He also played on the 1910 pennant-winning Cubs team. An outstanding player, Beaumont was the National League batting champ in 1902 (.357) and led the league in hits in 1902, 1903, 1904, and 1907. Beaumont batted over .300 seven times. In 1903 he led the league in runs scored, games played, plate appearances, at bats, hits, total bases, and singles. He ended his career with 1,759 hits, 955 runs, 617 RBI, and 254 stolen bases. Ginger Beaumont was inducted into the Wisconsin Athletic Hall of Fame in 1951, but is surely worthy of Cooperstown.

Born:
July 23, 1876
Rochester, WI

Died:
April 10, 1956
Burlington, WI

▷ Batted: LH
▷ Threw: RH
▷ Position: OF
▷ Career BA: .311

Teams:
Pittsburgh Pirates NL (1899–1906)
Boston Doves NL (1907–1909)
Chicago Cubs NL (1910)

Clarence Howeth Beaumont

Donie Bush

Born:
October 8, 1887
Indianapolis, IN

Died:
March 28, 1972
Indianapolis, IN

▷ Batted: Switch
▷ Threw: RH
▷ Position: SS
▷ Career BA: .250
▷ Managerial Record: 497–539

BUSH, DETROIT

An excellent contact hitter and superb shortstop, Owen "Donie" Bush epitomizes what every player should aspire to. He holds the MLB record for the most triple plays as well as the most putouts in a season by a shortstop (425). In his rookie year he helped lead the Tigers to the World Series and hit .318 in the fall classic. Bush later became an MLB manager, owned two minor league teams in the American Association (the Louisville Cardinals and the Indianapolis Indians), and scouted for the Red Sox and White Sox, devoting a total of 67 years to baseball. His 1927 Pirates with Harold "Pie" Traynor, Paul and Lloyd Waner, Kiki Cuyler, and Joe Cronin lost to the Yankees' Murderer's Row lineup. Bush scouted up to the age of 84, when he became ill. He passed away in 1972.

Teams:
Detroit Tigers AL (1908–1921)
Washington Senators AL (1921–1922; manager: 1923)
Pittsburgh Pirates NL (manager: 1927–1929)
Chicago White Sox AL (manager: 1930–1931)
Cincinnati Reds NL (manager: 1933)

Owen Joseph Bush

Gavvy Cravath

Clifford "Gavvy" or "Cactus" Cravath was one of the premier power hitters of the dead-ball era. He spent a good portion of his career in the minors, going up to the majors for brief stints with the Red Sox, the White Sox, and the Senators, and then back down to the Minneapolis Millers of the American Association,

Born:
March 23, 1881
Escondido, CA

Died:
May 23, 1963
Laguna Beach, CA

▷ Batted: RH
▷ Threw: RH
▷ Position: OF
▷ Career BA: .287
▷ Managerial Record: 91–137

Teams:
Boston Red Sox AL (1908)
Chicago White Sox AL (1909)
Washington Senators AL (1909)
Philadelphia Phillies NL (1912–1918; player/manager: 1919–1920)

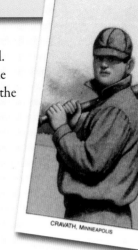

CRAVATH, MINNEAPOLIS

as pictured on his T206 card. At age 31, Cravath joined the Phillies and went on to lead the National League in homers six times. In 1915 he hit an amazing 24 round-trippers. His best year, however, was 1913, when he batted .341 and had 19 homers, 179 hits, and 128 RBI. At one time or another he led the league in on-base percentage, slugging percentage, hits, home runs, walks, and total bases. Cravath was player/manager of the Phillies in 1919 and 1920. He then returned to the minors for 2 years before becoming a coach for the Phillies.

Clifford Carlton Cravath

Bill Dahlen

DAHLEN, BOSTON NAT'L

DAHLEN, BROOKLYN

Teams:
Chicago Colts/Orphans NL (1891–1898)
Brooklyn Superbas/Dodgers NL (1899–1903; player/manager: 1910–1911; manager: 1912–1913)
New York Giants NL (1904–1907)
Boston Doves NL (1908–1909)

Born:
January 5, 1870
Nelliston, NY

Died:
December 5, 1950
Brooklyn, NY

▷ Batted: RH
▷ Threw: RH
▷ Position: SS
▷ Career BA: .272
▷ Managerial Record: 251–355

"Bad Bill" Dahlen was one of the toughest, hard-nosed infielders ever to play the game. An outstanding all-around player, Dahlen twice batted over .350, was always among the league fielding leaders, and was a base-stealing threat. He played on three National League pennant-winning teams and one World Series championship team (the 1905 Giants). A real power threat, Dahlen hit 15 home runs in 1894, and had a 42-game hitting streak that same year, eventually hitting in 70 of 71 games! As a manager, "Bad Bill" was tossed out of games 65 times, still a top-ten MLB record. Dahlen is on the short list for Cooperstown.

William Frederick Dahlen

Wild Bill Donovan

Sherry Magee

DONOVAN, DETROIT

DONOVAN, DETROIT

MAGEE, PHILA. NAT'L

Considered one of the most underrated players of all time, Sherry Magee could do it all. Known for his great hitting and fielding abilities, he was the National League batting champ in 1910, with a .331 average, and had a total of five .300-plus seasons. He was also the National League RBI leader in four different seasons, and hit 15 home runs on two different occasions, a very difficult feat in that era. With 2,169 hits, 441 stolen bases, and graceful outfield play, he is now being considered for the Hall of Fame by the Veterans Committee. He toiled in the minors for several years after his MLB career ended, retiring in 1926. Sherry Magee passed away after contracting pneumonia at the age of 44.

Sherwood Robert Magee

Born:
August 6, 1884
Clarendon, PA
Died:
March 13, 1929
Philadelphia, PA

▷ Batted: RH
▷ Threw: RH
▷ Position: OF
▷ Career BA: .291

Born:
October 13, 1876
Lawrence, MA
Died:
December 9, 1923
Forsyth, NY

▷ Batted: RH
▷ Threw: RH
▷ Position: P
▷ MLB Pitching Record: 186–139
▷ ERA: 2.69
▷ Managerial Record: 245–301

Teams:
Philadelphia Phillies NL (1904–1914)
Boston Braves NL (1915–1917)
Cincinnati Reds NL (1917–1919)

"Wild Bill" Donovan earned his nickname by usually finishing as one of the league leaders in bases on balls. In 1901 he led the league in wins with 25. An extremely durable pitcher, Donovan led the league in games pitched in 1901 (45) and complete games in 1903 (34). His best season was 1907, when he led the Tigers to the pennant with a 25–4 record, posting a 2.19 ERA. He was a player/manager in the majors until 1921. Donovan was killed in a train wreck in 1923 while managing in the minors. He was killed in the lower berth while George Weiss (future manager of the Yankees and the Mets, who was elected to the Hall of Fame in 1971) slept above him and was not injured.

William Edward Donovan

Teams:
Washington Senators NL (1898)
Brooklyn Superbas NL (1899–1902)
Detroit Tigers AL (1903–1912, 1918)
New York Yankees AL (player/manager: 1915–1916; manager: 1917)
Philadelphia Phillies NL (manager: 1921)

MAGIE. PHILA. NAT'L

MAGEE. PHILA. NAT'L

Chief Meyers

Nicknamed for his Native American heritage, Jack "Chief" Meyers backstopped three straight pennant winners for the New York Giants from 1911 to 1913, hitting above .300 in all three seasons, including .358 in 1912. In the 1912 World Series against the Red Sox, Meyers hit .357 in 28 at bats in a losing effort. He became a very popular player in New York, and performed on the vaudeville circuit with Christy Mathewson. He was considered one of the best students of the game, and finished in the top ten in National League MVP voting in 1911, 1912, and 1913, the three seasons he played in the World Series for the Giants. Meyers later played and managed for New Haven in the Eastern League before retiring from the game in 1920.

Teams:
New York Giants NL (1909–1915)
Brooklyn Robins NL (1916–1917)
Boston Braves NL (1917)

John Tortes Meyers

Born:
July 29, 1880
Riverside, CA
Died:
July 25, 1971
San Bernardino, CA

▷ Batted: RH
▷ Threw: RH
▷ Position: C
▷ Career BA: .291

Deacon Phillippe

Born:
May 23, 1872
Rural Retreat, VA
Died:
March 30, 1952
Avalon, PA

▷ Batted: RH
▷ Threw: RH
▷ Position: P
▷ MLB Pitching Record: 189–109
▷ ERA: 2.59

Teams:
Louisville Colonels NL (1899)
Pittsburgh Pirates NL (1900–1911)

Charles Louis Phillippe

Charles "Deacon" Phillippe is a player who should be on the bubble for Hall of Fame consideration. He was the winning pitcher for the Pirates in the first World Series game, won 20 games in at least six seasons, and still holds the record for the most decisions in the World Series with five. As a 27-year-old rookie, Phillippe pitched a no-hitter and won 21 games. A quiet, humble man, Phillippe earned his nickname for his demeanor, clean living, and because he was a church choirmaster in the off-season. He was noted for his pinpoint control, and no player in the last 110-plus years averaged fewer walks per nine innings pitched than he did. After posting a 189–109 record in 372 games and 2,607 innings pitched, "the Deacon" retired in 1911 at age 39.

Cy Seymour

the Reds, and he is still their career leader in batting average with .332. During WWI, Seymour worked in the shipyards. He died at age of 46 from tuberculosis.

Born:
December 9, 1872
Albany, NY
Died:
September 20, 1919
New York, NY

▷ Batted: LH
▷ Threw: LH
▷ Position: OF/P
▷ MLB Pitching Record: 61-56
▷ Career BA: .303

Teams:
New York Giants NL (1896–1900, 1906–1910)
Baltimore Orioles AL (1901–1902)
Cincinnati Reds NL (1902–1906)
Boston Braves NL (1913)

For the first 5 years of his MLB career, James "Cy" Seymour was a very good pitcher for the New York Giants, winning 25 games in 1898 to become the National League strikeout champion. However, Seymour was such a good hitter that he was switched to the outfield where his bat could be in the lineup every game. In 1905 Seymour was the National League batting champ, batting an amazing .377 with 219 hits and 121 RBI. Unfortunately, he just missed the Triple Crown that year because of his second-place finish in home runs. His best hitting years were with

James Bentley Seymour

George Stone

For the first 28 years of the American League, the batting title was won by a future Hall of Famer—such as Ty Cobb, Nap Lajoie, Tris Speaker, or Babe Ruth—in every season but one, that is. The 1906 AL batting champion was "Silent George" Stone. He played 2 games for Boston in 1903 before being traded to the Browns the day after Christmas in 1904. Stone hit with an exaggerated crouch, and Boston's Jimmy Collins felt it would limit his potential. In 1905, however, Stone led the league in hits with 189 and in 1906 he edged Nap Lajoie for the batting title, hitting .358 with 6 homers, 71 RBI, and 35 stolen bases. Stone also led the league that season in on-base percentage (.417) and slugging percentage (.501). He hit .320 in 1907, but after that his play declined sharply. Some say he contracted malaria in 1908, but Stone also suffered ankle and shoulder injuries during his last two seasons. In 1910, at age 33, he played his final MLB season.

Teams:
Boston Americans AL (1903)
St. Louis Browns AL (1905–1910)

George Robert Stone

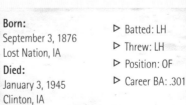

Born:
September 3, 1876
Lost Nation, IA
Died:
January 3, 1945
Clinton, IA

▷ Batted: LH
▷ Threw: LH
▷ Position: OF
▷ Career BA: .301

Jesse Tannehill

TANNEHILL, WASHINGTON

Jesse "Powder" Tannehill was one of the era's better two-way pitchers, winning 197 games (116 for Pittsburgh), hitting a career .256, playing 87 games in the outfield, and pinch-hitting 57 times. He won 20 or more games six times and led the National League with a 2.18 ERA in 1901. The next season was arguably his best, as Tannehill went 20–6 with a 1.95 ERA in 26 games for the Pirates. After a tough salary dispute with the notoriously frugal owner of the Pirates, Barney Dreyfuss, Tannehill jumped to the Highlanders in the American League in 1903. Pitching for the Red Sox in 1904, Jesse threw his only no-hitter against the White Sox, with his brother Lee Tannehill helping him out by going 0 for 3.

Teams:
Cincinnati Reds NL (1894, 1911)
Pittsburgh Pirates NL (1897–1902)
New York Highlanders AL (1903)
Boston Americans/Red Sox AL (1904–1908)
Washington Senators AL (1908–1909)

Jesse Niles Tannehill

Born:
July 14, 1874
Dayton, KY
Died:
September 22, 1956
Dayton, KY

▷ Batted: Switch
▷ Threw: LH
▷ Position: P
▷ MLB Pitching Record: 197–116
▷ ERA: 2.79

Fred Tenney

Fred Tenney started his notable career as a left-handed catcher, but soon became an innovator at first base for Boston. He pioneered the modern style of playing off first base, stretching for throws to help infielders beat close plays. He also originated the 3-6-3 double play. On the night of his senior dinner at Brown University, "The Soiled Collegian" got a frantic phone call from the Beaneaters looking for a fill-in catcher. After little sleep and a long train ride, Tenney made his

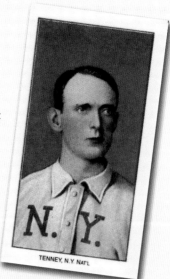

TENNEY, N.Y. NAT'L

MLB debut the next day, and finished the game despite fracturing a finger in the fifth inning. He topped .300 seven times in his first ten seasons. After an unsuccessful run as Boston's player/manager (202–402), Tenney went on to become a regular baseball correspondent for the *New York Times*, writing preseason previews and covering the World Series.

Frederick Tenney

Born:
November 26, 1871
Georgetown, MA
Died:
July 3, 1952
Boston, MA

▷ Batted: LH
▷ Threw: LH
▷ Position: 1B
▷ Career BA: .294
▷ Managerial Record: 202–402

Teams:
Boston Beaneaters/Doves/Rustlers NL (1894–1904; player/manager: 1905–1907, 1911)
New York Giants NL (1908–1909)

3

THE UNCOMMONS

Some Interesting Careers

THE PLAYERS IN THIS chapter had unique, colorful lives, some while they were still between the lines and some after their playing days were over.

These are not your average run-of-the-mill ballplayers; they all had something a little "different" in their approach to both the game and to life in general.

These are the uncommon players.

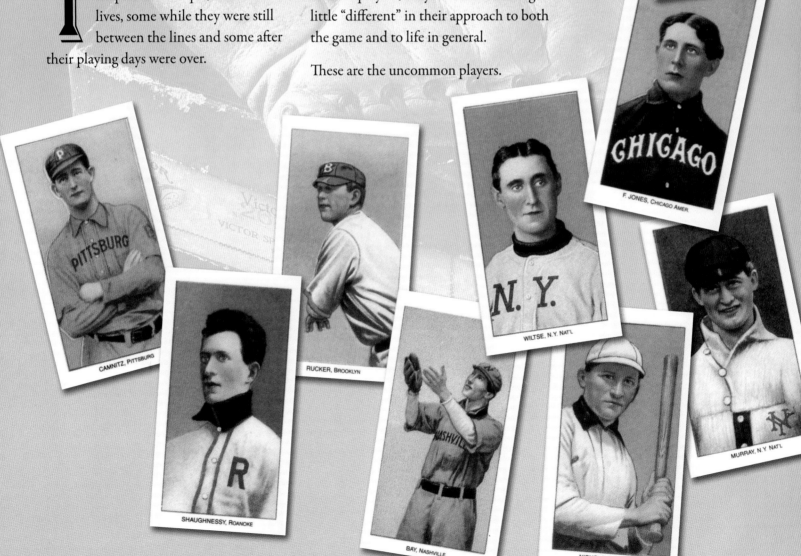

Ed Abbaticchio

Doc Adkins

Merle "Doc" Adkins was 29 when he began his pro career, playing in both the majors and minors as a rookie in 1902. Adkins pitched just 20 innings in 4 games for the Americans that year, and came back in 1903 to pitch only seven innings in 2 games for the Highlanders. He was a star in the minors, however, pitching from 1903 through 1912 for the Baltimore Orioles. He won 20 or more games four times. His best year was 1908, when he went 29–12, led the tough Eastern League in wins, and helped the Orioles win their first pennant. Adkins attended medical school while with the Orioles and became an M.D. in 1907. After he retired in 1914 with a 165–111 minor league record, Doc became a successful scout, discovering Ernie Shore. He later became a well-known doctor in Durham.

Merle Theron Adkins

Teams:
Boston Americans AL (1902)
New York Highlanders AL (1903)

Born:
August 5, 1872
Troy, WI
Died:
February 21, 1934
Durham, NC

▷ Batted: RH
▷ Threw: RH
▷ Position: P
▷ MLB Pitching Record: 1–1
▷ ERA: 5.00

Born:
April 15, 1877
Latrobe, PA
Died:
January 6, 1957
Fort Lauderdale, FL

▷ Batted: RH
▷ Threw: RH
▷ Position: 2B/SS
▷ Career BA: .254

Ed "Batty" Abbaticchio was the first major leaguer of Italian heritage. He was a good fielder with a mediocre bat. In 1908 his fielding percentage was .969, good for first in the league. His best year offensively was with Boston in 1905, when he hit .279 with 30 stolen bases and 170 hits in 610 at bats. Known mostly for his speed on the base paths, he swiped 20 or more bases three times and 30 or more bases twice. Abbaticchio left baseball for a year in 1906 to open a hotel, but was convinced to get back into the game, and later appeared in the 1909 World Series. In 1895, before his MLB days, he was one of the first professional football players, and is said to have developed the spiral punt. After his tour with the Doves in 1910, he went back to running his hotel until he retired in 1932.

Teams:
Philadelphia Phillies NL (1897–1898)
Boston Beaneaters/Doves NL (1903–1905, 1910)
Pittsburgh Pirates NL (1907–1910)

Edward James Abbaticchio

Born: Eduardo Giacomo Abbaticchio

Red Ames

A solid pitcher during his 17-year career, Leon "Red" Ames won 22 games in 1905 and pitched in three World Series with John McGraw's Giants (1905, 1911, 1912). He led the league in wild pitches in 1905 (30) and 1907 (20), and is tied with Walter Johnson for the most wild pitches in a career (156). If not for his wild pitching, Ames would have been considered a dominant pitcher, as he struck out 1,702 batters over his 17 years. He pitched a no-hitter on April 15, 1909, and *lost*, earning the nickname "Kalamity." After his MLB days, he played for the Kansas City Blues in the American Association. Ames then became player/manager of the Daytona Beach Islanders in the Florida State League in 1923, retiring after that season with a 49–47 minor league pitching record. He was inducted into the Trumbull County (Ohio) Sports Hall of Fame in 2005.

Teams:
New York Giants NL (1903–1913)
Cincinnati Reds NL (1913–1915)
St. Louis Cardinals NL (1915–1919)
Philadelphia Phillies NL (1919)

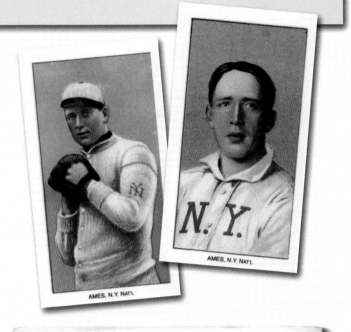

Born:
August 2, 1882
Warren, OH

Died:
October 8, 1936
Warren, OH

▷ Batted: Switch
▷ Threw: RH
▷ Position: P
▷ MLB Pitching Record: 183–167
▷ ERA: 2.63

Leon Kessling Ames

John Anderson

Norway native "Honest John" Anderson was an excellent hitter and was speedy on the base paths, although somewhat weak defensively. Even though he split the 1898 season between the Superbas and the Senators, he led the National League in slugging percentage (.494) and triples (22) that year. Anderson had an outstanding year in 1901, batting .330 for the Brewers. In 1906, with the Senators, he led the American League with 39 stolen bases. He batted over .300 five times in his career. After 14 years in the Bigs, "Honest John" finished with a .290 batting average in 6,341 at bats, with 49 home runs, 976 runs batted in, and 338 stolen bases. Anderson then played one season in the Eastern League with the Providence Grays, as pictured on his T206 card, before retiring in 1909 at age 35.

Teams:
Brooklyn Grooms/Superbas NL (1894–1898, 1899)
Washington Senators NL (1898), AL (1905–1907)
Milwaukee Brewers AL (1901)
St. Louis Browns AL (1902–1903)
New York Highlanders AL (1904–1905)
Chicago White Sox AL (1908)

Born:
December 14, 1873
Sarpsburg, Norway

Died:
July 23, 1949
Worcester, MA

▷ Batted: Switch
▷ Threw: RH
▷ Position: OF/1B
▷ Career BA: .290

John Joseph Anderson

Jake Atz

Jake Atz was one of the first Jewish players in major league baseball. He was a utility second baseman who later became one of the most successful minor league managers of his era. Atz played only 3 games for the Senators in 1902 but got another shot at the majors in 1907, playing part-time for the White Sox until he became starting second baseman in 1909. He returned to the minors in 1910 and started as manager in 1911 for the Providence Grays in the Eastern League. Atz managed the Fort Worth Panthers of the Texas League from 1914 to 1929, and again in 1933. Under his leadership, the Panthers won seven consecutive titles from 1919 to 1925. Atz managed a total of 27 years, 21 of them in the Texas League. He retired in 1941 with a 1,972–1,619 record and a .549 winning percentage. Jake Atz was inducted into the Texas Sports Hall of Fame in 1963 and the Texas League Hall of Fame in 2004.

John Jacob Atz

Born: Jacob Henry Atz

Born:	
July 1, 1879	▷ Batted: RH
Washington, D.C.	▷ Threw: RH
Died:	▷ Position: 2B
May 22, 1945	▷ Career BA: .218
New Orleans, LA	

Teams:
Washington Senators AL (1902)
Chicago White Sox AL (1907–1909)

Neal Ball

On July 19, 1909, Neal Ball had the distinction of pulling off the first unassisted triple play in major league history. A pretty good hitter, Ball's best year was 1911, when he batted .296 with 3 home runs. He did get the thrill of 1 at bat in the 1912 World Series for the Red Sox. Ball was considered a good, steady ballplayer by his peers. Around his time in the majors, he spent 14 seasons in the minors, where he once played in a game against Negro League star and future Hall of Famer Rube Foster. Ball played in the minors until 1924, mostly for the New Haven Murlins in the Eastern League. He also managed two seasons in the Eastern League for the Bridgeport Hustlers and the Pittsfield Hillies and one season for the Augusta Tygers in the South Atlantic League, before retiring in 1926 at the age of 45. After his return to private life, he worked as a hat salesman and a bowling alley manager.

Born:	
April 22, 1881	▷ Batted: RH
Grand Haven, MI	▷ Threw: RH
Died:	▷ Position: SS/2B
October 15, 1957	▷ Career BA: .251
Bridgeport, CT	

Teams:
New York Highlanders AL (1907–1909)
Cleveland Naps AL (1909–1912)
Boston Red Sox AL (1912–1913)

Cornelius Ball

Jack Barry

Born:
April 26, 1887
Meriden, CT
Died:
April 23, 1961
Shrewsbury, MA

▷ Batted: RH
▷ Threw: RH
▷ Position: SS/2B
▷ Career BA: .243
▷ Managerial Record: 90–62

Teams:
Philadelphia Athletics AL (1908–1915)
Boston Red Sox AL (1915–1919; player/manager: 1917)

"Black Jack" Barry had a great career as both a player and manager. He started in the Bigs right out of Holy Cross at age 21, and soon became part of Connie Mack's Athletics famous $100,000 infield. As part of the excellent infields of the A's and the Red Sox, he played on five American League pennant-winning teams and four World Series championship teams. Barry was known for his reliable glove and his leadership. He became player/manager for the Sox in 1917, winning 90 games, which was good for second in the league. He served in the military during WWI, missing the 1918 season, and retired soon after his return in 1919. Barry went on to coach for 40 years at his alma mater, Holy Cross, retiring with the highest winning percentage in the school's history. His 1924 team was undefeated and his 1952 team was the first and only New England team to win the NCAA championship.

John Joseph Barry

Harry Bay

Harry Bay was an outstanding athlete as well as a very colorful character. Only 5 feet 8 inches and 138 pounds, his slight build was an asset. Known as "Deerfoot" because of his speed, Bay was the American League stolen base champ in 1903 and 1904, and finished his major league career with 169 swipes. His best year offensively was 1905, when he batted .301 for the Naps. After Cleveland, Bay played four seasons in the Southern Association for the Nashville Volunteers. He was then player/manager for five different teams in three different leagues, finishing up with the Alton Blues in the Indiana-Illinois-Iowa League in 1917. Harry later became a well-known trumpet player and bandleader in Peoria. He also spent a few years in vaudeville before settling down to work in state government.

Harry Elbert Bay

Born:
January 17, 1878
Pontiac, IL
Died:
March 20, 1952
Peoria, IL

▷ Batted: LH
▷ Threw: LH
▷ Position: OF
▷ Career BA: .273

Teams:
Cincinnati Reds NL (1901–1902)
Cleveland Bronchos/Naps AL (1902–1908)

Beals Becker

Born:
July 5, 1886
El Dorado, KS
Died:
August 19, 1943
Huntington Park, CA

▷ Batted: LH
▷ Threw: LH
▷ Position: OF
▷ Career BA: .276

A hard-hitting outfielder, Beals Becker was usually among the leaders in home runs. He was the first player to hit 2 pinch-hit homers in one season, and he also set a record when he hit 2 inside-the-park jobs in one game. His best year was 1914, when he batted .325, hit 9 home runs, and led the league in singles. Beals played in three World Series, two with the Giants and one with the Phillies. A so-so fielder, Becker also had a hard time hitting lefties. He played 8 more years in the minors after his MLB days, 7 of them with the Kansas City Blues in the American Association, where he batted .367 in 1922 and won a championship in 1923.

Teams:
Pittsburgh Pirates NL (1908)
Boston Doves NL (1908–1909)
New York Giants NL (1910–1912)
Cincinnati Reds NL (1913)
Philadelphia Phillies NL (1913–1915)

David Beals Becker

Bill Bergen

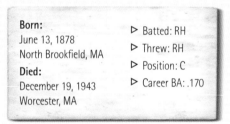

William Aloysius Bergen

Born:
June 13, 1878
North Brookfield, MA
Died:
December 19, 1943
Worcester, MA

▷ Batted: RH
▷ Threw: RH
▷ Position: C
▷ Career BA: .170

Teams:
Cincinnati Reds NL (1901–1903)
Brooklyn Superbas/Dodgers NL (1904–1911)

Bill Bergen had the distinction of being considered one of the best defensive catchers of all time . . . and one of the worst hitters of all time. A lifetime .170 hitter, Bergen is the only player in major league history with a minimum of 500 at bats and an on-base percentage under .200. Amazingly, Bergen once had 46 consecutive at bats without a hit. On the bright side, he was an outstanding catcher who once threw out six base stealers in a game. He went on to play three seasons in the minors for the Newark Indians and the Baltimore Orioles in the International League and the Scranton Miners in the New York State League, batting .205 in 614 at bats. He packed it in after the 1914 season when he was 36.

Bill Bernhard

Born:
March 16, 1871
Clarence, NY
Died:
March 30, 1949
San Diego, CA

▷ Batted: Switch
▷ Threw: RH
▷ Position: P
▷ MLB Pitching Record: 116–82
▷ ERA: 3.04

Teams:
Philadelphia Phillies NL (1899–1900)
Philadelphia Athletics AL (1901–1902)
Cleveland Bronchos/Naps AL (1902–1907)

William Henry Bernhard

BERNHARD, NASHVILLE

Nicknamed for his red hair, "Strawberry Bill" Bernhard didn't start playing pro ball until he was 28 years old. He was a consistent, steady pitcher who had a couple of excellent seasons. He was the first Cleveland pitcher to lead the American League in winning percentage, going 18–5 (.783) in 1902. Bernhard also went 23–13 in 1904, and won 15 or more games in five more seasons. He continued in the minors as player/manager, mainly for the Nashville Volunteers and the Memphis Turtles in the Southern Association, leading the Volunteers to the league pennant in 1908. After a short stint with the Salt Lake City Bees in the Pacific Coast League, Bernhard retired at age 46 after the 1917 season.

Bob Bescher

BESCHER, CINCINNATI

Teams:
Cincinnati Reds NL (1908–1913)
New York Giants NL (1914)
St. Louis Cardinals NL (1915–1917)
Cleveland Indians AL (1918)

A whiz on the base paths, Bob Bescher led the National League in stolen bases 4 straight years from 1909 to 1912. His 81 steals in 1911 stood as a National League record for more than half a century, and he stole 428 bases over his career. A decent hitter, his best year offensively was 1912, when he batted .281 and led the league with 120 runs scored. Bescher spent another 8 years in the minors after his major league days, playing for the Louisville Colonels and the Columbus Senators in the American Association, as well as the Wichita Falls Spudders and the Fort Worth Panthers in the Texas League. He retired after the 1925 season at 41 years old with a .277 minor league batting average. He died in an auto accident in 1942.

BESCHER, CINCINNATI

Born:
February 25, 1884
London, OH
Died:
November 29, 1942
London, OH

▷ Batted: Switch
▷ Threw: LH
▷ Position: OF
▷ Career BA: .258

Robert Henry Bescher

Joe Birmingham

Joe "Dode" Birmingham was an excellent center fielder with great range, but was only an average hitter. His best year offensively was 1911, when he batted .304 with 136 hits. His .289 batting average in 1909 was good for tenth in the league. After six seasons with the Naps, he was named manager at the age of 28 in 1912. The Naps finished third in the league in 1913 with an 86–66 record, but in 1914 they lost 102 games. He was replaced at the helm during the Naps' unsuccessful 1915 campaign, and ended his 4-year stint with a 170–191 record. Birmingham went on to manage and play for the Toronto Maple Leafs in the International League as well as the Pittsfield Hillies and the Albany Senators in the Eastern League. He retired in 1921 at 36 years old.

Team:
Cleveland Naps AL (1906–1911; player/manager: 1912–1914; manager: 1915)

Born:
August 6, 1884
Elmira, NY
Died:
April 24, 1946
Tampico, Mexico

▷ Batted: RH
▷ Threw: RH
▷ Position: OF
▷ Career BA: .253
▷ Managerial Record: 170–191

Joseph Leo Birmingham

Lena Blackburne

BLACKBURNE, PROVIDENCE

Russell Aubrey Blackburne

Born:
October 23, 1886
Clifton Heights, PA
Died:
February 29, 1968
Riverside, NJ

▷ Batted: RH
▷ Threw: RH
▷ Position: SS/3B/2B
▷ Career BA: .214
▷ Managerial Record: 99–133

Russell "Lena" Blackburne is known more for his Lena Blackburne Rubbing Mud than for his days as a player, coach, and manager. Prior to 1938, the options for dulling the shine on baseballs were dirt from the playing field or tobacco juice. Blackburne found that the muck from a special mud hole near the Delaware River worked without staining the ball. The location is still a secret, but Blackburne started a pretty good business; the mud is still used by major league baseball. A below average player, he played off and on in the minors through 1932 around his MLB tours, putting together a .283 batting average in 5,736 at bats in 14 minor league seasons. He played in the Eastern League for the Providence Grays in 1909, as pictured on his T206 card. He also managed and coached with various major and minor league teams, including the White Sox, the A's, the Toronto Maple Leafs in the International League, and the Lancaster Red Roses in the Interstate League.

Teams:
Chicago White Sox AL (1910, 1912, 1914–1915, 1927; manager: 1928–1929)
Cincinnati Reds NL (1918)
Boston Braves NL (1919)
Philadelphia Phillies NL (1919)

Bill Bradley

William Joseph Bradley

> **Born:**
> February 13, 1878
> Cleveland, OH
> **Died:**
> March 11, 1954
> Cleveland, OH
>
> ▷ Batted: RH
> ▷ Threw: RH
> ▷ Position: 3B
> ▷ Career BA: .271
> ▷ Managerial Record: 97–98

Teams:
Chicago Orphans NL (1899–1900)
Cleveland Blues/Bronchos/Naps AL (1901–1910; player/manager: 1905)
Brooklyn Tip-Tops FL (player/manager: 1914)
Kansas City Packers FL (1915)

Considered one of the best fielding third basemen in MLB history, Bill Bradley led the American League in fielding four times. Also a solid hitter, Bradley batted .340 in 1902 and was the first Cleveland player to hit for the cycle on September 24, 1902. He was player/manager for Cleveland in 1905 and for Brooklyn of the Federal League in 1914. Between his American League and Federal League tours, Bradley played for the Toronto Maple Leafs in the International League, batting .288 over three seasons. In 1916 he managed the Erie Sailors in the Interstate League. He then scouted for Cleveland for 25 years, retiring in 1953. Bill Bradley was elected to the Cleveland Indians Hall of Fame in 1957.

Kitty Bransfield

A slick-fielding first baseman with a nice bat, William "Kitty" Bransfield played for the Pirates during the years the team dominated baseball. After playing just 5 games in 1898 for Boston, 26-year-old Bransfield returned to the majors in 1901 to bat .295, and help the Pirates win the National League pennant by a comfortable 7 1/2 games. Honus Wagner was the shortstop on that great team. After the 1904 season, Bransfield was traded to the Phillies, where his career flourished. In 1908 he batted .304 and had his all-around best year. It took the Pirates about 15 years to find a first baseman as good as Bransfield, and fans referred to that period as "The Bransfield Curse." After his playing days, he umpired in the National League and the New England League and scouted for the Cubs. He also managed the Montreal Royals in the International League and the Waterbury Brasscos and the Hartford Senators in the Eastern League, leading the Brasscos to league championships in 1924 and 1925. Bransfield retired in 1927.

> **Born:**
> January 7, 1875
> Worcester, MA
> **Died:**
> May 1, 1947
> Worcester, MA
>
> ▷ Batted: RH
> ▷ Threw: RH
> ▷ Position: 1B
> ▷ Career BA: .270

Teams:
Boston Beaneaters NL (1898)
Pittsburgh Pirates NL (1901–1904)
Philadelphia Phillies NL (1905–1911)
Chicago Cubs NL (1911)

William Edward Bransfield

Ted Breitenstein

BREITENSTEIN, New Orleans

Ted Breitenstein is remembered for pitching a no-hitter in his first major league start. A dependable starter, he won 20 or more games three times. In 1893, he led the league with his 3.18 ERA. In 1895, however, he led the league with 30 losses, putting him third on the all-time list for losses in a season by a pitcher. He also lost 20 or more games another three times. Breitenstein pitched a second no-hitter on April 22, 1898, against the Pirates. He led the National League in starts and complete games twice. After his MLB days, he pitched 11 seasons in the minors, eight of them with the New Orleans Pelicans of the Southern Association, where he won 21 games in 1905 and 21 again in 1906. Breitenstein retired in 1911 with a 165–92 minor league record.

Born:
June 1, 1869
St. Louis, MO
Died:
May 3, 1935
St. Louis, MO

▷ Batted: LH
▷ Threw: LH
▷ Position: P
▷ MLB Pitching Record: 160–170
▷ ERA: 4.04

Teams:
St. Louis Browns/Cardinals NL (1891–1896, 1901)
Cincinnati Reds NL (1897–1900)

Theodore P. Breitenstein

Al Bridwell

BRIDWELL, N.Y. NAT'L

Al Bridwell was a steady player who could do a little bit of everything. In 1907 Bridwell led all shortstops with a .942 fielding percentage, and in 1911 he had the least strikeouts per at bat (18 K's). His best offensive year was 1909, when he batted .294 with 140 hits, 55 RBI, and 67 stolen bases. Bridwell's claim to fame is that on September 23, 1908, he hit the single off pitcher Jack Pfiester that started the play that became known as "Merkle's Boner." After two seasons in the renegade Federal League, he moved to the Southern Association to play for the Atlanta Crackers. He was player/manager of the Texas League's Houston Buffaloes in 1919, and then managed the Rocky Mount Tar Heels in the Virginia League in 1920 and the Spartanburg Pioneers in the South Atlantic League in 1921. He retired when he was 37 years old.

BRIDWELL, N.Y. NAT'L

Born:
January 4, 1884
Friendship, OH
Died:
January 23, 1969
Portsmouth, OH

▷ Batted: LH
▷ Threw: RH
▷ Position: SS
▷ Career BA: .255

Teams:
Cincinnati Reds NL (1905)
Boston Beaneaters/Doves/Rustlers/Braves NL (1906–1907, 1911–1912)
New York Giants NL (1908–1911)
Chicago Cubs NL (1913)
St. Louis Terriers FL (1914–1915)

Albert Henry Bridwell

George Browne

Born:
January 12, 1876
Richmond, VA
Died:
December 9, 1920
Hyde Park, NY

▷ Batted: LH
▷ Threw: RH
▷ Position: OF
▷ Career BA: .273

Teams:
Philadelphia Phillies NL (1901–1902, 1912)
New York Giants NL (1902–1907)
Boston Doves NL (1908)
Chicago Cubs NL (1909)
Washington Senators AL (1909–1910)
Chicago White Sox AL (1910)
Brooklyn Dodgers NL (1911)

A journeyman outfielder with a good bat, George Browne was at his peak with the Giants. Browne's best offensive season was 1903, when he batted .313, had 185 hits and 3 home runs, and led the league with 141 games played and 420 outs made. In 1904 he was the National League leader in runs scored with 99 and was fourth in the league in outs made with 449. He played in the 1905 World Series for the Giants, batting .293. Browne managed the Dubuque Tigers of the Western League in 1898 when he was only 22 years old, finishing third in the league with a 49–26 record.

George Edward Browne

Howie Camnitz

Howie "Red" Camnitz was the epitome of a solid workhorse pitcher, winning 20 or more games on three different occasions. The Kentucky curveball expert had four other seasons in which he won 15 or more games. His best year was 1909, when he went 25–6, was the National League winning percentage leader, and led the Pirates to the World Series.

He had seven seasons in which he pitched 200 or more innings. At the end of his career, he pitched for two seasons in the Federal League, retiring after the 1915 season. He came back in 1922 to manage the Winchester Dodgers in the Blue Grass League for one season. Camnitz went on to work in automotive sales for nearly 40 years until his death in 1960 at age 78.

Samuel Howard Camnitz

Born:
August 22, 1881
Covington, KY
Died:
March 2, 1960
Louisville, KY

▷ Batted: RH
▷ Threw: RH
▷ Position: P
▷ MLB Pitching Record: 133–107
▷ ERA: 2.75

Teams:
Pittsburgh Pirates NL (1904, 1906–1913)
Philadelphia Phillies NL (1913)
Pittsburgh Rebels FL (1914–1915)

Bill Carrigan

J. J. Clarke

Jay Justin Clarke

Bill Carrigan was a good backup catcher for the Boston Americans/Red Sox for ten seasons. Nicknamed "Rough" for his toughness behind the plate, he was superb defensively and had an above-average bat. Carrigan played on the 1912 Sox championship team, and in 1913 he became player/manager. He then led Boston to a second-place finish in 1914 and to World Series championships in 1915 and 1916. Managing the likes of Babe Ruth, Tris Speaker, Duffy Lewis, and Harry Hooper, Carrigan always felt blessed to have been in the right place at the right time. He came back in 1927 to manage but struggled for 3 years before retiring after the 1929 season to become a very successful banker. Bill Carrigan was elected to the Red Sox Hall of Fame in 2004.

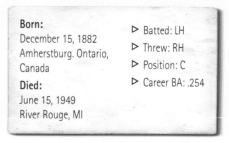

Born:
December 15, 1882
Amherstburg. Ontario, Canada
Died:
June 15, 1949
River Rouge, MI

▷ Batted: LH
▷ Threw: RH
▷ Position: C
▷ Career BA: .254

Teams:
Detroit Tigers AL (1905)
Cleveland Naps AL (1905–1910)
St. Louis Browns AL (1911)
Philadelphia Phillies NL (1919)
Pittsburgh Pirates NL (1920)

The highlight of J. J. "Nig" Clarke's career took place before he even got to the majors. On June 15, 1902, legend has it that he hit 8 home runs in one game playing for the Corsicana Oil Citys of the Texas League. Clarke is also noted for catching a perfect game on October 2, 1908, for the great Addie Joss. He was primarily a backup, and his best year was 1906, when he batted .358 with 179 at bats. His nickname was racially derogatory in nature due to his dark complexion. After his tour with St. Louis, Clarke played for the Indianapolis Indians of the American Association, the San Francisco Seals of the Pacific Coast League, the Houston Buffaloes of the Texas League, and the Memphis Chickasaws and the Mobile Sea Gulls of the Southern Association. When he was 36, he returned to the Bigs to catch for Philly. His last MLB game was in 1920, but Clarke then dabbled in the minors, retiring in 1925 at age 42 with a .266 minor league batting average.

Born:
October 22, 1883
Lewiston, ME
Died:
July 8, 1969
Lewiston, ME

▷ Batted: RH
▷ Threw: RH
▷ Position: C
▷ Career BA: .257
▷ Managerial Record: 489–500

Team:
Boston Americans/Red Sox AL (1906, 1908–1912;
player/manager: 1913–1916;
manager: 1927–1929)

William Francis Carrigan

Bill Clymer

CLYMER, COLUMBUS

William Johnston Clymer

Born:
December 18, 1873
Philadelphia, PA
Died:
December 26, 1936
Philadelphia, PA

▷ Batted: N/A
▷ Threw: N/A
▷ Position: SS
▷ Career BA: .000

Team:
Philadelphia Athletics AA (1891)

"Derby Day Bill" Clymer was only 17 years old in 1891 when he went 0 for 11 in his major league debut for Philadelphia of the American Association. The story, however, does not end there. Clymer went on to win 2,122 games as one of the greatest minor league managers of all time. Although he went 9-4 as player/manager of the Rochester Patriots in the Eastern League for 2 weeks in 1898, Clymer really began his managerial career in 1900 with the Atlantic League's Wilkes-Barre Barons, and he continued on as player/manager in the minors through 1908, batting .266. After his playing days Clymer managed until 1932 in the American Association, the New York State League, the International League, the Pacific Coast League, and the New York–Pennsylvania League. He managed the Columbus Senators in the American Association from 1904 to 1909 and again in 1920. He also managed the Buffalo Bisons in the International League in 1913 and 1914 and again in 1926 to 1930. Over 29 years as manager, he won seven championships and compiled a 2,122–1,762 record. Not bad for a player who only had 11 at bats!

Harry Coveleski

Harry "The Giant Killer" Coveleski had a meteoric run in the majors and then faded like a shooting star. The older brother of future Hall of Famer Stan Coveleski, he earned his nickname by beating the Giants three times in 5 days during a late-season playoff run in 1908. His first four seasons were fairly uneventful, but from 1914 through 1916 he won 65 games, after which he was ineffective again. His 2.34 ERA is still a Tigers' record. Covaseski was regarded as a player with unlimited potential who never really harnessed it. Around his time in the majors, he pitched seven seasons in the minors, mostly in the Southern Association, finishing up in 1919 with a 100–79 minor league pitching record. He managed the McAlester Miners in the Western Association in 1922. After retiring, Coveleski eventually opened a tavern called The Giant Killer in his hometown of Shamokin, Pennsylvania.

Born:
April 23, 1886
Shamokin, PA
Died:
August 4, 1950
Shamokin, PA

▷ Batted: Switch
▷ Threw: LH
▷ Position: P
▷ MLB Pitching Record: 81–55
▷ ERA: 2.39

Teams:
Philadelphia Phillies NL (1907–1909)
Cincinnati Reds NL (1910)
Detroit Tigers AL (1914–1918)

COVALESKI, PHILA. NAT'L.

Harry Frank Coveleski
Born: Harry Frank Kowalewski

Doc Crandall

CRANDALL, New York Nat'l

CRANDALL, N.Y. Nat'l

tour with the Braves, he pitched in the minors, mostly for the Los Angeles Angels in the Pacific Coast League. Crandall was player/manager of the Wichita Larks in the Western League for two seasons before he retired in 1929 with a 249–163 record for his 16 total minor league seasons. He came back in 1935 at age 47 to manage the Des Moines Demons in the Western League for one season.

Born:
October 8, 1887
Wadena, IN
Died:
August 17, 1951
Bell, CA

▷ Batted: RH
▷ Threw: RH
▷ Position: P
▷ MLB Pitching Record: 102–62
▷ ERA: 2.80

James "Doc" Crandall is considered baseball's first true relief pitcher. He was given his nickname because he usually came in to pitch in "emergency" situations. For five seasons he led the league in relief appearances, and helped the Giants to three pennants. Also an excellent pinch hitter, Crandall had a .285 lifetime average. In 1910 he posted a 17–4 record, batted .342 as a pinch hitter, and led the National League with 10 home runs. In 1915 he won 21 games in the short-lived Federal League. After his

Teams:
New York Giants NL (1908–1913)
St. Louis Cardinals NL (1913)
St. Louis Terriers FL (1914–1915)
St. Louis Browns AL (1916)
Boston Braves NL (1918)

James Otis Crandall

Birdie Cree

William "Birdie" Cree was a good ballplayer with an injury-plagued career. The 25-year-old rookie came up to the majors after two seasons with the Williamsport Millionaires in the Tri-State League, where he batted .332 in 1908. In his 7 years with New York, he was an excellent base stealer and a very good hitter. Cree's best year was 1911, when he batted .348 and stole 48 bases, good for third in the league, and ranked sixth in the MVP voting. As an outfielder, he had a very good arm, and was considered one of the best defensively. Toward the end of his career, Cree battled an ongoing weight problem that contributed to his injuries. Cree retired after the 1915 season at age 32 and went on to have a successful career in banking.

Born:
October 23, 1882
Khedive, PA
Died:
November 8, 1942
Sunbury, PA

▷ Batted: RH
▷ Threw: RH
▷ Position: OF
▷ Career BA: .292

William Franklin Cree

CREE, N.Y. AMER.

Team:
New York Highlanders/Yankees AL (1908–1915)

Lou Criger

Louis Criger

Born:
February 3, 1872
Elkhart, IN
Died:
May 14, 1934
Tucson, AZ

▷ Batted: RH
▷ Threw: RH
▷ Position: C
▷ Career BA: .221

Teams:
Cleveland Spiders NL (1896–1898)
St. Louis Perfectos/Cardinals NL (1899–1900)
Boston Americans/Red Sox AL (1901–1908)
St. Louis Browns AL (1909, 1912)
New York Highlanders AL (1910)

Lou Criger has the distinction of being the first catcher in Boston American League history. He was a very good defensive catcher who was weak offensively, although he did manage to bat .279 in 1898. He was the longtime batterymate of Hall of Famer Cy Young, catching for him for 12 years in Cleveland, St. Louis, and Boston. On May 5, 1904, he caught Young's perfect game, and he also caught a no-hitter on June 30, 1908. Criger also caught every inning in the first World Series in 1903. Between his tours with New York and St. Louis, Criger was player/manager for the Boyne City Boosters in the Michigan State League in 1911. After returning to the Browns, he retired in 1912 at 40 years old. Criger had played for so long that during the last four seasons of his 16-year career, he was one of the oldest players in the league.

Dode Criss

Born:
March 12, 1885
Sherman, MS
Died:
September 8, 1955
Sherman, MS

▷ Batted: LH
▷ Threw: RH
▷ Position: P/PH
▷ MLB Pitching Record: 3–9
▷ Career BA: .276

Team:
St. Louis Browns AL (1908–1911)

Dode Criss is regarded as baseball's first pinch-hit specialist. A pitcher by trade, although a weak one, Criss was the first player to pinch-hit 40 or more times in a season. His best year was 1908, his rookie year, when he batted .341 with 82 at bats. After four seasons in the majors, he went to the Houston Buffaloes in the Texas League, where he led the league in hits three times and pitched 3 no-hitters. He was definitely suited for the minors! Criss retired after the 1917 season with a .293 batting average and a 62–34 pitching record for the Buffaloes. Over a total of eight minor league seasons, he batted .308 and compiled a 93–59 pitching record. Dode Criss was inducted into the Texas League Hall of Fame in 2004, its first year of existence.

Dode Criss

Monte Cross

Teams:
Baltimore Orioles NL (1892)
Pittsburgh Pirates NL (1894–1895)
St. Louis Browns NL (1896–1897)
Philadelphia Phillies NL (1898–1901)
Philadelphia Athletics AL (1902–1907)

Born:
August 31, 1869
Philadelphia, PA
Died:
June 21, 1934
Philadelphia, PA

▷ Batted: RH
▷ Threw: RH
▷ Position: SS
▷ Career BA: .234

Montford Montgomery Cross

Monte Cross had a long steady career as a dependable shortstop with a very weak bat. He had the distinction of hitting the first home run of the 20th century, a 3-run homer on April 19, 1900. Kind of an early version of Mark Belanger, who had a similar career for the Orioles in the 1970s, Monte Cross was a pretty good fielder; his best overall season was 1897, when he batted .286 with 4 homers. He had 3,975 career putouts at the shortstop position. Cross played for the A's in the 1905 World Series against the Giants. After his lengthy MLB career, he played and managed in the minors, mostly for the American Association's Kansas City Blues and the Scranton Miners of the New York State League. Cross played part of the 1909 season for the Indianapolis Indians in the American Association, as pictured on his T206 card. He retired from the game at age 41 in 1911.

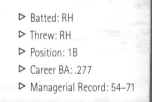

CROSS, INDIANAPOLIS

Harry Davis

H. DAVIS, PHILA. AMER.

A first baseman with a decent bat and some power, Harry Davis played for six different major league teams. In 1904 he batted .309 with 10 homers, a significant feat in the dead-ball era. He also batted over .300 four other times during his career. He was the American League leader in home runs from 1904 to 1907, and played on three Philadelphia World Series championship teams (1910, 1911, 1913). After his stint as player/manager of the Naps, he returned to the A's as player/coach through 1917. Davis then continued to coach for the A's and also did some scouting for them. He later worked in the Philadelphia tax department and then became a city councilor.

Harry H. Davis

Born:
July 19, 1873
Philadelphia, PA
Died:
August 11, 1947
Philadelphia, PA

▷ Batted: RH
▷ Threw: RH
▷ Position: 1B
▷ Career BA: .277
▷ Managerial Record: 54-71

DAVIS, PHILA. AMER.

Teams:
New York Giants NL (1895–1896)
Pittsburgh Pirates NL (1896–1898)
Louisville Colonels NL (1898)
Washington Senators NL (1898–1899)
Philadelphia Athletics AL (1901–1911, 1913–1917)
Cleveland Naps AL (player/manager: 1912)

Art Devlin

An outstanding athlete, Art Devlin was a great running back in college, excelled at baseball, and coached basketball and baseball. As a baseball player, he was a steady third baseman with a good glove and bat. His best season was 1906, when he batted .299 for the Giants. Devlin was the starting third baseman for the World Series champions in 1905, and led the league that year with 59 stolen bases. He also had four seasons with 30 or more thefts. After his tour with the Braves, he played and managed in the minors through 1918, finishing up with the Norfolk Tars in the Pacific Coast League. In the early 1920s, Devlin was the head baseball coach at Fordham University and in the late 1920s, he was the head basketball coach at the U.S. Naval Academy. He also coached with the Braves in 1926 and 1928.

Teams:
New York Giants NL (1904–1911)
Boston Braves NL (1912–1913)

Born:
October 16, 1879
Washington, D.C.
Died:
September 18, 1948
Jersey City, NJ

▷ Batted: RH
▷ Threw: RH
▷ Position: 3B
▷ Career BA: .269

Arthur McArthur Devlin

Bill Dinneen

William Henry Dinneen

Born:
April 5, 1876
Syracuse, NY
Died:
January 13, 1955
Syracuse, NY

▷ Batted: RH
▷ Threw: RH
▷ Position: P
▷ MLB Pitching Record: 170–177
▷ ERA: 3.01

Teams:
Washington Senators NL (1898–1899)
Boston Beaneaters NL (1900–1901)
Boston Americans AL (1902–1907)
St. Louis Browns AL (1907–1909)

"Big Bill" Dinneen was a very durable pitcher who, despite four 20-win seasons, was more highly regarded as an umpire after his tenure as a player. As a pitcher he won 3 of the 5 games in the first World Series in 1903. More incredibly, in 1904 he started 37 games and completed every one of them, an amazing 335 2/3 innings! As an umpire from 1909 to 1937, he was in eight World Series and was also one of the umpires for the first All-Star Game in 1933. The Hall of Fame placed Dinneen on the umpire Roll of Honor in 1946, and he was chosen to throw out the first pitch before Game 2 of the 1953 World Series in recognition of the 50th anniversary of his wins in the 1903 World Series.

Jiggs Donahue

Red Dooin

The career of John "Jiggs" Donahue, who got his nickname from his clog dancing, almost stopped before it really got started. In 1902 the Browns released the 22-year-old catcher after he hit .236 in 89 at bats. He rebuilt his career in 1903, playing first base with the American Association's Milwaukee Brewers and hitting .342 in 524 at bats with 7 home runs and 20 stolen bases. Donahue played first base when he returned to the majors for six more seasons. As first baseman for the 1906 World Series champion White Sox, he led the "Hitless Wonders" with his .257 batting average. Donahue led the league in fielding three times, and on May 31, 1908, he recorded 21 putouts in a 9-inning game. After his MLB days, Donahue was player/manager for the Texas League's Galveston Sand Crabs in 1911 before retiring from the game.

John Augustus Donahue

Born:
July 13, 1879
Springfield, OH
Died:
July 19, 1913
Columbus, OH

▷ Batted: LH
▷ Threw: LH
▷ Position: 1B
▷ Career BA: .255

Teams:
Pittsburgh Pirates NL (1900–1901)
Milwaukee Brewers AL (1901), AA (1902–1903)
St. Louis Browns AL (1902)
Chicago White Sox AL (1904–1909)
Washington Senators AL (1909)

Charles "Red" Dooin was one of the best defensive catchers of his era. Not a strong offensive force, one of Dooin's best seasons was 1904, when he hit .242 and finished third in the National League with 6 home runs. He led National League catchers in assists in 1908. Baseball legend says that he was the first catcher to wear shin guards, made of papier-mâché and worn under his socks (Roger Bresnahan was the first catcher to wear shin guards over his stockings). Dooin was offered a bribe to throw the 1908 World Series to the Giants but reported the offer to authorities. He was named the Phillies player/manager in 1910 and served in that position through the 1914 season, finishing second with the Phillies in 1913 and completing his tour with a 392–370 record. He later was player/manager for one season in the International League for the Reading Coal Barons in 1919. Dooin died of a heart attack at age 72.

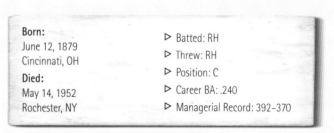

Born:
June 12, 1879
Cincinnati, OH
Died:
May 14, 1952
Rochester, NY

▷ Batted: RH
▷ Threw: RH
▷ Position: C
▷ Career BA: .240
▷ Managerial Record: 392–370

Teams:
Philadelphia Phillies NL (1902–1909; player/manager: 1910–1914)
New York Giants NL (1915, 1916)
Cincinnati Reds NL (1915)

Charles Sebastian Dooin

Mickey Doolan

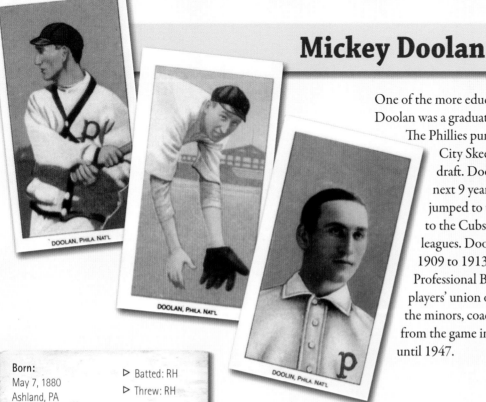

One of the more educated players of his era, Mickey "Doc" Doolan was a graduate of Villanova where he studied dentistry. The Phillies purchased him from the minor league Jersey City Skeeters after taking him in the 1904 Rule V draft. Doolan played shortstop in Philadelphia for the next 9 years, leading the league in fielding twice. He jumped to the Federal League in 1914 and was awarded to the Cubs in the Peace Agreement between the leagues. Doolan was team captain with the Phillies from 1909 to 1913 and was vice president of the Fraternity of Professional Baseball Players of America, the major league players' union of the day. He later managed two seasons in the minors, coached for the Cubs and the Reds, and retired from the game in 1932. Doolan then practiced dentistry until 1947.

Born:
May 7, 1880
Ashland, PA
Died:
November 1, 1951
Orlando, FL

▷ Batted: RH
▷ Threw: RH
▷ Position: SS
▷ Career BA: .230

Michael Joseph Doolan
Born: Michael Joseph Doolittle

Teams:
Philadelphia Phillies NL (1905–1913)
Baltimore Terrapins FL (1914–1915)
Chicago Whales FL (1915)
Chicago Cubs NL (1916)
New York Giants NL (1916)
Brooklyn Robins NL (1918)

Patsy Dougherty

Patsy Dougherty was one of the era's early scrappers, with a penchant for fighting. It is said that Boston sold him to New York because of his insubordination and that a fistfight with his Highlanders' manager Clark Griffith punched his ticket out of New York in 1906. White Sox manager Fielder Jones, who had previously brought him to the majors from the semipro ranks, then claimed Dougherty off waivers. Those 1906 White Sox were known as the "Hitless Wonders" but went on to win the World Series championship that season. Dougherty had earlier become the first player to hit 2 home runs in one World Series game with Boston in 1903. It was that season in which he led the league in at bats, runs scored, and hits, batting .331 with 4 home runs and 59 RBI. Dougherty stole 261 bases in his career, leading the league with 47 in 1908. After his playing days, Dougherty was president of the Interstate League and worked as a banker in Bolivar, New York.

Born:
October 27, 1876
Andover, NY
Died:
April 30, 19410
Bolivar, NY

▷ Batted: LH
▷ Threw: RH
▷ Position: OF
▷ Career BA: .284

Teams:
Boston Americans AL (1902–1904)
New York Highlanders AL (1904–1906)
Chicago White Sox AL (1906–1911)

Patrick Henry Dougherty

Slow Joe Doyle

Judd "Slow Joe" Doyle came up to the majors at age 24 after going 55–45 over five minor league seasons. Doyle earned his nickname from his extremely slow work on the mound and his deliberate stalling tactics. He was slow to recover from each outing as well, sometimes resting 8 to 10 days between appearances. Apparently some of that rest also came on the field's tarp, where Doyle was known to nap occasionally during games. Doyle threw shutouts in his first two major league starts, but his best season was 1907, when he went 11–11 in 29 games (23 starts) with a 2.65 ERA. He retired from the game after his five seasons in the majors.

Teams:
New York Highlanders AL (1906–1910)
Cincinnati Reds NL (1910)

Judd Bruce Doyle

Born:
September 15, 1881
Clay Center, KS
Died:
November 21, 1947
Tannersville, NY

▷ Batted: RH
▷ Threw: RH
▷ Position: P
▷ MLB Pitching Record: 22–21
▷ ERA: 2.85

Larry Doyle

"Laughing Larry" Doyle scored one of the more famous runs in early World Series history . . . or to be more exact, didn't score it. While playing for the Giants against the A's in the tenth inning of Game 5 of the 1911 World Series, Doyle scored from third on a fly out as night fell, but never touched home plate. Bill Klem, the home plate umpire, saw him miss the plate in the darkness but none of the A's did and no one tried to tag him. The A's had the last laugh, however, by closing out the Series in Game 6. A potent offensive player and solid defensive player, Doyle won three straight pennants with the Giants from 1911 to 1913, and won the National League batting title in 1915, leading the league in hits (189) and doubles (40). Doyle was named the NL MVP in 1912. He finished out his career as player/manager for the International League's Toronto Maple Leafs and the Southern Association's Nashville Volunteers, and retired in 1922.

Teams:
New York Giants NL (1907–1916, 1918–1920)
Chicago Cubs NL (1916–1917)

Born:
July 31, 1886
Caseyville, IL
Died:
March 1, 1974
Saranac Lake, NY

▷ Batted: LH
▷ Threw: RH
▷ Position: 2B
▷ Career BA: .290

Lawrence Joseph Doyle

Jack Dunn

DUNN, BALTIMORE

A fairly successful infielder and pitcher, Jack Dunn won 23 games in 1899 to help lead Brooklyn to a pennant. That season accounted for more than half of his career wins. Dunn's best offensive season was his last, 1904, when he hit .309 with his only home run in 1,622 career at bats. His biggest role in baseball history began in 1907 when as owner and manager, Dunn used his superior player-evaluation skills to build a minor league baseball juggernaut in Baltimore. Dunn's Orioles won 27 games in a row at one point, and were considered equal to the major league teams of the day. The Federal League's arrival in Baltimore forced him to sell off 12 of his Orioles, including a pitcher named George Ruth. Dunn got a very good price for Ruth, and called him his "$10,000 babe"—a nickname, and a legend, was born. Over 22 years, Dunn led his Orioles to an Eastern League pennant and seven consecutive International League pennants, while compiling a 1,959–1,408 record. He served as owner/manager until his sudden death in 1928.

Born:
October 6, 1872
Meadville, PA
Died:
October 22, 1928
Towson, MD

▷ Batted: RH
▷ Threw: RH
▷ Position: P/3B/SS
▷ MLB Pitching Record: 64–59
▷ Career ERA: 4.11
▷ Career BA: .245

Teams:
Brooklyn Bridegrooms/Superbas NL (1897–1900)
Philadelphia Phillies NL (1900–1901)
Baltimore Orioles AL (1901)
New York Giants NL (1902–1904)

John Joseph Dunn

Bull Durham

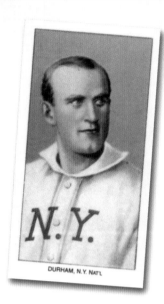

DURHAM, N.Y. NAT'L

Louis Raphael Durham

Born: Louis Raphael Staub

Louis "Bull" Durham needed four seasons to collect his career 29 innings pitched, but he could say he was undefeated in his career, going 2–0 with a 5.28 ERA. Most of Durham's notoriety was gained in the minors, however. In 1904 he had a respectable season for the Augusta Tourists of the South Atlantic League, pitching in front of a pretty good young player named Ty Cobb who was making his pro debut. In 1908, while pitching for the Indianapolis Indians in the American Association, Durham won 5 doubleheaders, collecting 5 shutouts in those 10 wins. Durham finished his pro career in 1913 in the Southern California League playing for Long Beach and Pasadena. From there it was an easy transition to his next career as an actor in silent films.

Teams:
Brooklyn Superbas NL (1904)
Washington Senators AL (1907)
New York Giants NL (1908–1909)

Born:
June 27, 1877
New Oxford, PA
Died:
June 28, 1960
Bentley, KS

▷ Batted: RH
▷ Threw: RH
▷ Position: P
▷ MLB Pitching Record: 2–0
▷ ERA: 5.28

Ted Easterly

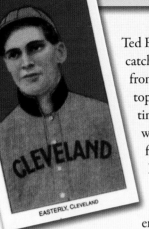

Ted Easterly was a good offensive catcher, hitting .300 over his career from the left side of the plate. He topped .300 for the season four times in the American League, which was good for two top-ten finishes. After jumping to the Federal League in 1914, he hit .335, finishing third in that league. But Easterly's enduring reputation was that of premier pinch hitter. He led the league in pinch hits in 1912, and is generally considered to be one of baseball's first pinch-hit specialists. After his major league career, Easterly played 4 more years in the minors for the Salt Lake City Bees, the Los Angeles Angels, and the Sacramento Senators of the Pacific Coast League and the Beaumont Exporters of the Texas League before retiring in 1920.

Born:	
April 20, 1885	▷ Batted: LH
Lincoln, NE	▷ Threw: RH
Died:	▷ Position: C
July 6, 1951	▷ Career BA: .300
Clearlake Highlands, CA	

Teams:
Cleveland Naps AL (1909–1912)
Chicago White Sox AL (1912–1913)
Kansas City Packers FL (1914–1915)

Theodore Harrison Easterly

Kid Elberfeld

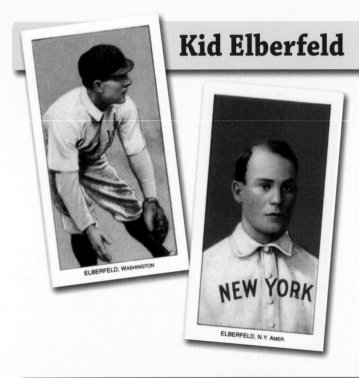

Norman "Kid" Elberfeld was known in his day as "The Tabasco Kid" because of his relentless jawing with the umpires. He was ejected from ballgames on a fairly regular basis for his insults and abuse. He was also an elite shortstop, and when Elberfeld and Honus Wagner were both in the minors, many considered Elberfeld a better prospect than Wagner. His best season was his first full season in 1901, when he hit .308 with 3 home runs, drove in 76 runs, and stole 23 bases. Elberfeld managed the Highlanders for part of the 1908 season and later managed 15 years in the minors, mostly in the Southern Association for the Chattanooga Lookouts and the Little Rock Travelers. He led the Travelers to second-place finishes in 1918 and 1919 and won the league championship in 1920. Elberfeld retired from the game in 1936 when he was 61 years old.

Norman Arthur Elberfeld

Born:	
April 13, 1875	▷ Batted: RH
Pomeroy, OH	▷ Threw: RH
Died:	▷ Position: SS
January 13, 1944	▷ Career BA: .271
Chattanooga, TN	▷ Managerial Record: 27–71

Teams:
Philadelphia Phillies NL (1898)
Cincinnati Reds NL (1899)
Detroit Tigers AL (1901–1903)
New York Highlanders AL (1903–1909;
player/manager: 1908)
Washington Senators AL (1910–1911)
Brooklyn Robins NL (1914)

Clyde Engle

ENGLE, N.Y. AMER.

Clyde "Hack" Engle had a pretty vanilla career in the majors, spiked with a few respectable seasons. In his first season, Engle set rookie records in hits (137) and RBI (71). Engle's place in baseball history was sealed in 1912 when his lazy fly ball in the tenth inning of the deciding game of the World Series was dropped by the Giants' Fred Snodgrass. Tris Speaker then singled Engle home to score the tying run. Speaker later scored on Larry Gardner's long fly ball, winning the championship for the Red Sox. After his tour in Cleveland, Engle managed the Topeka Savages in the Western League for one season. He then coached for the University of Vermont and for Yale University.

Teams:
New York Highlanders AL (1909–1910)
Boston Red Sox AL (1910–1914)
Buffalo Buffeds/Blues FL (1914–1915)
Cleveland Indians AL (1916)

Born:
March 19, 1884
Dayton, OH
Died:
December 26, 1939
Boston, MA

▷ Batted: RH
▷ Threw: RH
▷ Position: 1B/OF/3B
▷ Career BA: .265

Arthur Clyde Engle

Steve Evans

EVANS, ST. LOUIS NAT'L

Louis Richard Evans

Born:
February 17, 1885
Cleveland, OH
Died:
December 28, 1943
Cleveland, OH

▷ Batted: LH
▷ Threw: LH
▷ Position: OF/1B
▷ Career BA: .287

Teams:
New York Giants NL (1908)
St. Louis Cardinals NL (1909–1913)
Brooklyn Tip-Tops FL (1914–1915)
Baltimore Terrapins FL (1915)

Louis "Steve" Evans' best season was 1914 with the Brooklyn Tip-Tops of the Federal League. He finished second in the league in both batting (.348) and RBI (96) and third in the league in home runs (12). He hit just 4 home runs in 1915, splitting his season between Brooklyn and Baltimore, but his 34 doubles and 15 triples led the league. Evans set the record for being hit by pitches in 1910 with 31, a record that stood for 61 years. One of the game's biggest pranksters, Evans once took to the field at League Park in St. Louis with a parasol. After his MLB days and a two-season tour with the Toledo Iron Men of the American Association, Evans returned to private life in 1917 where he worked for the State of Ohio.

Bob Ewing

EWING, CINCINNATI

Teams:
Cincinnati Reds NL (1902–1909)
Philadelphia Phillies NL (1910–1911)
St. Louis Cardinals NL (1912)

George "Long Bob" Ewing was one of baseball's early workhorses, topping 280 innings pitched for four straight seasons, beginning in 1905, when he pitched 311 innings and posted his only 20-win season (20–11, 2.51). In that span, Ewing started 135 games and completed 111 of them, going 67–59. In 1907, Ewing and his trademark spitball made 37 starts and he threw 332 innings with a 1.73 ERA, going 17–19. Ewing moved on to the Phillies in 1910 at age 37, and went 16–14 with a 3.00 ERA that year. He pitched only 4 games for the Phillies in 1911 and only one inning for the Cards in 1912 before retiring. After his playing days Ewing returned to his farm in Wapakoneta to raise and race trotters, and he was later elected sheriff of Auglaize County. He was inducted into the Cincinnati Reds Hall of Fame in 2001.

George Lemuel Ewing

Born:
April 24, 1873
New Hampshire, OH

Died:
June 20, 1947
Wapakoneta, OH

▷ Batted: RH
▷ Threw: RH
▷ Position: P
▷ MLB Pitching Record: 124–118
▷ ERA: 2.49

Hobe Ferris

Despite the fact that Albert "Hobe" Ferris has baseball's all-time lowest on-base percentage for a player with more than 5,000 at bats (.265), he maintained a slugging percentage that was above league average over his 9-year career. Even though, as a rookie, he made 61 errors at second base after switching from shortstop in 1901 (the second-highest total in American League history), Ferris eventually became a premier defensive player. Ferris also holds the distinction of being the first player ejected from a game for fighting (1906), after he accused teammate Jack Hayden of loafing. However, his main claim to baseball fame is that he drove in all 3 runs in the Red Sox's 3–0 championship-deciding win in the first World Series in 1903. After his tour with the Browns, Ferris batted .281 in five seasons in the minors, mostly for the Minneapolis Millers of the American Association. He then retired from baseball and worked as a mechanic in Detroit.

FERRIS, ST. LOUIS AMER.

Teams:
Boston Americans/Red Sox AL (1901–1907)
St. Louis Browns AL (1908–1909)

Albert Sayles Ferris
Born: Albert Samuel Ferris

Born:
December 7, 1877
Trowbridge, England

Died:
March 18, 1938
Detroit, MI

▷ Batted: RH
▷ Threw: RH
▷ Position: 2B
▷ Career BA: .239

Art Fletcher

FLETCHER, N.Y.NAT'L

Art Fletcher burst out of the Texas League where he hit .273 with 35 stolen bases in 1908, his first pro season. He spent his next 2 years as a backup on John McGraw's Giants before earning the starting job in 1911. That year he helped the Giants win the pennant by hitting .319 with a .400 on-base percentage and 73 runs scored. From 1911 to 1920 he finished in the top four in the league in being hit by pitches. In 5 of the 6 years between 1913 and 1918, Fletcher led the league in this area, finishing second in 1915. His career number of 141 still stands in the top 25 on the all-time hit-by-pitch list. After his playing days, he managed the Phillies from 1923 to 1926 and in 1929 he managed the Yankees for 11 games. Fletcher went on to win several World Series rings as coach of the Murderer's Row Yankees under Miller Huggins.

Born:
January 5, 1885
Collinsville, IL
Died:
February 6, 1950
Los Angeles, CA

▷ Batted: RH
▷ Threw: RH
▷ Position: SS
▷ Career BA: .277
▷ Managerial Record: 237–383

Teams:
New York Giants NL (1909–1920)
Philadelphia Phillies NL (1920–1922; manager: 1923–1926)
New York Yankees AL (manager: 1929)

Arthur Fletcher

Russ Ford

Few people knew who Russ Ford was when the T206 set was released in 1909, but in the 1910 season Ford made his mark with an almost indelible rookie season. His 26 wins that year (26–6, 1.65 ERA) still stand as the American League rookie record. Ford's .813 winning percentage stood as a record for 24 years and his 8 shutouts stood as a Yankees' record for 68 years until Ron Guidry posted 9 in 1978. Ford was considered a spitball pitcher but actually was among the first to use an emery board to doctor the ball, a practice that was legal at the time. In 1914, Ford won 21 games for Buffalo, leading the Federal League with his .778 winning percentage, but his ongoing arm issues finally ended his MLB career in 1915. He returned to the minors in 1916, going 16–9 for the Western League's Denver Bears. After going just 3–3 in 1917 between the Bears and the American Association's Toledo Iron Men, Ford retired with a seven-season 107–71 minor league record.

Born:
April 25, 1883
Brandon, Manitoba, Canada
Died:
January 24, 1960
Rockingham, NC

▷ Batted: RH
▷ Threw: RH
▷ Position: P
▷ MLB Pitching Record: 99–71
▷ ERA: 2.59

Teams:
New York Highlanders/Yankees AL (1909–1913)
Buffalo Buffeds/Blues FL (1914–1915)

FORD, NEW YORK AMER.

Russell William Ford

John Ganzel

The long road of John Ganzel's pro career led to the first baseman essentially purchasing himself from the Highlanders to play for his own minor league club. The year was 1905 and Ganzel had already put in four-plus seasons in the majors. He hit .277 in 1903 for the Highlanders and .260 in 1904, finishing fourth in the American League with 6 home runs. The Highlanders lost the pennant on the last day of the 1904 season, and Ganzel purchased Grand Rapids of the Central League. He then paid New York $3,000 for his own release. He later managed the Reds and the Tip-Tops as well as the Rochester Bronchos/Hustlers of the Eastern League/International League and the Kansas City Blues of the American Association. Ganzel's Rochester Bronchos were league champs in 1909, 1910, and 1911. He was active in the Florida State League's Orlando franchise from 1938 until 1952. He was one of five brothers to play pro ball, and his nephew Foster "Babe" Ganzel played for the Senators for part of the 1927 and 1928 seasons.

Teams:

Pittsburgh Pirates NL (1898)
Chicago Orphans NL (1900)
New York Giants NL (1901)
New York Highlanders AL (1903–1904)
Cincinnati Reds NL (1907; player/manager: 1908)
Brooklyn Tip-Tops FL (manager: 1915)

John Henry Ganzel

Born:
April 7, 1874
Kalamazoo, MI
Died:
January 14, 1959
Orlando, FL

▷ Batted: RH
▷ Threw: RH
▷ Position: 1B
▷ Career BA: .251
▷ Managerial Record: 90–99

George Gibson

Born:
July 22, 1880
London, Ontario, Canada
Died:
January 25, 1967
London, Ontario, Canada

▷ Batted: RH
▷ Threw: RH
▷ Position: C
▷ Career BA: .236
▷ Managerial Record: 413–344

Teams:

Pittsburgh Pirates NL (1905–1916; manager: 1920–1922, 1932–1934)
New York Giants NL (1917–1918)
Chicago Cubs NL (manager: 1925)

Canadian born George "Mooney" Gibson had a distinguished career as a player and manager over a period of 21 years. He was only an average hitter, but he was a very good defensive catcher who developed young pitchers and was a workhorse behind the plate. During one stretch in 1909, he broke the record for catching consecutive games with 112; his streak finally ended at an amazing 140 games. Gibson was considered a field general by his teammates. After his playing days, he managed the Toronto Maple Leafs in the International League in 1919 before going back to Pittsburgh as manager. In the 1920s and 1930s, as manager for the Pirates and Cubs, he had some pretty good teams and ended 69 games over .500. Gibson became the first baseball player elected to the Canadian Sports Hall of Fame, was named Canada's best ballplayer for the first half of the century, and was elected to the Canadian Baseball Hall of Fame in 1987.

George C. Gibson

Dolly Gray

William "Dolly" Gray launched his career with the Los Angeles Angels in the Pacific Coast League. In his rookie season, he won 23 games, and followed that up with season wins of 24, 27, 32, and 26. He seemed destined for major league stardom, but unfortunately, once he got to the Senators, he never quite fulfilled his potential, winding up 36 games below .500 in his 3-year career. As a matter of fact, his winning percentage (.227) is one of the worst of all time. He returned to the Pacific Coast League to play through the 1913 season, posting a 153–94 career record. He then managed the Sherman Lions of the Texas Oklahoma League in 1914 and the Flint Vehicles of the Michigan-Ontario League in 1921, before retiring. He was elected to the Pacific Coast League Hall of Fame in 2008. Unfortunately he just didn't have enough to make it in the big leagues.

GRAY, WASHINGTON

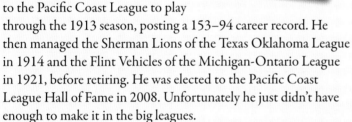

Born:
December 4, 1878
Houghton, MI
Died:
April 4, 1956
Yuba City, CA

▷ Batted: LH
▷ Threw: LH
▷ Position: P
▷ MLB Pitching Record: 15–51
▷ ERA: 3.52

Team:
Washington Senators AL (1909–1911)

William Denton Gray

Bill Hallman

Born:
March 15, 1876
Philadelphia, PA
Died:
April 23, 1950
Philadelphia, PA

▷ Batted: LH
▷ Threw: LH
▷ Position: OF
▷ Career BA: .235

Bill Hallman played parts of four seasons in the majors with the Brewers, White Sox, and Pirates. Hallman's only season as a regular outfielder came in 1901, the first year of the American League. That season, he earned the distinction of being the first AL outfielder to lead the league in errors with 26. Hallman also finished in the top ten in games played, at bats, doubles, and sacrifice hits, but that was his last season as an everyday player. His last year in the majors was 1907, but he played seven more seasons in the minors, three of them with the Kansas City Blues in the American Association. Although only a .235 career hitter in the major leagues, he hit .288 in his 11 minor league seasons.

Teams:
Milwaukee Brewers AL (1901)
Chicago White Sox AL (1903)
Pittsburgh Pirates NL (1906–1907)

William Harry Hallman

HALLMAN, KANSAS CITY

Topsy Hartsel

Bill Hinchman

HARTSEL, PHILA. AMER.

Born:
June 26, 1874
Polk, OH
Died:
October 14, 1944
Toledo, OH

▷ Batted: LH
▷ Threw: LH
▷ Position: OF
▷ Career BA: .276

Tully "Topsy" Hartsel finished in the league's top ten in walks in ten out of his 14 MLB seasons. In five of those seasons, he led the league. The main reason is that at 5 feet 5 inches and 155 pounds, Hartsel presented a small target for pitchers of the day. His 121 walks in 1905 remained a league record until pitchers started pitching around Babe Ruth in the 1920s. The diminutive leadoff hitter hit .276 over his big league career, leading the A's to four pennants in his ten seasons in Philly. He twice topped .400 in on-base percentage, leading the league both times, and twice topped 100 runs scored, leading the league with 109 in 1902. A respected baseball mind and gifted sign stealer, Hartsel was essentially an on-the-field coach to Connie Mack for most of his time with the A's. Hartsel went on to manage the American Association's Toledo Mud Hens from 1912 to 1914, and retired in Toledo to open an "automatic baseball" business. He later worked at the Community Traction Company until 1941 and managed their baseball team.

Teams:
Louisville Colonels NL (1898–1899)
Cincinnati Reds NL (1900)
Chicago Orphans NL (1901)
Philadelphia Athletics AL (1902–1911)

Tully Frederick Hartsel

HINCHMAN, CLEVELAND

Bill Hinchman came up to the majors from the Ilion Typewriters of the New York State League in 1905 at age 22. His first five seasons were not memorable offensively or defensively. In 1910 he returned to the minors as player/manager of the Columbus Senators of the American Association where he got hot, batting .309 in 1912, .297 in 1913, and .366 in 1914. He came back to the majors with a vengeance, posting a .307 average in 1915 and .315 in 1916 for the Pirates, good for fourth and third in the league, respectively. In 1916 he led the league with 16 triples, and his 76 RBI were good for third in the league. After his tour with the Pirates, Hinchman's bat was silent until 1931 when, at age 48, he returned to the game, playing for the Houston Buffaloes in the Texas League and the Jersey City Skeeters in the International League.

William White Hinchman

Teams:
Cincinnati Reds NL (1905–1906)
Cleveland Naps AL (1907–1909)
Pittsburgh Pirates NL (1915–1920)

Born:
April 4, 1883
Philadelphia, PA
Died:
February 20, 1963
Columbus, OH

▷ Batted: RH
▷ Threw: RH
▷ Position: OF
▷ Career BA: .261

Dick Hoblitzell

Danny Hoffman

HOBLITZELL, CINCINNATI

HOFFMAN, ST. LOUIS AMER.

Dick "Hobby" Hoblitzell was only 19 years old when the Reds purchased him late in the 1908 season from the Clarksburg Bees of the Western Pennsylvania League. As a rookie in 1909, he was considered a prodigy, batting .308, which was good for third place in the National League, behind the likes of Honus Wagner and Mike Mitchell. A solid first baseman, respected by both teammates and opponents, he was sold to the Red Sox in July 1914. He hit .319 that year to help the Sox become pennant contenders and played in the 1915 and 1916 World Series. Hoblitzell left the Sox to serve in the U.S. Army Dental Corps in WWI. After the war, he became player/manager of the South Atlantic League's Charlotte Hornets for several years, winning the league pennant in 1923. After retiring to run the family farm, he later hosted a radio sports show, was a newspaper sports columnist, an umpire for youth baseball, and was active in local politics.

Daniel John Hoffman

Born:
March 2, 1880
Canton, CT
Died:
March 14, 1922
Manchester, CT

▷ Batted: LH
▷ Threw: LH
▷ Position: OF
▷ Career BA: .256

Teams:
Philadelphia Athletics AL (1903–1906)
New York Highlanders AL (1906–1907)
St. Louis Browns AL (1908–1911)

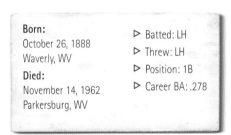

Born:
October 26, 1888
Waverly, WV
Died:
November 14, 1962
Parkersburg, WV

▷ Batted: LH
▷ Threw: LH
▷ Position: 1B
▷ Career BA: .278

Teams:
Cincinnati Reds NL (1908–1914)
Boston Red Sox AL (1914–1918)

Richard Carleton Hoblitzell

Outfielder Danny Hoffman began his solid 9-year major league career in 1903 with the Athletics at age 23. He found his best success early in his career, batting .299 for the A's in 1904 and .261 the following year. Unfortunately, in 1904, Hoffman was hit in the eye by a pitch from Boston's southpaw, Jesse Tannehill, seriously impairing his ability to hit against left-handed pitchers. Hoffman led the league with his 46 stolen bases in 1905, and helped the Athletics win the pennant that year. However, in 1906, the Athletics traded Hoffman to the New York Highlanders for Dave Fultz. It was with the Highlanders, in 1907, that he hit 5 homers, good for second place in the league. After his tour with the Browns, Hoffman played five seasons in the minors, three with the Wilkes-Barre Barons in the New York State League, after which he retired in 1915 as a career .284 minor league hitter.

Solly Hofman

HOFMAN, CHICAGO NAT'L

Arthur "Circus Solly" Hofman played most of his career with the Cubs, winning four pennants in 5 years starting in 1909. Initially a utility player, he settled into center field in 1909, where he earned his nickname with his acrobatic catches. A career .269 hitter, he hit .325 in 1910 with 24 doubles, 16 triples, and 3 home runs, finishing third in the National League in batting average, second in slugging percentage, and fourth in RBI with 86. He also stole 29 bases that season and 208 in his career. Hofman was the detonator in the famous "Merkle's Boner" play in 1908. He fielded Al Bridwell's apparent game-winning single and called out that Merkle had never touched second base. He then overthrew Evers into the crowd, raising the question of whether Evers had the actual game ball when he successfully executed the appeal. Hofman retired from the game after the 1916 season when he was 33 years old.

Born:
October 29, 1882
St. Louis, MO
Died:
March 10, 1956
St. Louis, MO

▷ Batted: RH
▷ Threw: RH
▷ Position: OF
▷ Career BA: .269

Teams:
Pittsburgh Pirates NL (1903, 1912–1913)
Chicago Cubs NL (1904–1912, 1916)
Brooklyn Tip-Tops FL (1914)
Buffalo Blues FL (1915)
New York Yankees AL (1916)

Arthur Frederick Hofman

Rudy Hulswitt

HULSWITT, ST. LOUIS NAT'L

Teams:
Louisville Colonels NL (1899)
Philadelphia Phillies NL (1902–1904)
Cincinnati Reds NL (1908)
St. Louis Cardinals NL (1909–1910)

Rudolph Edward Hulswitt

Born:
February 23, 1877
Newport, KY
Died:
January 16, 1950
Louisville, KY

▷ Batted: RH
▷ Threw: RH
▷ Position: SS
▷ Career BA: .253

Rudy Hulswitt hit .272 as a 25-year-old rookie for the Phillies in 1902 and followed that up with another solid season in 1903. Hulswitt hit just .247 that year, but doubled his doubles total to 22, adding 9 triples and 58 RBI in 519 at bats. He also, however, made his indelible mark on the National League by setting the shortstop record for errors in a season at 81, which still stands today. A badly injured shoulder cost him three seasons in the middle of his career, but he returned in 1908 to hit .228 for the Reds in 430 at bats at 31 years old. His playing time declined over the next two seasons and he retired in 1910 to play and manage off and on in the minors through 1941. He also coached and scouted for the Red Sox and the Dodgers into the 1930s.

Fielder Jones

A fine ballplayer and manager, Fielder Jones played with pennant-winners Brooklyn (1899, 1900) and Chicago (1901). There was no World Series in 1899 or 1901, but in 1900 Brooklyn took the win. Jones had a 70-game streak in reaching base at least once, and he hit over .300 six times. He batted .354 in 1896, but as a part-time player. His best year was 1901, when he batted .321. Considered one of the most intelligent managers of all time, Jones is known for leading the "Hitless Wonders" White Sox to the 1906 World Series championship solely on pitching, defense, and baserunning. The team batting average was .230. After his stint with the White Sox, he coached for Oregon State University and served as president of the Northwestern League from 1912 to 1914. He then managed the St. Louis Terriers and the St. Louis Browns before retiring to go into the lumber business in Oregon.

Fielder Allison Jones

Teams:
Brooklyn Bridegrooms/Superbas NL (1896–1900)
Chicago White Sox AL (1901–1903; player/manager: 1904–1908)
St. Louis Terriers FL (player/manager: 1914–1915)
St. Louis Browns AL (manager: 1916–1918)

Born:
August 13, 1871
Shinglehouse, PA

Died:
March 13, 1934
Portland, OR

▷ Batted: LH
▷ Threw: RH
▷ Position: OF
▷ Career BA: .285
▷ Managerial Record: 683–582

Teams:
Washington Senators AL (1901)
New York Highlanders AL (1903)
Brooklyn Superbas NL (1906–1910)

Timothy Joseph Jordan

Tim Jordan

One of the early power hitters of the game, Tim Jordan led the National League twice in home runs, smacking 12 for the Superbas in 1906 and then another 12 in 1908, a significant achievement during the dead-ball era. In 1906 he batted .262 with 118 hits to go along with his long balls. Defensively, Jordan was a very good first baseman. Although knee problems cut short his time in the majors, he went on to star in the minors through the 1916 season, playing mostly for the Toronto Maple Leafs in the International League, where he hit .330 with 20 home runs in 1911 and .312 with 19 homers in 1912. Jordan staged a comeback in 1920 to bat .256 in 238 at bats and 69 games for the International League's Syracuse Stars when he was 41 years old. He then retired, with a career .296 batting average in 4,614 at bats and 1,291 games over his 11 minor league seasons.

Born:
February 14, 1879
New York, NY.

Died:
September 13, 1949
Bronx, NY

▷ Batted: LH
▷ Threw: LH
▷ Position: 1B
▷ Career BA: .261

Ed Killian

"Twilight Ed" Killian did an awful lot in his 8-year career. A two-time 20-plus game winner, his 2.38 ERA is 24th on the all-time list. He also gave up fewer home runs than any pitcher in history, and actually once went 1,001 innings before coughing one up. His 1904 duel with pitching great Cy Young is considered one of the greatest pitching performances, by both men, of all time. Both Young and Killian pitched 14 scoreless innings before the Red Sox finally scored in the 15th. Killian also played in the 1907 and 1908 World Series, led the American League in shutouts with 8 in 1905, and had a 1.78 ERA in 1907. Killian played for the Toronto Maple Leafs in the Eastern League for two uneventful seasons before retiring in 1911 to work for the Ford Motor Company as a mechanic. He died from cancer at age 51.

Teams:
Cleveland Naps AL (1903)
Detroit Tigers AL (1904–1910)

Edwin Henry Killian

Born:
November 12, 1876
Racine, WI
Died:
July 18, 1928
Detroit, MI

▷ Batted: LH
▷ Threw: LH
▷ Position: P
▷ MLB Pitching Record: 102–78
▷ ERA: 2.38

Johnny Kling

Between 1906 and 1910 Johnny Kling was arguably the best defensive catcher in the game. In those four seasons, he helped the Cubs to four National League pennants and two World Series championships. Kling had a solid bat with a .271 career average. Not only was he a very good ballplayer, he also won the World Pocket Billiards championship, and actually took off the 1909 season to defend his title and open a billiards parlor in Kansas City. Over his 13 seasons, he had an outstanding .971 fielding percentage. As player/manager of the Braves in 1912, he finished in last place, even though he hit .317 that year. Kling became a successful real estate developer in Kansas City after his MLB days. He was the owner of the Kansas City Blues in the American Association from 1933 to 1937, and during his tenure he increased attendance to second in the league and banned segregated seating in the stadium.

John Kling

Born:
November 13, 1875
Kansas City, MO
Died:
January 31, 1947
Kansas City, MO

▷ Batted: RH
▷ Threw: RH
▷ Position: C
▷ Career BA: .271
▷ Managerial Record: 52–101

Teams:
Chicago Orphans/Cubs NL (1900–1911)
Boston Rustlers/Braves NL (1911; player/manager: 1912)
Cincinnati Reds NL (1913)

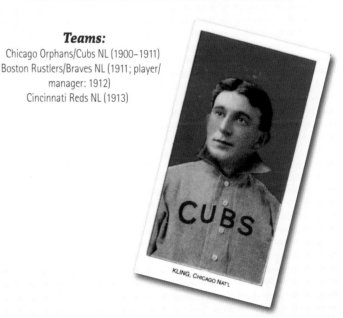

Ed Konetchy

Ed "The Candy Kid" Konetchy was a very steady, durable first baseman for six different teams over his 15-year MLB career. He had a memorable year in 1910, when he batted .302 and had a 20-game hitting streak. Konetchy led the league in doubles in 1911 and had some MVP voting consideration in both 1911 and 1912. He managed to bang out an impressive 2,150 hits over his time in the majors. He played for the Texas League's Fort Worth Panthers for three seasons, slamming 41 homers in 1925 and 21 in 1926, and winning the pennant in 1925. Konetchy also managed six seasons in the minors, three of them with the Lacrosse Black Hawks of the Wisconsin State League, before retiring in 1942. He is remembered for being a hero in 1911 when the Cards were involved in a train crash. Twelve people died, but more would have perished if he had not carried many of the injured to safety.

Teams:
St. Louis Cardinals NL (1907–1913)
Pittsburgh Pirates NL (1914)
Pittsburgh Rebels FL (1915)
Boston Braves NL (1916–1918)
Brooklyn Robins NL (1919–1921)
Philadelphia Phillies NL (1921)

Born:
September 3, 1885
La Crosse, WI
Died:
May 27, 1947
Fort Worth, TX

▷ Batted: RH
▷ Threw: RH
▷ Position: 1B
▷ Career BA: .281

Edward Joseph Konetchy

Arlie Latham

Arlie Latham joined the St. Louis Browns as they were about to win four consecutive American Association pennants, from 1885 to 1888. An expert base stealer, he was known as a fun-loving third baseman who taunted and teased opponents relentlessly from the dugout and as a third-base coach. As MLB's first full-time coach, Latham's antics resulted in the official introduction of the coaches' box as a way to confine him. Latham may have cost the Browns a fifth-straight pennant in 1889 when an umpire refused to call a game for darkness, which would have given the Browns a win that could have clinched the title. Latham lit 12 candles in the dugout in protest, and lit them again after the umpire blew them out. The umpire then forfeited the game to Brooklyn, who went on to win the pennant that year. After playing for the Pirates and Reds, Latham returned to the Browns as player/manager in 1896. During his stint as player and third-base coach for the Giants in 1909, Latham had the distinction of being the oldest player in the major leagues at age 49.

Teams:
Buffalo Bisons NL (1880)
St. Louis Browns AA/NL (1883–1889; player/manager: 1896)
Chicago Pirates PL (1890)
Cincinnati Reds NL (1890–1895)
Washington Senators NL (1899)
New York Giants NL (1909)

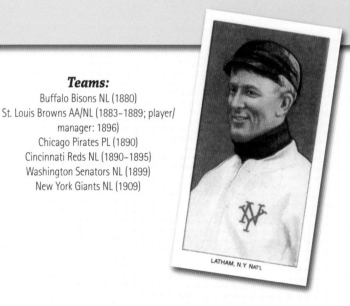

Born:
March 15, 1860
West Lebanon, NH
Died:
November 29, 1952
Garden City, NY

▷ Batted: RH
▷ Threw: RH
▷ Position: 3B
▷ Career BA: .269
▷ Managerial Record: 0–3

Walter Arlington Latham

Tommy Leach

In 1903, Tommy Leach played in the first World Series game, and hit 4 triples, which is still an MLB record. Because of his speed, he was converted from the infield to the outfield and excelled defensively. Nicknamed "Wee Tommy" because of his slight build, Leach led the National League in home runs in 1902 with 6, and twice led the league in runs scored. He batted over .300 twice and had over 2,000 hits in his career. Leach managed in the Florida State League from 1920 through 1928, mostly for the Tampa Smokers, and later scouted for the Boston Braves from 1935 to 1941. Leach retired to Florida and went into the citrus business.

Teams:
Louisville Colonels NL (1898–1899)
Pittsburgh Pirates NL (1900–1912, 1918)
Chicago Cubs NL (1912–1914)
Cincinnati Reds NL (1915)

Born:
November 4, 1877
French Creek, NY
Died:
September 29, 1969
Haines City, FL

▷ Batted: RH
▷ Threw: RH
▷ Position: OF/3B
▷ Career BA: .269

Thomas William Leach

Lefty Leifield

Teams:
Pittsburgh Pirates NL (1905–1912)
Chicago Cubs NL (1912–1913)
St. Louis Browns AL (1918–1920)

Albert "Lefty" Leifield was a solid, durable pitcher who had his best years with the Pirates. After going 26–9 in 1905 for the Des Moines Underwriters in the Western League, the 21-year-old southpaw came up to Pittsburgh. There he had a 20-win season in 1907, and he won 15 or more games five times. His 2.47 lifetime ERA was outstanding. 1909 was his best year, when he had a 19-win season for the World Series champion Pirates. After being released in 1913, Leifield pitched in the minors, going 21–19 in the Pacific League for the San Francisco Seals in 1914. He then went 17–14 in 1915 and 19–14 in 1916 for the American Association's St. Paul Saints. In 1918 Leifield returned to St. Louis to pitch and coach until 1920. After his playing days, he coached for the Browns, managed the Oklahoma City Indians in the Western League in 1929, and returned to St. Paul to manage the Saints from 1930 to 1932.

Born:
September 5, 1883
Trenton, IL
Died:
October 10, 1970
Alexandria, VA

▷ Batted: LH
▷ Threw: LH
▷ Position: P
▷ MLB Pitching Record: 124–97
▷ ERA: 2.47

Albert Peter Leifield

Paddy Livingston

LIVINGSTONE, PHILA. AMER.

Paddy Livingston had a long career between the majors and the minors, but his MLB days lasted only seven seasons. A pretty good catcher with a very weak bat, he was a friendly and gregarious fellow. Livingston is most known for making the throw to Frank "Home Run" Baker to catch Ty Cobb stealing third base in August 1909. The play was captured on film, showing Cobb coming in spikes high. Baker was injured on the play, and the now-famous photo hangs in the Hall of Fame. Around his MLB tours, he played seven seasons in the minors, four of them with the Indianapolis Indians of the American Association. He was player/manager for the 1917 Milwaukee Brewers in the American Association before retiring as a player with a .313 minor league batting average. Livingston then coached for the A's and later worked for the city of Cleveland, retiring in 1963. He lived to age 97, and was the last surviving player from the American League's first season (1901).

Teams:
Cleveland Blues AL (1901)
Cincinnati Reds NL (1906)
Philadelphia Athletics AL (1909–1911)
Cleveland Naps AL (1912)
St. Louis Cardinals NL (1917)

Born:
January 14, 1880
Cleveland, OH
Died:
September 19, 1977
Cleveland, OH

▷ Batted; RH
▷ Threw: RH
▷ Position: C
▷ Career BA: .209

Patrick Joseph Livingston

Hans Lobert

Born:
October 18, 1881
Wilmington, DE
Died:
September 14, 1968
Philadelphia, PA

▷ Batted: RH
▷ Threw: RH
▷ Position: 3B
▷ Career BA: .274
▷ Managerial Record: 42–111

Teams:
Pittsburgh Pirates NL (1903)
Chicago Cubs NL (1905)
Cincinnati Reds NL (1906–1910)
Philadelphia Phillies NL (1911–1914; manager: 1938, 1942)
New York Giants NL (1915–1917)

John Bernard Lobert

John Lobert, or "Hans Number 2," as he was nicknamed by Honus Wagner (Hans Number 1, of course), was a reliable third baseman for several different teams for 14 seasons. Probably the fastest player in the game, he stole 40 or more bases four times and 20 or more bases nine times. Lobert also batted .300 or better four times. After his playing days, he spent eight years as coach of the U.S. Military Academy at West Point. He then managed the Bridgeport Bears in the Eastern League, finishing in second place from 1929 through 1931. Lobert managed the Jersey City Skeeters in the International League in 1932 before returning to work for the Phillies from 1934 to 1941, managing the team for 2 games at the end of the 1938 season. He took over as skipper of the 1942 Phillies when he was 60 years old, and proceeded to lose 109 games. He then coached for the Reds for 2 years and scouted for the Giants until his death at age 86.

LOBERT, CINCINNATI

Harry Lord

Harry Lord began his MLB career with the Boston Americans in 1907 while attending Bates College. In 1908, after graduation, he rejoined the team, which had been renamed the Boston Red Sox. Although he did fairly well in his rookie year, he really took off in 1909, batting .311 with 36 stolen bases. Lord had a stellar 9-year career in the majors. His best year was 1911, when he batted .321 for the White Sox and stole 43 bases. A decent fielder with a strong arm, Lord was a starter at third base for most of his career. He managed to swipe 206 bases over that period. He became player/manager of the Buffalo Buffeds in the Federal League for 1 year in 1915, delivering a 60–49 record. He was then player/manager in the Eastern League for the Lowell Grays in 1916 and the Portland Duffs in 1917 before managing the Jersey Skeeters in the International League in 1918.

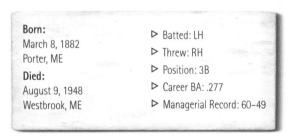

Born:
March 8, 1882
Porter, ME
Died:
August 9, 1948
Westbrook, ME

▷ Batted: LH
▷ Threw: RH
▷ Position: 3B
▷ Career BA: .277
▷ Managerial Record: 60–49

Teams:
Boston Americans/Red Sox AL (1907–1910)
Chicago White Sox AL (1910–1914)
Buffalo Buffeds FL (player/manager: 1915)

Harry Donald Lord

Harry Lumley

Harry Garfield Lumley

Born:
September. 29, 1880
Forest City, PA
Died:
May 22, 1938
Binghamton, NY

▷ Batted: LH
▷ Threw: LH
▷ Position: OF
▷ Career BA: .274
▷ Managerial Record: 55–98

Team:
Brooklyn Superbas NL (1904–1910; player/manager: 1909)

In the 20th century only one rookie led his league in triples and homers, and his name was Harry "Judge" Lumley. As a 23-year-old rookie in 1904, Lumley also finished second only to Honus Wagner in total bases and second only to "Bad Bill" Dahlen in RBI. He developed into one of the most feared sluggers of his era and Brooklyn's most popular player. By the time Lumley was included in the T206 set in 1909, his once-bright career was in full decline due to ongoing weight issues and resulting injuries. An injured ankle led to a .216 average in 1908, and he only played 55 games in 1909 due to a shoulder injury, hitting .250 with no homers as the Superbas' player/manager. He went just 55–98 (.359) as Brooklyn's manager, and was replaced in 1910 by Bill Dahlen. Lumley was player/manager of the Binghamton Bingoes in the New York State League for three seasons. He retired in 1913 as a career .335 minor league hitter and ran a tavern in Binghamton.

Carl Lundgren

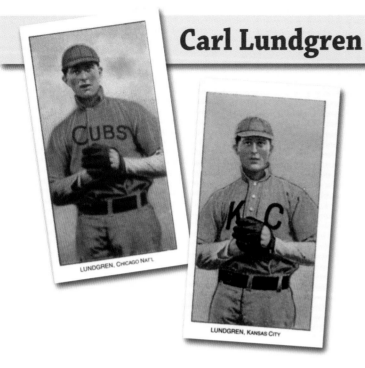

LUNDGREN, CHICAGO NAT'L

LUNDGREN, KANSAS CITY

Carl Lundgren was a very talented pitcher who played for the Cubs for his entire MLB career. Nicknamed "The Human Icicle" because he was so effective when pitching in cold weather, Lundgren played on two World Series championship teams with the Cubs (1907, 1908) and helped them win the National League pennant in 1906. His best year was 1907 when he went 18–7, but he had several other very good years going 17–9 in 1904, 13–5 in 1905, and 17–6 in 1906. His 2.42 career ERA was outstanding. Unfortunately, other Cubs pitchers, such as Mordecai Brown, Ed Reulbach, and Orval Overall, were even better and overshadowed him. Lundgren dabbled in the minors through 1912, going 26–22 over three seasons. He then coached for the University of Michigan for seven seasons before coaching at his alma mater, the University of Illinois Urbana-Champaign, until his death in 1934 at the age of 54.

Born:
February 16, 1880
Marengo, IL
Died:
August 21, 1934
Marengo, IL

▷ Batted: RH
▷ Threw: RH
▷ Position: P
▷ MLB Pitching Record: 91–55
▷ ERA: 2.42

Team:
Chicago Orphans/Cubs NL (1902–1909)

Carl Leonard Lundgren

Nick Maddox

Nick Maddox had a short but effective major league career, throwing a no-hitter as a rookie and winning 23 games his second year. His 2.29 ERA was outstanding. Unfortunately, he faded into the sunset pretty quickly. His MLB record was 5–1, 23–8, 13–8, 2–3—and then out. Maddox then pitched for the Kansas City Blues and the Louisville Colonels of the American Association and the Wichita Witches of the Western League. He had an excellent first season back in the minors, going 22–13 for Kansas City in 1911. However, he struggled for the remainder of his pro career, finally retiring in 1914 at age 27 with a 48–49 record compiled over five minor league seasons.

Nicholas Maddox

MADDOX, PITTSBURG

Team:
Pittsburgh Pirates NL (1907–1910)

Born:
November 9, 1886
Govanstown, MD
Died:
November 27, 1954
Pittsburgh, PA

▷ Batted: LH
▷ Threw: RH
▷ Position: P
▷ MLB Pitching Record: 43–20
▷ ERA: 2.29

George McBride

George "Pinch" McBride was the prototypical great-glove, no-bat player. Even with an anemic .218 lifetime batting average, he played in the big leagues for 16 seasons because he was one of the best—if not *the* best—shortstop in the American League for several years. Known for his great range and acrobatic fielding plays, McBride led the American League in fielding for four straight seasons (1912–1915). From all indications, he only hit well in clutch situations, thus earning his nickname, "Pinch." Late in the 1921 season, while managing the Senators, McBride was seriously injured when he was hit in the face with a ball, which led to his retirement. He coached for the Detroit Tigers in the mid- to late 1920s before returning to Milwaukee, where he had started his career with his hometown team in 1901.

Teams:
Milwaukee Brewers AL (1901)
Pittsburgh Pirates NL (1905)
St. Louis Cardinals NL (1905–1906)
Washington Senators AL (1908–1920; manager: 1921)

Born:
November 20, 1880
Milwaukee, WI
Died:
July 2, 1973
Milwaukee, WI

▷ Batted: RH
▷ Threw: RH
▷ Position: SS
▷ Career BA: .218
▷ Managerial Record: 80–73

George Florian McBride

Moose McCormick

Nicknamed because of his stature, Harry "Moose" McCormick became baseball's first elite pinch hitter. John McGraw created that niche for McCormick because he was too slow to be an everyday outfielder. He is most known for scoring what would have been the winning run against the Cubs in 1908 if not for Fred Merkle's infamous "bonehead play" that cost the Giants that year's pennant. He did collect 413 at bats for the Giants in 1909, hitting .291 with 3 homers and 27 RBI. After 1909, he left MLB for 2 years, returning to hit .294 in 119 at bats in 99 games in 1912 and 1913. McCormick was once daydreaming on deck, looked up to see an errant outfield throw coming at him, and hit the ball right out of the park. After his MLB days, he was player/manager of the Chattanooga Lookouts in the Southern Association in 1914 and 1915. McCormick saw action in WWI, coached at Bucknell and West Point, and was director of physical education and training at Mitchell Field, Long Island, for the Army Air Force in World War II.

Born:
February 28, 1881
Philadelphia, PA
Died:
July 9, 1962
Lewisburg, PA

▷ Batted: LH
▷ Threw: LH
▷ Position: OF
▷ Career BA: .285

Teams:
New York Giants NL (1904, 1908–1909, 1912–1913)
Pittsburgh Pirates NL (1904)
Philadelphia Phillies NL (1908)

Harry Elwood McCormick

Matty McIntyre

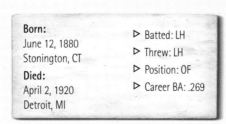

For over 500 games, Matty McIntyre was the left field complement to the Tigers' famed outfield pairing of Ty Cobb and Sam Crawford. As the Tigers' leadoff hitter, he scored 412 runs in 7 years, mostly in front of Cobb and Crawford. Many considered McIntyre the most valuable Tigers player during the team's three consecutive pennant-winning seasons. He battled with Ty Cobb throughout their tour together, and battled with Tigers' management as well, until he was finally sold to the White Sox in 1910. Although he was still hampered by a severely broken ankle suffered in 1907 and a 1909 bout of appendicitis, McIntyre became a popular player in Chicago, hitting .323 in 569 at bats, with 52 RBI and 17 stolen bases in 1911. After collecting only 84 at bats in 1912, his MLB career came to an end. He played in the minors through 1917, finishing up as player/manager of the Mobile Sea Gulls in the Southern Association. McIntyre died of Bright's disease (nephritis) in 1920 at age 39.

Born:
June 12, 1880
Stonington, CT
Died:
April 2, 1920
Detroit, MI

▷ Batted: LH
▷ Threw: LH
▷ Position: OF
▷ Career BA: .269

Teams:
Philadelphia Athletics AL (1901)
Detroit Tigers AL (1904–1910)
Chicago White Sox AL (1911–1912)

Matthew Martin McIntyre

Fred Merkle

In 1908, Fred Merkle was 19 years old, the youngest player in the National League. He only had 35 MLB games under his belt when he became part of one of the most controversial plays in baseball history. On September 23, 1908, while running from first, he allegedly failed to touch second base on an apparent game-winning hit against the Cubs. As fans stormed the field, thinking the game was won, Johnny Evers of the Cubs retrieved the ball (or, to hear some tell it, *a* ball) and touched second base. Umpire Hank O'Day called Merkle out, nullifying the winning run, and called the game a draw, which led to a playoff game for the pennant. The Giants lost. Many question whether Evers actually had the game ball when he touched second base, and various arguments about "Merkle's Boner" continue to this day. At 6 feet 1 inch, and 190 pounds, Merkle was one of the fastest big men in the game, and stole 20 or more bases on eight occasions. He was seventh in MVP voting in 1911 with a .283 batting average, 12 home runs, 84 RBI, and 49 stolen bases. After his MLB days, Merkle managed the Reading Keystones in the International League before retiring from the game in 1927.

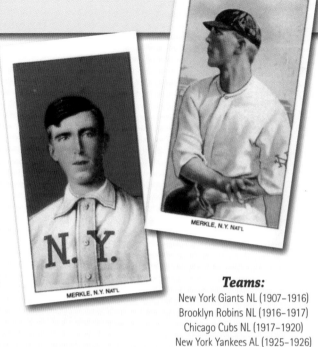

Teams:
New York Giants NL (1907–1916)
Brooklyn Robins NL (1916–1917)
Chicago Cubs NL (1917–1920)
New York Yankees AL (1925–1926)

Frederick Charles Merkle

Born:
December 20, 1888
Watertown, WI
Died:
March 2, 1956
Daytona Beach, FL

▷ Batted: RH
▷ Threw: RH
▷ Position: 1B
▷ Career BA: .273

Clyde Milan

Known as "Deerfoot" because of his amazing speed, Clyde Milan had a solid 16-year career in the majors, banging out 2,100 hits and stealing 495 bases. He was the stolen-base champ in 1912 with 88, which was a single-season record until Ty Cobb broke it in 1915. He led the league again in 1913 with 75 stolen bases. Over his career he had a total of five seasons with 40 or more stolen bases. Milan still ranks 37th on the all-time steals list. He batted over .300 on four different occasions, and 1911 was his best year, when he batted .315. As player/manager of the Senators in 1922 he put together a 69–85 managerial record. Milan managed in the minors from 1924 to 1937, mostly in the Southern Association, and led the Birmingham Barons to the league championship in 1931. He returned to the Senators to coach from 1938 to 1952.

Team:
Washington Senators AL (1907–1921; player/manager: 1922)

Jesse Clyde Milan

Born:
March 25, 1887
Linden, TN
Died:
March 3, 1953
Orlando, FL

▷ Batted: LH
▷ Threw: RH
▷ Position: OF
▷ Career BA: .285
▷ Managerial Record: 69–85

Dots Miller

Fred Mitchell

Fred Mitchell did a little of everything during his MLB career. A sub-.500 pitcher and a poor hitter, he had a high baseball IQ, which helped him as a manager. After coaching for the Boston Braves from 1914 to 1916, Mitchell became manager of the Chicago Cubs in 1917 and led his Cubs to a National League pennant win in 1918. He finished his stint as the Cubs' manager with a 308–269 record. He then managed the Boston Braves for three seasons, finishing with a 186-274 record. Around his MLB days, Mitchell played six seasons in the minors, four of them with the Eastern League's Toronto Maple Leafs, as pictured on his T206 card. After his stint with the Braves Mitchell coached at Harvard University until 1939. He died in 1970 at the age of 92.

John "Dots" Miller was Honus Wagner's double-play partner from 1909 to 1911 and they clicked for 160 twin killings in that span (while Johnny Evers of "Tinker to Evers to Chance" fame turned 101). Miller was a pretty fair hitter as well, finishing in the top seven in the league in RBI in five of his 12 seasons with Pittsburgh, St. Louis, and Philly. He turned into the prototypical utility man in St. Louis, earning 500-plus at bats for four straight seasons while playing every infield position. He finished in the top ten in National League MVP voting in 1913 and 1914. Miller retired after the 1921 season, and in 1922, as a 35-year-old rookie manager, he managed the San Francisco Seals of the Pacific Coast League to the league championship. During his second season as the Seals manager, he developed pulmonary tuberculosis and died 3 days before his 37th birthday in 1923.

Born:
September 9, 1886
Kearny, New Jersey
Died:
September 5, 1923
Saranac Lake, NY

▷ Batted: RH
▷ Threw: RH
▷ Position: 1B/2B/SS/3B
▷ Career BA: .263

Born:
June 5, 1878
Cambridge, MA
Died:
October 13, 1970
Newton, MA

▷ Batted: RH
▷ Threw: RH
▷ Position: P/C
▷ MLB Pitching Record: 31–49
▷ ERA: 4.10
▷ Managerial Record: 494–543

Frederick Francis Mitchell

Born: Frederick Francis Yapp

Teams:
Boston Americans AL (1901–1902)
Philadelphia Athletics AL (1902)
Philadelphia Phillies NL (1903–1904)
Brooklyn Superbas NL (1904–1905)
New York Highlanders AL (1910)
Boston Braves NL (1913; manager: 1921–1923)
Chicago Cubs NL (manager: 1917–1920)

Teams:
Pittsburg Pirates NL (1909-1913)
St. Louis Cardinals NL (1914-1919)
Philadelphia Phillies NL (1920-1921)

John Barney Miller

Carlton Molesworth

Pat Moran

Carlton Molesworth

Born:
February 15, 1876
Frederick, MD

Died:
July 25, 1961
Frederick, MD

▷ Batted: LH
▷ Threw: LH
▷ Position: P
▷ MLB Pitching Record: 0–2
▷ ERA: 14.62

Team:
Washington Senators MLB NL (1895)

Why Carleton Molesworth played only 4 major league games in his career is a mystery. After pitching only 16 innings for the Senators in 1895 at 19 years old, he came back in 1901 as a minor league outfielder. That year he played in the New York State League for the Schenectady Electricians and the Cortland Wagonmakers before joining the Chattanooga Lookouts in the Southern Association. A quality player/manager in the Southern Association, he had some very good offensive seasons, batting over .300 eight times during his 13-year minor league career. In 1905, while with the Montgomery Senators, he led the SOUA in batting with a .313 average. Molesworth joined the Birmingham Barons in 1906, became player/manager in 1908, and then manager only from 1915 to 1922. He led the Barons to pennants in 1912 and 1914 and amassed a 1,098–977 record over his 15 seasons at the helm.

Between playing and managing, Pat Moran spent 23 years in the majors. All in all, he was a much better manager than a player. A decent catcher defensively, Moran was proficient at handling pitchers. His best offensive year was 1903, when he batted .262 and had 7 home runs, good for second in the league. As a manager, he had many winning seasons. He led the Phillies to the World Series in 1915, losing 4–1 to the Red Sox. In 1919 he managed the winning Reds in the infamous World Series against the Chicago "Black Sox." After reporting to spring training in 1924, Moran became ill from Bright's disease and passed away soon after, cutting short his successful career as an MLB manager.

Born:
February 7, 1876
Fitchburg, MA

Died:
March 7, 1924
Orlando, FL

▷ Batted: RH
▷ Threw: RH
▷ Position: C
▷ Career BA: .235
▷ Managerial Record: 748–586

Teams:
Boston Beaneaters NL (1901–1905)
Chicago Cubs NL (1906–1909)
Philadelphia Phillies NL (1910–1914; manager: 1915–1918)
Cincinnati Reds NL (manager: 1919–1923)

Patrick Joseph Moran

George Moriarty

MORIARTY, DETROIT

One of the most colorful characters of the era, George Moriarty was a steady ballplayer, an outstanding umpire, and a combative tiger on the field. Primarily a third baseman, he was strong at all infield positions. He had 248 stolen bases in his career to go along with his .251 career batting average. As an American League umpire from 1917 to 1940, he officiated in five World Series and an All-Star Game. He was very well respected and never backed down from any manager. He was even known to participate in fisticuffs periodically with both players and skippers. Moriarty is also known for ejecting more players from the World Series than any other umpire. A mentor to the great Hank Greenberg, he led the charge to stop anti-Semitic catcalls by both fans and opposing players. He took a 2-year break from umpiring to manage the Tigers (1927, 1928) and later scouted for the Tigers until 1958.

Teams:
Chicago Cubs NL (1903–1904)
New York Highlanders/Yankees AL (1906–1908)
Detroit Tigers AL (1909–1915; manager: 1927–1928)
Chicago White Sox AL (1916)

Born:
July 7, 1884
Chicago, IL
Died:
April 8, 1964
Miami, FL

▷ Batted: RH
▷ Threw: RH
▷ Position: 3B
▷ Career BA: .251
▷ Managerial Record: 150–157

George Joseph Moriarty

George Mullin

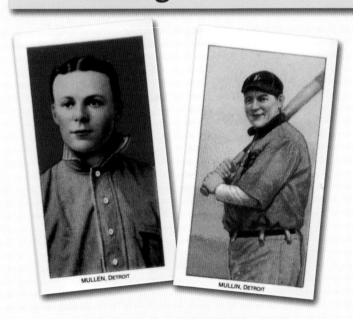

MULLEN, DETROIT

MULLIN, DETROIT

MULLIN, DETROIT

Born:
July 4, 1880
Toledo, OH
Died:
January 7, 1944
Wabash, IN

▷ Batted: RH
▷ Threw: RH
▷ Position: P
▷ MLB Pitching Record: 228–196
▷ ERA: 2.82

Burly fireballer "Wabash George" Mullin helped the Tigers win three consecutive pennants from 1907 to 1909 behind Ty Cobb and manager Hughie Jennings. Sixty-six of his 228 career wins came in that span, including a career-high, league-leading 29 wins in 1909. That year he went 29–8, with a 2.22 ERA. He also pitched a July 4 no-hitter against the Browns in 1912. He holds the Tigers' record for innings pitched and has the second-most runs in team history. Mullin won 20 or more games on five different occasions. After his MLB days, he coached in the minors until 1921, and then retired to become a policeman in Wabash, Indiana.

Teams:
Detroit Tigers AL (1902–1913)
Washington Senators AL (1913)
Indianapolis Hoosiers FL (1914)
Newark Pepper FL (1915)

George Joseph Mullin

Danny Murphy

Philadelphia native Danny Murphy spent most of his career playing in his hometown for the Athletics. A stellar second baseman and part-time outfielder, Murphy contributed to five pennant and three Series wins during his tour with the A's. In 1911, when he was 34 years old, he batted a lofty .329 with 167 hits. He batted over .300 on seven different occasions, the last three times as a part-time player. Murphy was one of those ballplayers who did his job every day with no fanfare and was a credit to the game. After his tour in Brooklyn, Murphy managed the New Haven Murlins in the Eastern League from 1916 to 1919, the first 2 years as player/manager. He then returned to the A's as coach until 1924.

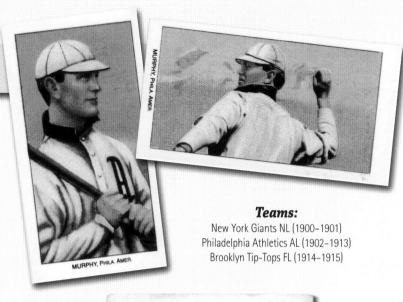

Daniel Francis Murphy

Teams:
New York Giants NL (1900–1901)
Philadelphia Athletics AL (1902–1913)
Brooklyn Tip-Tops FL (1914–1915)

Born:
August 11, 1876
Philadelphia, PA
Died:
November 22, 1955
Jersey City, NJ

▷ Batted: RH
▷ Threw: RH
▷ Position: 2B/OF
▷ Career BA: .289

Teams:
St. Louis Cardinals NL (1906–1908)
New York Giants NL (1909–1915, 1917)
Chicago Cubs NL (1915)

Born:
March 4, 1884
Arnot, PA
Died:
December 4, 1958
Sayre, PA

▷ Batted: RH
▷ Threw: RH
▷ Position: OF
▷ Career BA: .270

Red Murray

John "Red" Murray was a player's player. He is one of only three players to twice finish in the top five in both home runs and stolen bases. The other two to accomplish this feat were Honus Wagner and Ty Cobb. In 1907 Murray hit a 471-foot blast, an absolutely incredible feat considering it was the dead-ball era. He played on four pennant-winning Giants teams and was the home run champ in 1909. He is tied with Honus Wagner for the most MLB home runs from 1907 to 1909 (21). Defensively, Murray was considered one of the best right fielders in the league. With a rifle for an arm, he led the league in assists on several occasions. Although not as famous as Speaker, Cobb, and the rest, Murray certainly would have a place on most All-Star teams. After retiring from the game, Murray settled in Elmira, New York, where he owned a tire store and was recreation director for 18 years. He was inducted into the Elmira Baseball Hall of Fame in 1961.

John Joseph Murray

Simon Nicholls

Bill O'Hara

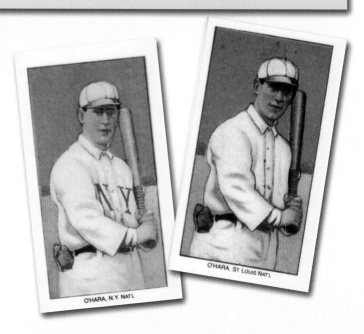

Simon Burdette Nicholls

Born:
July 18, 1882
Germantown, MD
Died:
March 12, 1911
Baltimore, MD

▷ Batted: LH
▷ Threw: RH
▷ Position: SS
▷ Career BA: .251

Teams:
Detroit Tigers AL (1903)
Philadelphia Athletics AL (1906–1909)
Cleveland Naps AL (1910)

Simon Nicholls' major league baseball career was brief, just two full seasons with the A's (he hit .302 in one of them) and very small parts of four more with Detroit, Philadelphia, and Cleveland. His life was brief as well, ending at 29 years old as a result of typhoid fever and pelvic peritonitis, just a week after the birth of his second child. Nicholls was playing at the time for the Baltimore Orioles, then in the Eastern League. The day before the 1911 season opened, the World Series champion Athletics were in Baltimore for an exhibition game on "Simon Nicholls Day." It is said that more than 5,000 fans turned out to honor their Orioles captain, raising $3,000 for the support of his widow and children. Prior to his baseball career, Nicholls graduated from Maryland Agricultural College, now the University of Maryland.

Born:
August 14, 1883
Toronto, Ontario, Canada
Died:
June 15, 1931
Jersey City, NJz

▷ Batted: LH
▷ Threw: RH
▷ Position: OF
▷ Career BA: .232

Teams:
New York Giants NL (1909)
St. Louis Cardinals NL (1910)

Canadian-born Bill O'Hara played two seasons in the majors with 360 of his 380 career at bats coming in center field with the Giants in 1909. That season he hit .236 with a home run, 30 RBI, and 31 swipes. After his brief MLB career, he went back to the minors to play six seasons for the Toronto Maple Leafs in the International League. The Toronto native joined the Canadian armed forces in WWI, serving briefly as a pilot and then with the 24th Canadian Battalion. In July 1916, he saw action in the Battle of the Somme, one of the bloodiest days in British military history. O'Hara received the Military Cross for his bravery and for putting his baseball skills to good use to accurately hurl grenades for the British during that battle. Wounded in action, he later became a fur trapper in northern Canada. He returned to baseball to manage for Toronto in 1927 and 1928.

William Alexander O'Hara

Rube Oldring

Rube Oldring was a fleet-footed, slick-fielding outfielder who played for four Athletics pennant-winners. He batted a career high .308 in 1910 but was benched in the World Series that year due to a leg injury suffered in the last of several exhibition games organized by Connie Mack against an American League All-Star squad to prepare for the Cubs. Oldring made one of early baseball's most legendary catches in Game 4 of the 1913 World Series, and the fans voted him the A's MVP that year. After his MLB days, he was player/manager in the minors through the mid-1920s, mostly in the Virginia League. He finished up with the Richmond Colts, winning the Virginia League championship in 1926 with an 83–68 record. He bought a farm after retiring from the game.

Teams:
New York Highlanders AL (1905)
Philadelphia Athletics AL (1906–1916, 1918)
New York Yankees AL (1916)

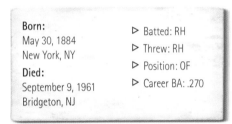

Born:
May 30, 1884
New York, NY
Died:
September 9, 1961
Bridgeton, NJ

▷ Batted: RH
▷ Threw: RH
▷ Position: OF
▷ Career BA: .270

Reuben Henry Oldring

Charley O'Leary

Charley O'Leary played in the majors from 1904 to 1934—sort of. He really played only from 1904 to 1913, but in 1934, when he was 51, the St. Louis Browns called him out of retirement. In a pinch-hitting appearance, he stroked a single and later scored a run. Prior to that, he was a weak-hitting shortstop with a good glove who started for the Tigers and later became a good utility player. During the off-season, he had a zany vaudeville act with his teammate Germany Schaefer, which was quite popular. He managed the Indianapolis Indians in the American Association and the San Antonio Bronchos in the Texas League before coaching for the Yankees under Miller Huggins in the 1920s for all those great Ruth–Gehrig championship teams. He went on to coach the Cubs and the Browns before being called back to play in 1934.

Teams:
Detroit Tigers AL (1904–1912)
St. Louis Cardinals NL (1913)
St. Louis Browns AL (1934)

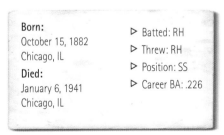

Born:
October 15, 1882
Chicago, IL
Died:
January 6, 1941
Chicago, IL

▷ Batted: RH
▷ Threw: RH
▷ Position: SS
▷ Career BA: .226

Charles Timothy O'Leary

Al Orth

"Smilin' Al" Orth was also known as "The Curveless Wonder" during his 15-year career. Relying on changing speeds and his uncanny control instead of velocity or any kind of breaking pitch, Orth amassed 204 career wins, winning 14 or more games in 11 seasons, including 2 years with 20-plus wins. His pitches were completely without zip, however, as Ossee Schreckengost of the Athletics once demonstrated by catching Orth's pitch barehanded while batting against him. In New York in 1906, Orth had his best season, going 27–17 with a 2.34 ERA. He struck out 133 that year and 121 in 1905 after Jack Chesbro taught him the spitball. Orth was pretty good with the bat as well, and still ranks seventh all-time in hits by a pitcher with 389. He was used as a pinch hitter 78 times in his career. Orth later became part owner of the Lynchburg Shoemakers in the Virginia League in 1908 and served as player/manager for parts of the 1908 and 1909 seasons. He was a National League umpire from 1912 to 1917, and also coached for Washington and Lee University and the Virginia Military Institute. During WWI Orth worked with U.S. troops in France as a YMCA athletic director.

ORTH, LYNCHBURG

Teams:
Philadelphia Phillies NL (1895–1901)
Washington Senators AL (1902–1904)
New York Highlanders AL (1904–1909)

Albert Lewis Orth

Born:
September 5, 1872
Tipton, IN
Died:
October 8, 1948
Lynchburg, VA

▷ Batted: LH
▷ Threw: RH
▷ Position: P
▷ MLB Pitching Record: 204–189
▷ ERA: 3.37

Orval Overall

OVERALL, CHICAGO NAT'L

OVERALL, CHICAGO NAT'L

OVERALL, CHICAGO NAT'L

Before Orval Overall's MLB days, he pitched for the University of California at Berkeley and was captain of their football team. It might not surprise you that "Double O" lasted just—you guessed it—7 years in the majors. But they were a great 7 years. His career 2.24 ERA is 13th best in major league history. Overall was a Tigers nemesis during their three straight World Series appearances; he beat them once in the 1907 Series and twice in 1908, including the Game 5 clincher—a 3-hit shutout in which he struck out four batters in the first inning, the only time that has happened in World Series history. Unfortunately, his arm started to give him trouble in 1911, shortening his career. He attempted a comeback in 1913, but ended up retiring that year. He was nicknamed "The Big Groundhog" because his birthday was on February 2. In 1918 he unsuccessfully ran for Congress. He then became a very influential banker in Fresno.

Teams:
Cincinnati Reds NL (1905–1906)
Chicago Cubs NL (1906–1910, 1913)

Orval Overall

Born:
February 2, 1881
Farmersville, CA
Died:
July 14, 1947
Fresno, CA

▷ Batted: Switch
▷ Threw: RH
▷ Position: P
▷ MLB Pitching Record: 108–71
▷ ERA: 2.23

Frank Owen

Freddy Parent

Frank "Yip" Owen had several very good years with the White Sox, winning 20 or more games 3 straight years. Born in Ypsilanti, Michigan (hence the nickname), he replaced Doc White in the 1906 World Series and pitched for six innings, not being involved in the decision. His best year was 1904, when he went 21–15 with a sparkling 1.94 ERA. Owen then came back in 1905 to go 21–13, and 22–13 in 1906. He managed to fan 443 batters over his career. Overall, he was a dependable, consistent pitcher. After his major league days, Owen dabbled in the minors, playing three seasons in the American Association for the Toledo Mud Hens and the Kansas City Blues. He retired in 1911 when he was 31 years old.

Teams:
Detroit Tigers AL (1901)
Chicago White Sox AL (1903–1909)

Born:
December 23, 1879
Ypsilanti, MI
Died:
November 24, 1942
Dearborn, MI

▷ Batted: Switch
▷ Threw: RH
▷ Position: P
▷ MLB Pitching Record: 82–67
▷ ERA: 2.55

Frank Malcolm Owen

Frederick Alfred Parent

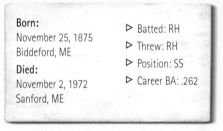

Born:
November 25, 1875
Biddeford, ME
Died:
November 2, 1972
Sanford, ME

▷ Batted: RH
▷ Threw: RH
▷ Position: SS
▷ Career BA: .262

Teams:
St. Louis Perfectos NL (1899)
Boston Americans/Red Sox AL (1901–1907)
Chicago White Sox AL (1908–1911)

Freddy Parent was the starting shortstop in the first World Series in 1903. A dependable, steady player, he was also the first shortstop in Boston Red Sox history. A star in the minors, he got his big chance in 1901, and proceeded to bat .306 for Boston. He was an outstanding bunter and base stealer, as well as a spray hitter. Parent led the league in outs made in 1902, 1905, and 1906. He had a tendency to crowd the plate, which resulted in a multitude of beanings that shortened his career. After his MLB stint, Parent played in the minors until 1918, when he became player/manager of the Springfield Ponies in the Eastern League. He then managed the Lewiston Red Sox in 1919 and later managed the Lawrence Merry Macks in the New England League in 1927. In the early 1920s he was head coach at Colby College. He then served as junior varsity coach at Harvard University in the late 1920s before returning to Maine and living to age 96. He was inducted into the Maine Baseball Hall of Fame in 1969.

Dode Paskert

George "Dode" Paskert carved out a solid 15-year MLB career, wowing fans and peers alike with his tremendous outfield range and overall speed. Known as an elite defensive player, he was underrated as a hitter. Paskert made several appearances on the offensive leader boards, highlighted by his .315 average in 1912, good for ninth in the National League. He finished in the top ten in runs six times, doubles four times, hits twice, RBI once, and he even finished sixth in home runs in 1916 with 8. He stole 293 career bases and finished 14th in NL MVP voting in 1912, when he hit .315 with 102 runs, 43 RBI, and 36 stolen bases. In 1917, at the age of 35, the Cubs traded home run champ Cy Williams to the Phillies straight up for Paskert. Also known as "Honey Boy" for his sweet ballplaying ability, he continued to play in the minors, mostly for the Columbus Senators in the American Association, until he finally retired in 1927 at the age of 46.

George Henry Paskert

Teams:
Cincinnati Reds NL (1907–1910, 1921)
Philadelphia Phillies NL (1911–1917)
Chicago Cubs NL (1918–1920)

Born:
August 28, 1881
Cleveland, OH
Died:
February 12, 1959
Cleveland, OH

▷ Batted: RH
▷ Threw: RH
▷ Position: OF
▷ Career BA: .268

Jack Pfiester

Jack "The Giant Killer" Pfiester had a lifetime ERA of 2.02, good for third all-time for pitchers who have thrown 1,000 or more innings. His nickname was a result of his dominance over the New York Giants. He amassed a 15–5 record against them over the course of his career. Pfiester's devastating curveball was his out pitch. In a feat unheard of in the game today, he struck out 17 batters in 15 amazing innings on May 30, 1906. He was also on the mound the day that the Giants' Fred Merkle failed to touch second base, and thus avoided a loss in the World Series. Considered one of the elite pitchers in the game, he had one 20-win season with the Cubs and pitched in four World Series. Pfiester dabbled in the minors after his MLB career until he was 38 years old, pitching for the Louisville Colonels in the American Association and the Sioux City Indians in the Western League. He retired in 1916 with a six-season 88–69 minor league record.

Teams:
Pittsburgh Pirates NL (1903–1904)
Chicago Cubs NL (1906–1911)

John Albert Pfiester
Born: John Albert Hagenbush

Born:
May 24, 1878
Cincinnati, OH
Died:
September 3, 1953
Loveland, OH

▷ Batted: RH
▷ Threw: LH
▷ Position: P
▷ MLB Pitching Record: 71–44
▷ ERA: 2.02

Ollie Pickering

PICKERING, MINNEAPOLIS

Ollie Pickering was a pretty good outfielder who played for eight seasons in the majors for six different teams. His best year was 1901, when he batted .309 with 169 hits and 102 runs scored. His main claim to fame is that he was the first batter in the new American League in 1901. Now that's a great trivia question! Around his MLB days, he played and managed 12 seasons in the minors. In 1905 he played for the Columbus Senators of the American Association and batted .327 as their leading hitter. He later played for 11 different teams in eight different leagues and managed five of them, finally retiring in 1922. As pictured on his T206 card, he played for the Minneapolis Millers in the American Association in 1909 and 1910.

Teams:
Louisville Colonels NL (1896–1897)
Cleveland Spiders NL (1897)
Cleveland Blues/Bronchos AL (1901–1902)
Philadelphia Athletics AL (1903–1904)
St. Louis Browns AL (1907)
Washington Senators AL (1908)

Born:
April 9, 1870
Olney, IL
Died:
January 20, 1952
Vincennes, IN

▷ Batted: LH
▷ Threw: RH
▷ Position: OF
▷ Career BA: .272

Oliver Daniel Pickering

Doc Powers

POWERS, PHILA. AMER.

Michael Riley Powers

Born:
September 22, 1870
Pittsfield, MA
Died:
April 26, 1909
Philadelphia, PA

▷ Batted: RH
▷ Threw: RH
▷ Position: C
▷ Career BA: .216

Teams:
Louisville Colonels NL (1898–1899)
Washington Senators NL (1899)
Philadelphia Athletics AL (1901–1905, 1906–1909)
New York Highlanders AL (1905)

A good defensive catcher, Michael "Doc" Powers became Eddie Plank's personal batterymate because of his talent for calling a ballgame. Powers attended the University of Notre Dame, was a licensed physician (thus the nickname), and was a "can't-miss" prospect. He was a marginal hitter, and his best year was 1901, when he batted .251. On April 12, 1909, he was injured when he crashed into a wall chasing a foul popup. He died three weeks later as a result of internal injuries and complications from the mishap. Some say that he was the inspiration for the character "Bump" Bailey in Bernard Malamud's *The Natural* (and its film adaptation), who died after crashing into a wall. In any event, it is ironic—and tragic—that Doc Powers chose to play baseball rather than practice medicine.

Jack Quinn

Jack Quinn's career was long and notable. The Austrian-Hungarian born pitcher didn't throw his first pitch until he was 25, but went on to play 23 seasons. A proficient spitballer, he was allowed to throw the pitch even after it was banned in 1920. Quinn helped the Yankees to their first pennant in 1921, and won the World Series with the A's in 1929 and 1930. Longevity was his stock in trade. He holds records as the oldest player to win an MLB game (49) and to start a World Series game (46). He also holds the AL record as the oldest player to hit a home run (47). Quinn was the oldest MLB player for five of his last seven seasons. He threw his last MLB pitch at age 50 in 1933, wrapping up his career with 247 wins, a 3.29 ERA, and 1,329 strikeouts.

John Picus Quinn

Born: Joannes Pajkos

Teams:

New York Highlanders/Yankees AL (1909–1912, 1919–1921)
Boston Braves NL (1913)
Baltimore Terrapins FL (1914–1915)
Chicago White Sox AL (1918)
Boston Red Sox AL (1922–1925)
Philadelphia Athletics AL (1925–1930)
Brooklyn Robins/Dodgers NL (1931–1932)
Cincinnati Reds NL (1933)

Born:
July 1, 1883
Stefurov, Austria-Hungary
(now Slovakia)
Died:
April 17, 1946
Pottsville, PA

▷ Batted: RH
▷ Threw: RH
▷ Position: P
▷ MLB Pitching Record: 247–218
▷ ERA: 3.29

Ed Reulbach

"Big Ed" Reulbach played basketball and football for Notre Dame in addition to starring as captain of their baseball team. After joining the Cubs, he went 60–15 on the mound from 1906 to 1909, leading the National League in winning percentage all three seasons. His eyesight was so poor that his catchers painted their gloves white so that he could see them. Despite that, the 6-foot 1-inch right-hander went 182–106 over his 13-year career. He is still the only pitcher in MLB history to pitch 2 complete game shutouts in a doubleheader, played against the Dodgers on September 26, 1908. Reulbach owns one of only five 1-hit games thrown in the World Series, turning the trick for the Cubs against the White Sox, their crosstown rivals, in Game 2 in 1906. He died in 1961, the last living member of the 1908 World Series champion Cubs team.

Edward Marvin Reulbach

Teams:

Chicago Cubs NL (1905–1913)
Brooklyn Dodgers/Robins NL (1913–1914)
Newark Peppers FL (1915)
Boston Braves NL (1916–1917)

Born:
December 1, 1882
Detroit, MI
Died:
July 17, 1961
Glens Falls, NY

▷ Batted: RH
▷ Threw: RH
▷ Position: P
▷ MLB Pitching Record: 182–106
▷ ERA: 2.28

Claude Ritchey

RITCHEY, BOSTON NAT'L

One of the best second basemen in this era of baseball, Claude Ritchey played 13 seasons in the National League with the Reds, the Colonels, the Pirates, and the Doves. Ritchey was traded from Louisville to Pittsburgh in December 1899 as part of a 16-player trade that included Rube Waddell, Jack Chesbro, and Honus Wagner. He then spent four seasons as the right side of the Bucs' double-play combination with Wagner. Nicknamed "Little All Right" because of his slight build, Ritchey played second base for the Pirates in the first World Series in 1903, hitting .148 with one stolen base. He led National League second basemen in fielding percentage five times and led the league once in games played and in sacrifices. Ritchey retired to his hometown of Emlenton after the 1909 season at the age of 35 with a .273 average and 18 career home runs. He then worked for the Emlenton Refining Company, which later became Quaker State Oil.

Born:
October 5, 1873
Emlenton, PA
Died:
November 8, 1951
Emlenton, PA

▷ Batted: Switch
▷ Threw: RH
▷ Position: 2B
▷ Career BA: .273

Teams:
Cincinnati Reds NL (1897)
Louisville Colonels NL (1898–1899)
Pittsburgh Pirates NL (1900–1906)
Boston Doves NL (1907–1909)

Claude Cassius Ritchey

Claude Rossman

ROSSMAN, DETROIT

Modern baseball has seen a handful of strange cases where a major league player simply lost the ability to throw a baseball, but the founding father of the syndrome has to be Claude Rossman. A big contributor at first base for the Tigers' 1907 and 1908 pennant-winning seasons, he was skilled at laying down bunts with Ty Cobb at first, often allowing Cobb to advance from first to third. He hit .294 in 1908 with 2 homers and 71 RBI, good for fourth in the AL in slugging percentage, sixth in batting average, fifth in RBI, and third in total bases. He was out of MLB a year later because he often froze in the field when he had to throw the ball from his first-base position, allowing runners to advance while he refused to risk a throw. However, Rossman was able to put together five good seasons as an outfielder in the minors for the American Association's Minneapolis Millers, batting .356 in 1911, .322 in 1912, and .302 in 1913. His health then deteriorated and he retired from the game in 1914. His "freezing" quirk foreshadowed a decline in neurological and mental health, which eventually led to his death at 46 in a Poughkeepsie mental hospital.

Teams:
Cleveland Naps AL (1904, 1906)
Detroit Tigers AL (1907–1909)
St. Louis Browns AL (1909)

Claude R. Rossman

Born:
June 17, 1881
Philmont, NY
Died:
January 16, 1928
Poughkeepsie, NY

▷ Batted: LH
▷ Threw: LH
▷ Position: 1B
▷ Career BA: .283

Nap Rucker

Nap Rucker came up to Brooklyn after starring in the South Atlantic League, going 27–9 with a 1.95 ERA in 1906 for the Augusta Tourists when he was 21. His MLB pitching record is deceptive. He holds the Dodgers' record for the most shutouts (38) and the most strikeouts (16) in a 9-inning game. He also threw a no-hitter against Boston in 1908. Rucker surely would have had a very good record if he had played on better teams. In 1910 he led the National League in shutouts (6), complete games (27), and innings pitched (320). He led the league in shutouts (6) again in 1912. After his career, Rucker became a successful Georgia businessman, owning two cotton plantations and a wheat mill. He was a bank investor, served as mayor of Roswell, Georgia, from 1935 to 1936, and became the water commissioner after his term as mayor. He also scouted for the Dodgers for many years. He was inducted into the Georgia Sports Hall of Fame in 1967.

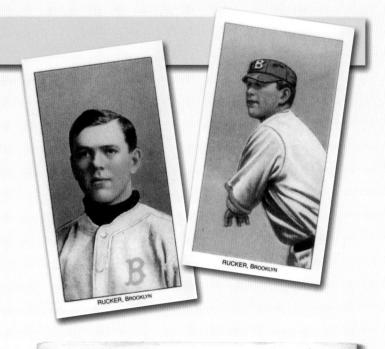

RUCKER, Brooklyn

RUCKER, Brooklyn

Team:
Brooklyn Superbas/Dodgers/Robins NL (1907–1916)

George Napoleon Rucker

Born:
September 30, 1884
Crabapple, GA
Died:
December 19, 1970
Alpharetta, GA

▷ Batted: RH
▷ Threw: LH
▷ Position: P
▷ MLB Pitching Record: 134–134
▷ ERA: 2.42

Dick Rudolph

RUDOLPH, Toronto

Fordham University alum Dick Rudolph pitched only 3 games as a rookie and 1 game in 1911 for the Giants. From 1907 to 1913 he pitched mostly for the Toronto Maple Leafs in the Eastern/International League, where he went 25–10 in 1912 and 120–71 overall, before joining the Braves. He had a sparkling 26–10 record in 1914, followed by 22 wins in 1915 and 19 wins in 1916. During the 1914 season, he was the best pitcher on a team that won the World Series. Not bad! The Braves were up against his old team the Giants that year. Just before the Series began, the Giants had "Rudolph Day" in the Bronx to honor Dick Rudolph—and jinx him for the Series. But he got the last laugh with a 5–3 opening victory. After his long tour with the Braves, he managed the 1928 Waterbury Brasscos in the Eastern League and the 1930 Portland Mariners in the New England League before retiring. Later he volunteered at Fordham as the freshman baseball coach. He was elected to the International League Hall of Fame in 1948.

Teams:
New York Giants NL (1910–1911)
Boston Braves NL (1913–1927)

Richard Rudolph

Born:
August 25, 1887
New York, NY
Died:
October 20, 1949
Bronx, NY

▷ Batted: RH
▷ Threw: RH
▷ Position: P
▷ MLB Pitching Record: 121–108
▷ ERA: 2.66

Germany Schaefer

SCHAEFER, DETROIT

SCHAEFER, WASHINGTON

Herman "Germany" Schaefer is the only player in MLB history who actually stole first base. While trying to beat the White Sox for the Senators on August 4, 1911, Schaefer was on first and Clyde Milan was on third with the winning run in the ninth. They tried a delayed double steal but catcher Fred Payne did not throw to second to get Schaefer. On the next pitch, Schaefer "stole" first, running back to the base to taunt Payne that he was going to steal second again. He did so on the next pitch but got caught before he could reach second base. Milan ran for home but was not in time to score. The practice was outlawed after that. Known for his pranks and showmanship on the field, Schaefer used humor to rattle the opposing team. It is said that a vaudeville act he performed with Tigers teammate Charley O'Leary was the inspiration for MGM's *Take Me Out to the Ball Game* (1949) with Gene Kelly and Frank Sinatra. Although he was battling pulmonary tuberculosis, Schaefer was hired to scout for the Giants in 1919. Unfortunately he passed away soon after while scouting in upstate New York.

Herman A. Schaefer

Teams:
Chicago Cubs NL (1901–1902)
Detroit Tigers AL (1905–1909)
Washington Senators AL (1909–1914)
Newark Peppers FL (1915)
New York Yankees AL (player/coach 1916)
Cleveland Indians AL (player/coach 1918)

Born:
February 4, 1876
Chicago, IL
Died:
May 16, 1919
Saranac Lake, NY

▷ Batted: RH
▷ Threw: RH
▷ Position: 2B
▷ Career BA: .257

Ossee Schreck

SCHRECK, COLUMBUS

A good catcher and first baseman, Ossee Schreck was solid defensively and had a pretty good bat. In 1899 he batted .290, followed by a couple of seasons where he topped the .300 mark. He had a very strong arm, and was stellar at both positions that he played. In a part-time role, Schreck's best year was 1902, when he batted .324 with 284 at bats for Philly. He was Rube Waddell's batterymate for the A's, and the two became fast friends both on the field and in the pub. When drinking started to impact his performance, he weaned himself off the booze by drinking milkshakes with a splash of sherry. He played his last MLB game in 1908. He then dabbled in the American Association for two seasons, playing for the Columbus Senators in 1909 and the Louisville Colonels in 1910 before retiring from the game. He passed away 4 years later at the age of 39 from kidney disease.

Teams:
Louisville Colonels NL (1897)
Cleveland Spiders NL (1898–1899)
St. Louis Perfectos NL (1899)
Boston Americans AL (1901)
Cleveland Bronchos AL (1902)
Philadelphia Athletics AL (1902–1908)
Chicago White Sox AL (1908)

Born:
April 11, 1875
New Bethlehem, PA
Died:
July 9, 1914
Philadelphia, PA

▷ Batted: RH
▷ Threw: RH
▷ Position: C/1B
▷ Career BA: .271

Ossee Freeman Schreckengost

Born: Ossee Freeman Schrecongost

Wildfire Schulte

Shag Shaughnessy

SCHULTE, CHICAGO NAT'L

Teams:
Chicago Cubs NL (1904–1916)
Pittsburgh Pirates NL (1916–1917)
Philadelphia Phillies NL (1917)
Washington Senators AL (1918)

Born:
September 17, 1882
Cohocton, NY
Died:
October 2, 1949
Oakland, CA

▷ Batted: LH
▷ Threw: RH
▷ Position: OF
▷ Career BA: .270

Frank "Wildfire" Schulte is one of only four players in MLB history to post a 20-20-20-20 season (compiling 20 doubles, triples, home runs, and stolen bases) in 1911, and that is no dead-ball era stat line. Willie Mays was the next player to accomplish the feat in 1957, and it wasn't done again until Curtis Granderson and Jimmy Rollins turned the trick in 2007. Schulte was also the first National League MVP in 1911, when he led the league in home runs, RBI, extra base hits, total bases, and slugging percentage. He stole home 22 times in his career, and was among the first to use the "thin-handled" 40-ounce bats that were the precursors of today's bats. One of his many eccentricities was his habit of searching the streets to find hairpins, which he believed predicted how well he'd hit that day. After his MLB days, Schulte played in the International League and Pacific Coast League through 1922 and also managed the Binghamton Bingoes in 1919.

Frank M. Schulte

SHAUGHNESSY, ROANOKE

What is Francis "Shag" Shaughnessy best-known for? If your favorite league has a playoff system where the first-place team plays the lowest-qualifying team, you can thank Shag Shaughnessy, who came up with the now-familiar playoff format in 1933. The Shaughnessy playoff system is used all over the world now, most notably in minor league baseball, probably because he served as president of the International League from 1936 to 1960. He also coached for the Tigers (1928), was GM for the Montreal Royals, introduced the option play in football as a coach at Yale and Cornell Universities, and was men's hockey coach and football coach at McGill University. Before accomplishing all of that, Shaughnessy collected 32 major league at bats with the Senators and A's before managing in the minors for 19 years. As player/manager of the Roanoke Tigers of the Virginia League, he won the league championship in 1909. He later won the Central League championship with the Fort Wayne Railroaders in 1912 and the Canadian League championship in 1913, 1914, and 1915 with the Ottawa Senators. He retired in 1936 with a career 1,189–1,053 managerial record. He was part of the inaugural class elected to the International League Hall of Fame in 1947, was inducted into the Canadian Football Hall of Fame in 1963, the Canadian Baseball Hall of Fame in 1983, and the McGill University Sports Hall of Fame in 1997.

Born:
April 8, 1883
Amboy, IL
Died:
May 15, 1969
Montreal, Québec, Canada

▷ Batted: RH
▷ Threw: RH
▷ Position: OF
▷ Career BA: .281

Teams:
Washington Senators AL (1905)
Philadelphia Athletics AL (1908)

Francis Joseph Shaughnessy

Jimmy Sheckard

Jimmy Sheckard was a players' player who put together a solid 17-year major league career. In 1901 he batted a lofty .354 with 11 home runs and 104 runs batted in. A five-tool player, Sheckard led the National League in stolen bases twice with 77 in 1899 and 67 in 1903. He was also the NL home run champ in 1903 with 9, making him the first player to lead the league in homers and swipes in the same season. An outstanding outfielder, he set a single-season record for double plays in 1899 and again in 1911. Sheckard played in four World Series with the Cubs. After coaching for the Cubs, he was athletic director at the Great Lakes Naval Training Station during WWI. He later coached for Franklin and Marshall College before managing the Lancaster Red Sox in the Interstate League in 1932. He died at age 68 after being hit by a car.

Teams:
Brooklyn Bridegrooms/Superbas NL (1897–1898, 1900–1902, 1903–1905)
Baltimore Orioles NL (1899)
Baltimore Orioles AL (1902)
Chicago Cubs NL (1906–1912)
St. Louis Cardinals NL (1913)
Cincinnati Reds NL (1913)

SHECKARD, CHICAGO NAT'L

SHECKARD, CHICAGO NAT'L

Samuel James Tilden Sheckard

Born:
November 23, 1878
Chanceford Township, PA
Died:
January 15, 1947
Lancaster, PA

▷ Batted: LH
▷ Threw: RH
▷ Position: OF
▷ Career BA: .274

Jimmy Slagle

SLAGLE, BALTIMORE

The pride of Worthville, Pennsylvania, a tiny town with less than 100 residents even today, Jimmy "Rabbit" Slagle was a talented National League outfielder. In 1900 with the Phillies, he was the National League leader in outs made (436) and sacrifice hits (27).

With the Cubs, he led the league in games played (155) in 1905, and played center field during the Cubs' pennant-winning years of 1906 to 1908. A very dependable hitter, he batted .315 in 1902 and .298 in 1903. Slagle also stole 40 bases in 1902 and had 273 thefts over his solid career. An above-average outfielder, he had 2,692 putouts in 3,010 chances. After his tour with the Cubs, Slagle played two seasons in the Eastern League for the Baltimore Orioles, batting .268 between 1909 and 1910. He then retired to Chicago where he owned a laundry business. A monument now stands in Worthville to its most famous citizen, who was always proud of his roots.

Teams:
Washington Senators NL (1899)
Philadelphia Phillies NL (1900–1901)
Boston Beaneaters NL (1901)
Chicago Orphans/Cubs NL (1902–1908)

Born:
July 11, 1873
Worthville, PA
Died:
May 10, 1956
Chicago, IL

▷ Batted: LH
▷ Threw: RH
▷ Position: OF
▷ Career BA: .268

James Franklin Slagle

Frank Smith

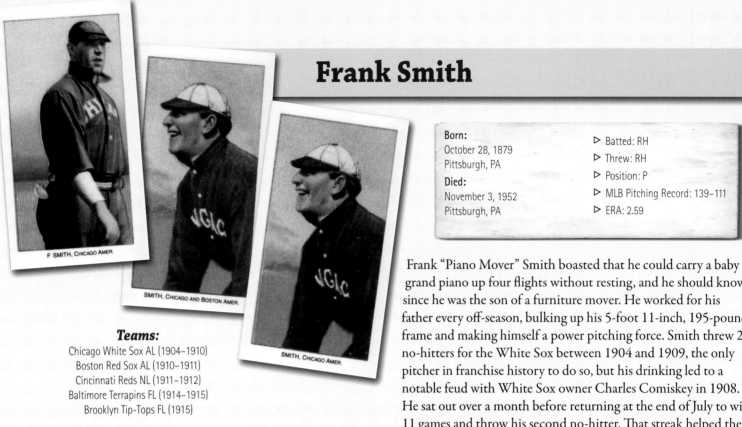

SMITH, CHICAGO AND BOSTON AMER.

F. SMITH, CHICAGO AMER.

SMITH, CHICAGO AMER.

Teams:
Chicago White Sox AL (1904–1910)
Boston Red Sox AL (1910–1911)
Cincinnati Reds NL (1911–1912)
Baltimore Terrapins FL (1914–1915)
Brooklyn Tip-Tops FL (1915)

Frank Elmer Smith

Born: October 28, 1879 Pittsburgh, PA	▷ Batted: RH
	▷ Threw: RH
	▷ Position: P
Died: November 3, 1952 Pittsburgh, PA	▷ MLB Pitching Record: 139–111
	▷ ERA: 2.59

Frank "Piano Mover" Smith boasted that he could carry a baby grand piano up four flights without resting, and he should know since he was the son of a furniture mover. He worked for his father every off-season, bulking up his 5-foot 11-inch, 195-pound frame and making himself a power pitching force. Smith threw 2 no-hitters for the White Sox between 1904 and 1909, the only pitcher in franchise history to do so, but his drinking led to a notable feud with White Sox owner Charles Comiskey in 1908. He sat out over a month before returning at the end of July to win 11 games and throw his second no-hitter. That streak helped the White Sox in the pennant race until the final day of the season. In 1909 he put together a 25–17 record while leading the American League in games played, games started, and complete games. Smith retired to the family moving business in 1916 after two seasons in the Federal League.

Fred Snodgrass

Fred "Snow" Snodgrass will forever be remembered as the outfielder who dropped a routine fly ball in the tenth inning of the deciding game of the 1912 World Series, helping the Red Sox win the game. People forget, however, that he was a very solid ballplayer with a good bat and glove over the course of his career. He batted .321 in 1910, .294 in 1911, and .291 in 1913 and was always considered a good team player and a credit to the game. He went on to become a successful banker, and a city councilor and then mayor of Oxnard, California, but could never live down the "Snodgrass Muff," his infamous World Series play. A similar thing happened to another player in another era during the 1986 World Series. That man was also a very good player and a credit to the game. Both players deserve better.

SNODGRASS, N.Y. NAT'L.

SNODGRASS, N.Y. NAT'L.

Teams:
New York Giants NL (1908–1915)
Boston Braves NL (1915–1916)

Frederick Carlisle Snodgrass

Born: October 19, 1887 Ventura, CA	▷ Batted: RH
	▷ Threw: RH
	▷ Position: OF/1B/C
Died: April 5, 1974 Ventura, CA	▷ Career BA: .275

Jake Stahl

Jake Stahl was one of the most feared hitters of the time, but his low-key manner kept him from becoming a baseball icon. After one season, the Red Sox sold him to Washington where, at 26, he became the youngest manager in American League history. Fired after a change in ownership, Stahl asked to be traded back to Boston, but was traded instead to the White Sox. Stahl refused to report and sat out 1907 as head coach at Indiana University. After a short tour with the Highlanders in 1908, Stahl was back in Boston where he anchored the team until his first retirement in 1910. After a year in banking, Stahl returned as player and manager in 1912 at the request of his father-in-law, W. F. Mahan, who was then part owner of the team. He led the Sox to a World Series championship in 1912, but 9 months later he was fired because a broken foot kept him from playing. Stahl returned to banking, then served in WWI, and returned to banking yet again to become the president of a successful bank in Chicago. He died from tuberculosis at age 43.

Teams:
Boston Americans/Red Sox AL (1903, 1908–1910; player/manager: 1912–1913)
Washington Senators AL (1904; player/manager: 1905–1906)
New York Highlanders AL (1908)

Garland Stahl

Born:
April 13, 1879
Elkhart, IL
Died:
September 18, 1922
Monrovia, CA

▷ Batted: RH
▷ Threw: RH
▷ Position: 1B
▷ Career BA: .261
▷ Managerial Record: 263–270

Oscar Stanage

Oscar Harland Stanage

Born:
March 17, 1883
Tulare, CA
Died:
November 11, 1964
Detroit, MI

▷ Batted: RH
▷ Threw: RH
▷ Position: C
▷ Career BA: .234

Teams:
Cincinnati Reds NL (1906)
Detroit Tigers AL (1909–1920, 1925)

Oscar Stanage had an interesting career as a catcher. Known to have the strongest arm in the league, he set the American League record in 1911 for assists by a catcher (212), which still stands, and he is in the top 20 of all time in that category. Stanage also led the league in games caught that year, with an amazing 141 games. On the other side of the coin, he was a weak hitter, and surprisingly, a poor defensive catcher. He had 41 errors in 1911, which is a record, and he is in the top ten for most errors at his position. His best year offensively was 1911, when he batted .264. At age 42, Stanage was one of the oldest players in the American League when he made his last MLB appearance while coaching for the Tigers. He then managed the Evansville Hubs of the Illinois-Indiana-Iowa League, finishing 72–66 in 1926, and coached for the Pirates from 1927 to 1931.

Harry Steinfeldt

George Stovall

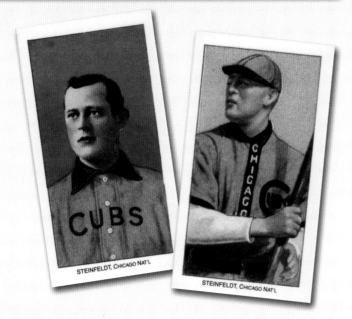

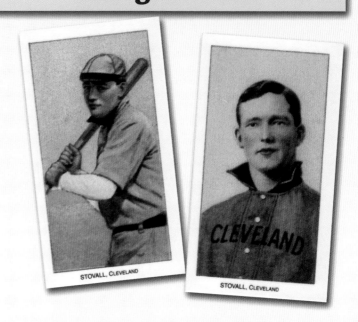

Harry Steinfeldt was the fourth member of the "Tinker to Evers to Chance" infield, and in 1906 led the 116-game-winning Cubs, as well as the entire National League, in RBI and hits. He also batted an excellent .327 that year. Steinfeldt had four World Series appearances with the Cubs, from 1906 to 1910, and won two of them. While with the Reds, he led the league with 32 doubles in 1903. As a fielder, Steinfeldt was considered one of the best, even though he never made it to the Hall of Fame. Steinfeldt managed in the minors during the 1912 season for the Meridian Metropolitans in the Cotton States League. After struggling with ill health for several years, he died at age 36 from, according to his death certificate, a cerebral hemorrhage.

Born:
September 29, 1877
St. Louis, MO
Died:
August 17, 1914
Bellevue, KY

▷ Batted: RH
▷ Threw: RH
▷ Position: 3B
▷ Career BA: .267

Teams:
Cincinnati Reds NL (1898–1905)
Chicago Cubs NL (1906–1910)
Boston Doves NL (1911)

Harry M. Steinfeldt

George Thomas Stovall

Born:
November 23, 1877
Leeds, MO
Died:
November 5, 1951
Burlington, IA

▷ Batted: RH
▷ Threw: RH
▷ Position: 1B
▷ Career BA: .265
▷ Managerial Record: 313–376

Teams:
Cleveland Naps AL (1904–1910; player/manager: 1911)
St. Louis Browns AL (player/manager: 1912–1913)
Kansas City Packers FL (player/manager: 1914–1915)

George "Firebrand" Stovall played 955 games at first base for the Cleveland Indians, second only to Hal Trosky. His nifty scoop of a low throw sealed the final out of Addie Joss's perfect game in 1908. Joss died less than 3 years later and Stovall organized a 1-day player's strike so Joss's teammates could attend his funeral. A popular player, he became the Naps' manager in 1911 before being sold to the Browns as player/manager. Stovall was the first player to sign with the Federal League in 1914 and he recruited fellow players for the new league. He was later named president of the Association of Professional Ball Players of America. He managed the 1917 Vernon Tigers in the Pacific Coast League and the 1922 Jacksonville Indians in the Florida State League. He also coached for Loyola, scouted for Pittsburgh, and worked in the shipyards during WWI and WWII. His brother Jesse Stovall pitched for the Naps and the Tigers from 1903 to 1904.

Sammy Strang

STRANG, BALTIMORE

Samuel Nicklin Strang

Born: Samuel Strang Nicklin

Born:
December 16, 1876
Chattanooga, TN

Died:
March 13, 1932
Chattanooga, TN

▷ Batted: Switch
▷ Threw: RH
▷ Position: 3B/2B/OF/SS
▷ Career BA: .269

Teams:
Louisville Colonels NL (1896)
Chicago Orphans NL (1900, 1902)
New York Giants NL (1901, 1905–1908)
Chicago White Sox AL (1902)
Brooklyn Superbas NL (1903–1904)

Speedy Sammy Strang, nicknamed "The Dixie Thrush," was a very valuable player as a starter and a utility man. Some speculate that John McGraw coined the term "pinch hitter" because Strang always came through in the "pinch" when he came up to bat. He led the league in on-base percentage in 1906 with .423. A base-stealing threat, he had 46 swipes in 1903. He played on the Giants' 1905 championship team. After his MLB days, Strang played for the Baltimore Orioles in the Eastern League from 1908 through 1910. He also coached at Georgia Tech in 1902 and at the U.S. Military Academy from 1909 to 1917. Strang was manager and president of the Chattanooga Lookouts of the Southern Association from 1919 to 1921 and manager in 1925.

Gabby Street

STREET, WASHINGTON

Nicknamed for his constant chatter behind the plate, Charles "Gabby" Street was Walter Johnson's catcher for four seasons. He was also famous for one of the more entertaining feats in baseball history, catching a ball dropped from the Washington Monument in 1908. A good defensive catcher with a weak bat, he played for several teams but was more famous as a manager. Also known as "The Old Sarge," he led the Cards to two pennants in 1930 and 1931 and a World Series championship in 1931. Street also managed in the minors for 13 years for eight teams in five leagues, winning the Western Association championship with his 1922 Joplin Miners. After years managing in the minors and the majors, he ended up in the broadcast booth, where he excelled as a color commentator for the Cards. He mentored the young Harry Caray, and worked until his death in 1951.

Born:
September 30, 1882
Huntsville, AL

Died:
February 6, 1951
Joplin, MO

▷ Batted: RH
▷ Threw: RH
▷ Position: C
▷ Career BA: .208
▷ Managerial Record: 365–332

Teams:
Cincinnati Reds NL (1904–1905)
Boston Beaneaters NL (1905)
Washington Senators AL (1908–1911)
New York Highlanders AL (1912)
St. Louis Cardinals NL (manager: 1929–1933; player/manager: 1931)
St. Louis Browns AL (manager: 1938)

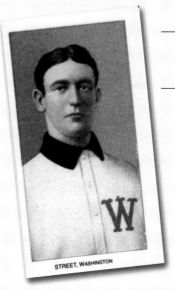

STREET, WASHINGTON

Charles Evard Street

Billy Sullivan

Ed Summers

William Joseph Sullivan Sr.

Born:
February 1, 1875
Oakland, WI
Died:
January 28, 1965
Newberg, OR

▷ Batted: RH
▷ Threw: RH
▷ Position: C
▷ Career BA: .213
▷ Managerial Record: 78–74

Born:
December 5, 1884
Ladoga, IN
Died:
May 12, 1953
Indianapolis, IN

▷ Batted: Switch
▷ Threw: RH
▷ Position: P
▷ MLB Pitching Record: 68–45
▷ ERA: 2.42

Team:
Detroit Tigers AL (1908–1912)

Teams:
Boston Braves NL (1899–1900)
Chicago White Sox AL (1901–1914; player/manager: 1909)
Detroit Tigers AL (1916)

"Kickapoo Ed" Summers pitched five seasons with the Tigers, from 1908 to 1912, going 65–48 with a 2.42 career ERA. His rookie season was his best, when he went 24–12 with a 1.64 ERA, good for fourth in the league. That year, the Tigers won the second of three consecutive American League pennants. He went 19–9 in 1909 with a 2.24 ERA, but his success in his first two seasons didn't translate to the World Series, where he went 0–4 with a 5.73 ERA in four appearances between the 1908 and 1909 World Series. Summers hit just .162 for his career over 352 at bats, but did collect 2 major league home runs, both in the same game in 1910. He started suffering from rheumatism during the 1911 season and was out of the majors a year later at age 27. He played for the Eastern League's Providence Grays in 1914 before retiring from the game for good.

Billy Sullivan is statistically among the worst-hitting catchers in major league history. With Sullivan behind the plate, however, the White Sox won two pennants and very nearly two more, and never finished lower than fourth between 1901 and 1911. In 1903 and 1910, the 2 years in his prime that he played fewer than 89 games due to injury, the White Sox played sub-.500 ball and finished seventh and sixth. Ty Cobb called Sullivan "the best catcher ever to wear shoe leather." The first player to catch 1,000 games, Sullivan was the patent holder on the first inflatable chest protector for catchers. After his tour with the Tigers, Sullivan retired to his apple and nut farm in Newberg, Oregon. When his son Billy Jr. caught in the 1940 World Series, it was the first time in MLB history that a father and son had both competed in the Fall Classic.

Oron Edgar Summers

Bill Sweeney

Bill Sweeney spent seven of his eight major league seasons in Boston, hitting .280 in his run with the Doves/Rustlers/Braves with 10 homers and 350 RBI. In his first four seasons in the majors, he played every position except pitcher, but he played the majority of his games at second and third base. From 1911 to 1913, Sweeney was an impact player in the National League. He finished sixth in the league in batting in 1911, hit .344 in 1912, good for third in the league, and received MVP votes in all three of those seasons, finishing sixth in the balloting in 1912. After seven seasons in Boston, Sweeney was traded to the Cubs in February 1914 for Johnny Evers. The Braves went on to win the World Series championship the next season. After his playing days, he owned and operated a successful Boston-area insurance company. He also coached for Boston College for one season in 1916.

Born:
March 6, 1886
Covington, KY
Died:
May 26, 1948
Cambridge, MA

▷ Batted: RH
▷ Threw: RH
▷ Position: 2B/3B/SS
▷ Career BA: .272

SWEENEY, BOSTON NAT'L

Teams:
Chicago Cubs NL (1907, 1914)
Boston Doves/Rustlers/Braves NL (1907–1913)

William John Sweeney

Lee Tannehill

L. TANNEHILL, CHICAGO AMER.

TANNEHILL, CHICAGO AMER.

Lee Tannehill can win you a drink at virtually any bar in America, but it has nothing to do with his hitting. Tannehill carved out a 10-year career with the White Sox despite hitting a mere .220 lifetime with just 3 homers (2 of which came in his rookie season). He slugged just .273 in his career, topping .300 in slugging percentage in only two seasons. He was the poster child for "The Hitless Wonders," as the White Sox of his day were known, but he also was one of the most highly regarded defensive players of his generation. Tannehill primarily played third base (668 games) but he played 367 games at shortstop, thus becoming the answer to the all-time baseball trivia stumper: Who is the only shortstop in major league history to convert 2 unassisted triple plays in the same game? The game was played on August 4, 1911, against the Washington Senators. After his tour with the Sox, he played in the minors through the 1918 season. He also managed the 1916 South Bend Benders in the Central League and the 1917 Jacksonville Roses in the South Atlantic League. He retired when he was 37 years old.

Born:
October 26, 1880
Dayton, KY
Died:
February 16, 1938
Live Oak, FL

▷ Batted: RH
▷ Threw: RH
▷ Position: 3B
▷ Career BA: .220

Team:
Chicago White Sox AL (1903–1912)

Lee Ford Tannehill

Dummy Taylor

Ira Thomas

TAYLOR, BUFFALO

THOMAS, PHILA. AMER.

Luther "Dummy" Taylor got his nickname because he was deaf, "dummy" being an acceptable term for deaf people in that era. One of the unsung heroes of baseball, he was a good pitcher with a career record north of .500. Although he lost 27 games for the Giants in 1901, he won 21 games in 1904, 16 in 1905, and 17 in 1906. Out of respect for Taylor, his Giants teammates learned sign language, and they used the signs in games until opposing teams figured out what they were doing. He was well liked and was also quite a comic, often entertaining the fans by mocking the umpires in mime behind their backs. After his MLB tour, Taylor played in the minors through 1915, spending the 1909 and 1910 seasons in the Eastern League with the Buffalo Bisons, as pictured on his T206 card. He then umpired in the minors from 1916 until 1938. He later worked and coached at three schools for the deaf in the Midwest. Taylor was inducted into the Kansas Baseball Hall of Fame in 2006.

Ira Felix Thomas

Born:
January 22, 1881
Ballston Spa, New York
Died:
October 11, 1958
Philadelphia, PA

▷ Batted: RH
▷ Threw: RH
▷ Position: C
▷ Career BA: .242

Teams:
New York Highlanders AL (1906–1907)
Detroit Tigers AL (1908)
Philadelphia Athletics AL (1909–1915)

At 6 feet 2 inches Ira Thomas was not your typical catcher, but he caught 450 MLB games over ten seasons, seven under Connie Mack in Philadelphia. As team captain and catcher for the A's, he won four pennants and three World Series, but only caught as many as 100 games once, in 1911. Thomas hit .273 that season, slugged .340, collected 150 assists behind the plate, and finished eighth in American League MVP voting. After his playing days, he coached for the A's and was owner/manager of the Texas League's Shreveport Gassers in 1923 and 1924. In 1925, Thomas found his niche as chief scout for the A's, discovering Lefty Grove and Al Simmons, among others. He scouted for the A's until he moved back east to scout for the Yankees at age 75 in 1956.

Teams:
New York Giants NL (1900–1902, 1903–1908)
Cleveland Bronchos AL (1902)

Born:
February 21, 1875
Oskaloosa, KS
Died:
August 22, 1958
Jacksonville, IL

▷ Batted: RH
▷ Threw: RH
▷ Position: P
▷ MLB Pitching Record: 116–106
▷ ERA: 2.75

Luther Haden Taylor

John Titus

"Silent John" Titus, nicknamed for his quiet demeanor, was a good, steady, dependable player for both the Phillies and the Braves. With an uncanny eye for taking pitches, he sometimes stood at the plate and just pulled in his stomach without moving at an inside pitch. However, he ranks 74th on the all-time hit-by-pitch list. Over 11 major league seasons, Titus was hit a total of 94 times, and in 1909 he led the league when he was hit 16 times. Both a good hitter and fielder, he had several .300-plus seasons, and in 1912 he batted .325 for the Braves. His trademark was the toothpick he always had in his mouth, even when he was batting. After his MLB days, Titus played for the Kansas City Blues in the American Association, batting .311 between the 1914 and 1915 seasons. He retired from the game when he was 39 years old.

Teams:
Philadelphia Phillies NL (1903–1912)
Boston Braves NL (1912–1913)

John Franklin Titus

Born:
February 21, 1876
St. Clair, PA
Died:
January 8, 1943
St. Clair, PA

▷ Batted: LH
▷ Threw: LH
▷ Position: OF
▷ Career BA: .282

Terry Turner

Terrence Lamont Turner

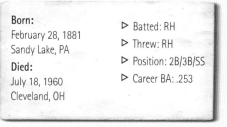

Born:
February 28, 1881
Sandy Lake, PA
Died:
July 18, 1960
Cleveland, OH

▷ Batted: RH
▷ Threw: RH
▷ Position: 2B/3B/SS
▷ Career BA: .253

Teams:
Pittsburgh Pirates NL (1901)
Cleveland Naps/Indians AL (1904–1918)
Philadelphia Athletics AL (1919)

Terry "Cotton Top" Turner was a no-nonsense, hard-nosed, fundamentally solid player. He is still Cleveland's all-time leader in games played, with 1,619 collected over 15 seasons. At 5 feet 8 inches, and 149 pounds, Turner was once described by a sportswriter as "a little rabbit of a man with the guts of a commando." Known for how well he played three infield positions, he led American League shortstops in fielding percentage on four different occasions, broke up 3 no-hitters, and ruined Chief Bender's shot at a perfect game. Turner's best year was 1912, when he batted .308. He led the league in sacrifice hits in 1914. He stole 25 or more bases four times and had a career high of 31 swipes in 1910. Most important, Turner is known for pioneering the headfirst slide. He returned to private life in Cleveland in 1919, where he was a chief superintendent of the Cleveland Street Department until his retirement in 1952. He was selected to the Top 100 Greatest Indians' roster in 2001.

Jack Warhop

Here's a great baseball trivia question: Who was the pitcher who gave up Babe Ruth's first career homer? Yes, Jack Warhop has that dubious distinction, giving up the first of Ruth's 714 jacks on May 6, 1915. Warhop also led the American League in hit batsmen in 1909 and 1910 and home runs allowed in 1914 and 1915. He had a pretty tough career, ending up almost 30 games below .500. In 1914 he pitched a heartbreaker against the White Sox, when his 12-inning shutout turned into a 1–0 loss in the 13th inning. After his tour with the Yankees, Warhop worked the circuit in the minors, pitching for eight different teams in five different leagues. He also managed the Norfolk Tars in the Virginia League in 1921. He retired after the 1928 season at age 42 with a 155–70 minor league pitching record.

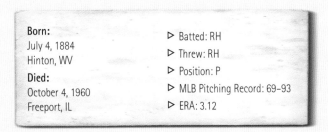

Born:
July 4, 1884
Hinton, WV
Died:
October 4, 1960
Freeport, IL

▷ Batted: RH
▷ Threw: RH
▷ Position: P
▷ MLB Pitching Record: 69–93
▷ ERA: 3.12

Team:
New York Highlanders/Yankees AL (1908–1915)

John Milton Warhop

Jake Weimer

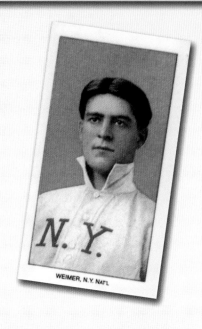

Jacob Weimer

Born:
November 29, 1873
Ottumwa, IA
Died:
June 19, 1928
Chicago, IL

▷ Batted: RH
▷ Threw: LH
▷ Position: P
▷ MLB Pitching Record: 97–69
▷ ERA: 2.23

Teams:
Chicago Cubs NL (1903–1905)
Cincinnati Reds NL (1906–1908)
New York Giants NL (1909)

Southpaw "Tornado Jake" Weimer was 29 years old when he broke into the majors in 1903. He was already a seasoned veteran after seven seasons in the minor leagues. As a major league rookie, Weimer went 20–8 with a 2.30 ERA for the Cubs. He threw 3 shutouts that season, beating Giants' ace Christy Mathewson in two of them. The next year, he went 20–14 with a 1.91 ERA, and in 1905 he posted an 18–12, 2.26 ERA record. Because the Cubs had plenty of pitching talent and sorely needed help at third base, Weimer was traded to the Reds for Harry Steinfeldt in 1906. With their "Tinker to Evers to Chance" infield complete, the Cubs then won three straight pennants. Weimer won 20 for the Reds in 1906 but burned out quickly after that.

Doc White

A graduate of Georgetown Dental School, Guy "Doc" White was a very good pitcher who led the American League in 1906 with his 1.52 ERA. He was also first in the league in 1907 with 27 wins. White had four seasons in which his ERA was below 2 and his lifetime 2.39 ERA is 26th on the all-time list. He won 15 or more games on eight different occasions, and in September 1909 he pitched 5 straight shutouts. White worked in his dental practice in the off-season, earning his nickname. He also wrote and published some music that became popular at the time and had a short stint in vaudeville. After his tour with the Sox, he played in the minors through 1917 and then managed the Texas League's Waco Navigators in 1919 and the Muskegon Muskies of the Central League in 1920. White then became a coach and physical education teacher for his alma mater, Central High in Washington, D.C., for the next 28 years. During that time he also coached at the University of Maryland.

Guy Harris White

Teams:
Philadelphia Phillies NL (1901–1902)
Chicago White Sox AL (1903–1913)

Born:
April 9, 1879
Washington, D.C.
Died:
February 19, 1969
Silver Spring, MD

▷ Batted: LH
▷ Threw: LH
▷ Position: P
▷ MLB Pitching Record: 189–156
▷ ERA: 2.39

Ed Willett

When Ed Willett joined the Tigers in 1906 and went 1–8 in nine starts over two seasons, few envisioned how important he would become to a Tigers team that would win three straight pennants from 1906 to 1909. He went 15–8 with a 2.28 ERA in 1908 despite an injured ankle. He then had his best season in the majors in 1909, going 21–10 with a 2.34 ERA. He made two relief appearances in the 1909 World Series, pitching 7.2 scoreless innings and allowing just 3 hits. Willett was the best fielding pitcher of his era by far. In 1910 he recorded 113 assists in 224 innings pitched, or more than 4.5 assists per nine innings. In 247 career games, Willett started 202 games and finished 142. After his tour in the Federal League, he pitched in the minors through 1919, going 20–19 over four seasons. He then managed the 1922 Grand Island Champions and the 1923 Beatrice Blues in the Nebraska State League.

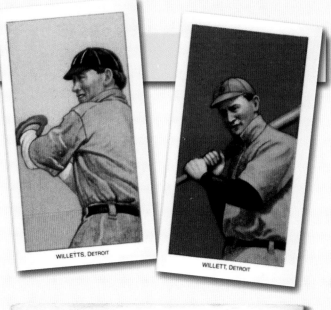

Teams:
Detroit Tigers AL (1906–1913)
St. Louis Terriers FL (1914–1915)

Born:
March 7, 1884
Norfolk, VA
Died:
May 10, 1934
Wellington, KS

▷ Batted: RH
▷ Threw: RH
▷ Position: P
▷ MLB Pitching Record: 102–99
▷ ERA: 3.08

Robert Edgar Willett

Jimmy Williams

Owen Wilson

WILLIAMS, ST. LOUIS AMER.

WILSON, PITTSBURG

James Thomas Williams

Born:
December 20, 1876
St. Louis, MO
Died:
January 16, 1965
St. Petersburg, FL

▷ Batted: RH
▷ Threw: RH
▷ Position: 2B
▷ Career BA: .275

Teams:
Pittsburgh Pirates NL (1899–1900)
Baltimore Orioles/New York Highlanders AL (1901–1907)
St. Louis Browns AL (1908–1909)

Jimmy Williams still holds the Pirates' franchise record hitting streak at 27 games, which he strung together in 1899, his rookie season. That year he also hit 28 triples, a rookie record that also still stands today. He hit 9 homers that season, but his nickname of "Home Run" Williams was given to him in 1897 when he was with the St. Joseph Saints of the Western Association and hit 22 home runs before a July injury scuttled the season. In 1901 John McGraw persuaded Williams to leave the Pirates and become one of the original Baltimore Orioles, and he also became an original Highlander when the franchise was sold to New York. The year the T206 set was issued was the last of his 11 seasons in the majors. Williams then played in the American Association for the Minneapolis Millers through 1915, batting .306 over four seasons. He coached and scouted for the Cincinnati Reds in the 1930s and later worked for the Honeywell Company in Minneapolis.

Owen "Chief" Wilson's slashing batting style was a perfect fit for the expanse of Forbes Field in Pittsburgh. Wilson set what may be one of the most unbreakable records in baseball in 1912, when he posted 36 triples. That season the Pirates totaled 129 triples as a team, which is also the MLB record. Wilson was not streamlined at 6 feet 2 inches, and 185 pounds, or particularly speedy, but he drove the ball to the gaps, hitting 59 career homers in nine seasons, 31 of which were inside the park. Originally known as "Tex," his Pirates teammates called him "Chief" because manager Fred Clarke thought he looked like a chief of the Texas Rangers. Wilson was said to have a tremendous throwing arm and he occasionally demonstrated his considerable prowess with a lariat. Wilson had started his pro career in the Texas League in 1905, and in 1917 he returned to that league for one season to play for the San Antonio Bronchos, after which he retired to his family ranch in Bertram, Texas.

Teams:
Pittsburgh Pirates NL (1908–1913)
St. Louis Cardinals NL (1914–1916)

Born:
August 21, 1883
Austin, TX
Died:
February 22, 1954
Bertram, TX

▷ Batted: LH
▷ Threw: RH
▷ Position: OF
▷ Career BA: .269

John Owen Wilson

Hooks Wiltse

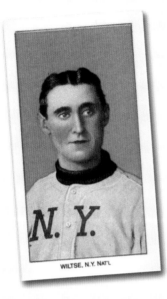

WILTSE, N.Y. NAT'L

WILTSE, N.Y. NAT'L

WILTSE, N.Y. NAT'L

While playing for the Giants, George "Hooks" Wiltse and future Hall of Famer Christy Mathewson became one of the greatest "righty-lefty" pitching duos of all time. A solid pitcher, Wiltse won 20 or more games two times. In 1908, he pitched a 10-inning no-hitter, just missing out on a perfect game. Hooks had a sparkling 2.47 lifetime ERA, which ranks him in the top 50 in MLB history. His brother Lewis "Snake" Wiltse also played in the majors. After the Federal League, he spent 11 seasons playing and managing in the International League, mostly for the Buffalo Bisons and the Reading Pretzels, retiring in 1926. He also coached the Yankees in 1925. Wiltse retired to Syracuse, where he worked in real estate sales, was an alderman in the early 1930s, and served as deputy assessor from 1934 to 1944. He was elected to the International League Hall of Fame in 1952.

George Leroy Wiltse

Teams:
New York Giants NL (1904–1914)
Brooklyn Tip-Tops FL (1915)

Born:
September 7, 1879
Hamilton, NY
Died:
January 21, 1959
Long Beach, NY

▷ Batted: RH
▷ Threw: LH
▷ Position: P
▷ MLB Pitching Record: 139–90
▷ ERA: 2.47

THE BAD BOYS OF BASEBALL

HISTORY IS LITTERED with people from all walks of life and professions who for one reason or another either never capitalized on the special talents they had, or threw it away for greed, ego, or other reasons. Some, on the other hand, just never took their profession seriously, or let their tempers get in the way.

The same holds true for some of the players in the T206 collection. We call these the infamous men of the collection. Some almost ruined their careers, some ruined themselves, and others nearly ruined the game of baseball. Of course, this same scenario still exists 100 years later . . . only the names have changed.

Meet the bad boys of baseball.

Frank Bowerman

"Sleepy" Bill Burns

BOWERMAN, BOSTON NAT'L

BURNS, CHICAGO AMER

Frank Eugene Bowerman

Born:
December 5, 1868
Romeo, MI

Died:
November 30, 1948
Romeo, MI

▷ Batted: RH
▷ Threw: RH
▷ Position: C
▷ Career BA: .251
▷ Managerial Record: 22–54

Teams:
Baltimore Orioles NL (1895–1898)
Pittsburgh Pirates NL (1898–1899)
New York Giants NL (1900–1907)
Boston Doves NL (1908; player/manager: 1909)

Frank Bowerman was a tough, hard-nosed catcher who was a backup to catching greats Roger Bresnahan and Wilbert Robinson. When needed, he played several other positions in the infield and even pitched a game for the Giants in 1904. Bowerman was also the first to catch the great Christy Mathewson. Known for his rough style of play and fiery temper, he regularly got into fights with players and umpires, and sometimes even with fans. It is said that he picked a fight with his Pirates' manager Fred Clarke, resulting in a black eye for Clarke, and in 1903 he was arrested after punching a heckler in the face. Bowerman managed the Doves briefly in 1909, but got the ax because of his temper. He finished the 1909 season in the American Association with the Indianapolis Indians and continued to play in the minors through 1911. Bowerman managed the London Tecumsehs in the Canadian League in 1912 before retiring from the game.

"Sleepy Bill" Burns is noted more for his involvement in the infamous 1919 World Series "Black Sox" scandal than for his pitching abilities. According to all accounts, Burns was the middleman between Chicago players Eddie Cicotte, Chick Gandil, and New York gambler Arnold Rothstein. At that time, Burns had been out of the majors for 7 years, but had played a bit for the Oakland Oaks in the Pacific Coast League. After the scandal became public, he served as a witness for the prosecution at the trial in return for immunity. As an MLB pitcher, he never won more than 8 games, but he did have a 1.69 ERA his rookie year. His only winning season was 1907, when he went 24–17 for the Pacific Coast League's Los Angeles Angels before graduating to the majors. As a player, Burns had a very sleepy career. He managed the Mineral Well Resorters in the West Texas League in 1920 before leaving baseball.

Born:
January 27, 1880
San Saba, TX

Died:
June 6, 1953
Ramona, CA.

▷ Batted: Switch
▷ Threw: LH
▷ Position: P
▷ MLB Pitching Record: 30–52
▷ ERA: 2.72

Teams:
Washington Senators AL (1908–1909)
Chicago White Sox AL (1909–1910)
Cincinnati Reds NL (1910–1911)
Philadelphia Phillies NL (1911)
Detroit Tigers AL (1912)

William Thomas Burns

Hal Chase

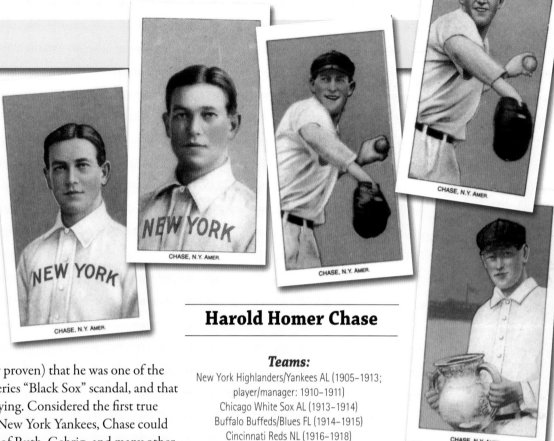

CHASE, N.Y. AMER.

CHASE, N.Y. AMER.

CHASE, N.Y. AMER.

CHASE, N.Y. AMER.

CHASE, N.Y. AMER.

"Prince Hal" Chase is considered one of the greatest first basemen ever to play the game. He was also the most notoriously corrupt. An excellent hitter and fielder, we can only wonder what might have been if he had not been addicted to gambling, betting for and against teams that he played on. He batted over .300 six times, and won the National League batting crown in 1916 with his .339 average. There were claims (never proven) that he was one of the middlemen in the 1919 World Series "Black Sox" scandal, and that at times he "laid down" when playing. Considered the first true star of the team that became the New York Yankees, Chase could have been up there with the likes of Ruth, Gehrig, and many other Yankees' greats. In his later years, when he was drifting from job to job, Chase admitted that he had gambled on games while he was a player and claimed that he was remorseful. His justification was that he hadn't been paid enough money. His punishment is that he never made the Hall of Fame even though some say he was one of the greatest fielding first basemen of all time.

Harold Homer Chase

Teams:
New York Highlanders/Yankees AL (1905–1913;
player/manager: 1910–1911)
Chicago White Sox AL (1913–1914)
Buffalo Buffeds/Blues FL (1914–1915)
Cincinnati Reds NL (1916–1918)
New York Giants NL (1919)

Born:
February 13, 1883
Los Gatos, CA
Died:
May 18, 1947
Colusa, CA

▷ Batted: RH
▷ Threw: LH
▷ Position: 1B
▷ Career BA: .291
▷ Managerial Record: 86–80

Eddie Cicotte

CICOTTE, BOSTON AMER.

Knuckleballer Eddie Cicotte might have made it to the Hall of Fame if he had not been involved in the infamous "Black Sox" scandal of 1919. Along with seven other players, he was banned from baseball for life for allegedly throwing the World Series. A master of trick pitches (the knuckleball, spitball, and shine ball), Eddie "Knuckles" Cicotte was a dominant pitcher. In 1917 he led the American League in wins (28) and ERA (1.53), leading the White Sox to the World Series championship, and he led the league in wins again in 1919 with 29. There is speculation that he was involved in the scandal because owner Charles Comiskey kept him out of the lineup so he would not win 30 games, which would have triggered a $10,000 bonus. In any event, he took the dive and was banned for life after the 1920 season. He later played for some renegade teams under a pseudonym.

Born:
June 19, 1884
Springwells, MI
Died:
May 5, 1969
Detroit, MI

▷ Batted: Switch
▷ Threw: RH
▷ Position: P
▷ MLB Pitching Record: 208–149
▷ ERA: 2.38

Teams:
Detroit Tigers AL (1905)
Boston Red Sox AL (1908–1912)
Chicago White Sox AL (1912–1920)

Edward Victor Cicotte

Mike Donlin

DONLIN, N.Y. NAT'L

DONLIN, N.Y. NAT'L

Teams:
St. Louis Perfectos/Cardinals NL (1899–1900)
Baltimore Orioles AL (1901)
Cincinnati Reds NL (1902–1904)
New York Giants NL (1904–1906, 1908, 1911, 1914)
Boston Rustlers NL (1911)
Pittsburgh Pirates NL (1912)

Born:
May 30, 1878
Peoria, IL

Died:
September 24, 1933
Hollywood, CA

▷ Batted: LH
▷ Threw: LH
▷ Position: OF
▷ Career BA: .333

DONLIN, N.Y. NAT'L

"Turkey Mike" Donlin could have been in the Hall of Fame if not for his extravagant lifestyle. A notorious drinker and playboy, his off-field antics drastically altered a career that could have been great. Donlin batted over .300 in ten of his 12 seasons. His best year was 1905, when he was team captain and batted a lofty .356 to help the Giants win the World Series. He also led the league with his 124 runs scored that year. Donlin was a power hitter, finishing in the top ten in home runs for five seasons. Nicknamed "Turkey" for his red neck and strutting style of walking, Donlin cut short his own career. He ended up in prison for public drunkenness in 1902, causing the Orioles to release him. He also took several seasons off to act in vaudeville with his first wife, and had lost his edge by the time he returned to the game. He managed the Memphis Chickasaws in the Southern Association in 1917, and later scouted for the Boston Braves and New York Giants. Donlin dabbled in silent movies after his baseball career went silent.

Michael Joseph Donlin

Jerry Downs

Jerry "Red" Downs was one of the sadder stories of this era. A decent minor leaguer, he made it to the big leagues in 1907. On May 2, he was starting center fielder for the Tigers, playing next to Ty Cobb. For most of that season, however, he played second base. He played in the 1907 and 1908 World Series, although he was a very lackluster hitter. Downs played in the minors for 9 years after being sent down to the American Association's Minneapolis Millers in 1909. He returned for one more MLB stint in 1912, playing for the Cubs as a sub for the injured Joe Tinker. He managed the San Francisco Seals of the Pacific Coast League in 1917 and faded from baseball soon after. The Great Depression hit him hard, and in March 1932, Downs was arrested for robbing a jewelry store in Los Angeles and convicted. He spent 3 1/2 years in San Quentin. At the time of his arrest, he admitted that his drinking had ruined his major and minor league careers and had gotten him "into this jam."

Teams:
Detroit Tigers AL (1907–1908)
Brooklyn Dodgers NL (1912)
Chicago Cubs NL (1912)

Jerome Willis Downs

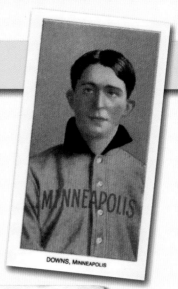

DOWNS, MINNEAPOLIS

Born:
August 22, 1883
Neola, IA

Died:
October 19, 1939
Council Bluffs, IA

▷ Batted: RH
▷ Threw: RH
▷ Position: 2B
▷ Career BA: .227

Jean Dubuc

Jean Joseph Octave Arthur Dubuc

Born:
September 15, 1888
St. Johnsbury, VT
Died:
August 28, 1958
Fort Myers, FL

▷ Batted: RH
▷ Threw: RH
▷ Position: P
▷ MLB Pitching Record: 85–76
▷ ERA: 3.04

Teams:
Cincinnati Reds NL (1908–1909)
Detroit Tigers AL (1912–1916)
Boston Red Sox AL (1918)
New York Giants NL (1919)

Jean "Chauncey" Dubuc is best known for his indirect involvement in the "Black Sox" scandal of 1919. A former teammate claimed Dubuc received a telegram from Sleepy Bill Burns, the alleged middleman between the gamblers and the White Sox players, who was also a former teammate of Dubuc's. The telegram read "Bet on the Cincinnati team today." Some claim Dubuc was one of the players banned from baseball for life, but others point out that he went to Canada for the 1921 season, and thus escaped the commissioner's notice. As an MLB player Dubuc won 17 games twice for the Tigers and finished with 85 wins. He played for several more years in the minors, playing his last game in 1926 at the age of 37 as manager of the Manchester Blue Sox in the New England League. He later managed the New Bedford Whalers in the Northeastern League in 1934. Dubuc went on to coach baseball and hockey for Brown University and also scouted for the Detroit Tigers, signing Birdie Tebbetts and Hank Greenberg among others.

Chick Gandil

Charles "Chick" Gandil will forever be known as the ringleader of the fixing of the 1919 World Series. Gandil was the alleged go-between and pitchman for Joseph "Sport" Sullivan, who masterminded the plan for the White Sox to throw the Series. When he was 17 years old, Gandil ran away from home to play baseball along the Mexican border. To help make ends meet, he boxed professionally as a heavyweight for $150 a fight. He bounced around in the minors for 4 years before his MLB debut in 1910. Gandil finished sixth in MVP voting in 1913, when he ranked eighth in batting average (.318) and RBI and seventh in hits. He started his second tour with the White Sox in 1917 and won the World Series with them that year. Gandil's final game was on September 28, 1919, when he retired and returned to California. Commissioner Landis banned him from baseball for life in 1920. Gandil continued to deny his involvement in the scandal until he died.

Born:
January 19, 1888
St. Paul, MN
Died:
December 13, 1970
Calistoga, CA

▷ Batted: RH
▷ Threw: RH
▷ Position: 1B
▷ Career BA: .277

Teams:
Chicago White Sox AL (1910, 1917–1919)
Washington Senators AL (1912–1915)
Cleveland Indians AL (1916)

Charles Arnold Gandil

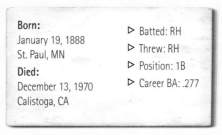

Rube Kroh

KROH, CHICAGO NAT'L

Maverick southpaw Floyd "Rube" Kroh's best year was 1909, when he went 9–4 for the Cubs. However, he was benched for most of the 1910 season for insubordination. Besides curfew violations, he violated his contract by pitching an illegal game for a New Jersey team, after which the Cubs released him. His 2.20 ERA was very good and he could have been a top-notch pitcher if he played by the rules and didn't fight club management. Kroh had a long minor league career before and after his MLB years. He had five 15-win seasons in the minors, posting three of them in the Southern Association for the Nashville Volunteers from 1914 to 1916. He enlisted in the army in 1917 and was injured in action in France. Upon his return, Kroh dabbled in the minors until 1922, but several operations on his right leg, injured in the war, did not succeed in returning him to good playing shape. Unable to play well, he stayed in baseball as an umpire in the minors.

Born:
August 25, 1886
Friendship, NY
Died:
March 17, 1944
New Orleans, LA

▷ Batted: LH
▷ Threw: LH
▷ Position: P
▷ MLB Pitching Record: 14–9
▷ ERA: 2.20

Teams:
Boston Americans/Red Sox AL (1906–1907)
Chicago Cubs NL (1909–1910)
Boston Braves NL (1912)

Floyd Myron Kroh

Dan McGann

McGANN, MILWAUKEE

Dennis Lawrence McGann

Born:
July 15, 1871
Shelbyville, KY
Died:
December 13, 1910
Louisville, KY

▷ Batted: Switch
▷ Threw: RH
▷ Position: 1B
▷ Career BA: .284

Teams:
Boston Beaneaters/Doves NL (1896, 1908)
Baltimore Orioles NL (1898)
Brooklyn Superbas NL (1899)
Washington Senators NL (1899)
St. Louis Cardinals NL (1900–1901)
Baltimore Orioles AL (1902)
New York Giants NL (1902–1907)

One of the early game's best first basemen, Dan "Cap" McGann averaged close to 70 RBI and 30 stolen bases in his first 8 years and led National League first basemen in fielding percentage for six seasons. He and teammate (and future manager) John McGraw were close friends and drinking buddies. Their most notable years as teammates were the Giants' pennant-winning years of 1904 and 1905. A top-ten league leader in RBI, slugging percentage, home runs, and stolen bases, McGann was adept at getting hit by pitches, and is seventh all-time on the hit-by-pitch list with 230. McGann and McGraw came to blows in 1908, which was his final MLB season. He then played two seasons in the American Association for the Milwaukee Brewers. In December 1910 McGann was found dead in his hotel room with a bullet in his chest and a gun in his hand. The death was ruled a suicide, but his sisters believed he was murdered for a diamond ring he wore worth $800.

Larry McLean

George McQuillan

MCLEAN, CINCINNATI

McQUILLAN, PHILA. NAT'L

McQUILLAN, PHILA. NAT'L

John Bannerman McLean

Teams:
Boston Americans AL (1901)
Chicago Cubs NL (1903)
St. Louis Cardinals NL (1904, 1913)
Cincinnati Reds NL (1906–1912)
New York Giants NL (1913–1915)

John McLean took to using the name "Larry" early in his career after someone mentioned he resembled Nap (Larry) Lajoie. A huge presence at 6 feet 5 inches and 230 pounds, he would often become a raging bull due to a losing battle with the bottle. This led to suspensions, brawls, and eventually his untimely death. McLean hit .298 in 1910 while driving in 71 runs and was a .262 career hitter with 298 RBI. He went 6 for 12 in his only World Series appearance with the Giants in 1913. His career ended in 1915 when he staggered up to John McGraw outside their St. Louis hotel and accused the Giants' coaching staff of trying to cheat him out of his $1,000 bonus. A fight ensued; he was cut from the team the next day, and never played in the majors again. In 1921, 39-year-old John McLean climbed over the bar in a Boston speakeasy to attack a bartender and was shot and killed.

Born:
July 18, 1881
Fredericton, New
Brunswick, Canada

Died:
March 24, 1921
Boston, MA

▷ Batted: RH
▷ Threw: RH
▷ Position: C
▷ Career BA: .262

Called "The Giant Killer" for his domination over New York, George McQuillan started his major league career in 1907 by pitching 25 consecutive innings without giving up a run. That record stood for 101 years, until 2008, when the A's Brad Ziegler went 39.1 scoreless innings to open his career. McQuillan posted a 1.69 ERA his first four seasons, including 1908, when he went 23–17 with a 1.53 ERA. He helped lead the Phillies to their 1915 pennant and is still their career ERA leader. Starting in 1909, however, he struggled with alcoholism and was labeled unreliable and out of condition. The Reds sent him to Hot Springs, Arkansas, in 1910 to dry out, but they released him in 1911 since his skills were declining. After a few years with the American Association's Columbus Senators, McQuillan made it back to the Bigs, but was a mediocre pitcher at best. He worked in the minors until 1926, mostly for Columbus, retiring with a 15-season 179–160 minor league pitching record. He later managed a furniture store in Columbus.

Teams:
Philadelphia Phillies NL (1907–1910, 1915–1916)
Cincinnati Reds NL (1911)
Pittsburgh Pirates NL (1913–1915)
Cleveland Indians AL (1918)

Born:
May 1, 1885
Brooklyn, NY

Died:
March 30, 1940
Columbus, OH

▷ Batted: RH
▷ Threw: RH
▷ Position: P
▷ MLB Pitching Record: 85–89
▷ ERA: 2.38

George Watt McQuillan

Bugs Raymond

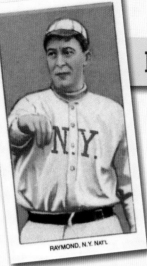

John McGraw once said that Arthur "Bugs" Raymond was the best pitcher he ever tried to manage. Considered one of the best spitball pitchers of the era, Raymond was also one of the game's biggest boozers. Teammate Rube Marquard once said that Bugs didn't spit on the ball, he just breathed on it and it came up drunk. His best season was 1909, when he went 18–12 with 2.47 ERA, despite quitting the Giants with six weeks left in the season to tend bar. Sadly, many felt the more he drank, the better he pitched, feeding his habit. McGraw tried to help Raymond beat his addiction, sending him away for treatment, but he was kicked out of the program for horsing around. Finally admitting defeat, McGraw kicked Raymond off the team in 1911 after he left the Giants' bullpen during a game to go to a local bar. Raymond went back to Chicago and played in the United States League for the Chicago Green Sox for a short time in 1912. In

September of that year, 30-year-old Bugs Raymond died of head injuries suffered in a brawl during a game at the same sandlot field in Chicago where he had played baseball as a kid.

Teams:
Detroit Tigers AL (1904)
St. Louis Cardinals NL (1907–1908)
New York Giants NL (1909–1911)

Born:
February 24, 1882
Chicago, IL
Died:
September 7, 1912
Chicago, IL

▷ Batted: RH
▷ Threw: RH
▷ Position: P
▷ MLB Pitching Record: 45–57
▷ ERA: 2.49

Arthur Lawrence Raymond

Boss Schmidt

Charles "Boss" Schmidt had a powerful physique from working in the coal mines before his baseball days. He was starting catcher for the Tigers during their three consecutive pennant seasons between 1907 and 1909, even though he committed 5 errors and allowed 16 stolen bases in the 1908 World Series. Schmidt is known for his series of fights with teammate Ty Cobb, and he once knocked Cobb unconscious in the Tigers' clubhouse. A skilled fighter, Schmidt reportedly fought an exhibition with heavyweight champion Jack Johnson. He declared himself the toughest player in the game, and to prove it he often caught without shin guards and pounded nails into the floor with his bare fists. After his MLB tour, Schmidt played and managed for several different teams in the minor leagues through the 1927 season.

Born:
September 12, 1880
Coal Hill, AR
Died:
November 14, 1932
Altus, AR

▷ Batted: Switch
▷ Threw: RH
▷ Position: C
▷ Career BA: .243

Team:
Detroit Tigers AL (1906–1911)

Charles Schmidt

Dolly Stark

Heinie Zimmerman

STARK, SAN ANTONIO

ZIMMERMAN, CHICAGO NAT'L

Monroe Randolph Stark

Born:
January 19, 1885
Ripley, MS
Died:
December 1, 1924
Memphis, TN

▷ Batted: RH
▷ Threw: RH
▷ Position: SS
▷ Career BA: .238

Teams:
Cleveland Naps AL (1909)
Brooklyn Superbas/Dodgers NL (1910–1912)

Monroe "Dolly" Stark had already played for four minor league teams over four seasons when he was called up from the Texas League's San Antonio Bronchos to play for the Naps in 1909. The 24-year-old rookie batted .200 in 19 games and 60 at bats that year before returning to the minors. In his four MLB seasons he played in 127 games, hit .238 in 378 at bats, and drove in 30 runs, scored 90, and stole 14 bases. After his stint with Brooklyn, Stark again returned to the minors to play for nine teams in as many seasons. He also managed in four of those seasons, mainly for the Augusta Dollies in the South Atlantic League. The 39-year-old Ripley, Mississippi native was gunned down in a bar fight in Memphis in December 1924.

Henry "Heinie" Zimmerman, or "The Great Zim," was the National League home run champ in 1912 with 14 homers. That same year, he also led the league in batting average (.372), slugging percentage (.571), and seven other categories. In 1916 and 1917 he led the league in RBI. An excellent all-around player, Zimmerman played on two World Series championship teams in 1907 and 1908. However, his big ego and spendthrift ways took a toll on his career. In 1916 the Cubs suspended him for "laying down" and then traded him to the Giants. After a few good years in New York, his performance became erratic, causing speculation that he was dishonest. John McGraw suspended Zimmerman in 1919, along with Hal Chase, for attempting to fix games, and Zimmeran was indicted for bribery. He was then permanently banned from baseball in 1921 for a host of suspected acts of corruption. Zimmerman operated a mob-connected speakeasy in New York in the late 1920s and was indicted for tax evasion in the 1930s.

Born:
February 9, 1887
New York, NY
Died:
March 14, 1969
New York, NY

▷ Batted: RH
▷ Threw: RH
▷ Position: 3B/2B
▷ Career BA: .295

Teams:
Chicago Cubs NL (1907–1916)
New York Giants NL (1916–1919)

Henry Zimmerman

5

THE MINOR LEAGUERS

MANY OF THE SO-CALLED "minor leaguers" in the T206 collection had major league experience, but they were minor leaguers when the T206 set came out. In the true spirit of the national pastime, if they made an appearance in a major league game, we consider them major league players.

The players on the following pages, however, are the players who never made it to the Bigs for one reason or another. They were the true minor leaguers.

BASTIAN, San Antonio

MANION, Columbia

NATTRESS, Buffalo

GUIHEEN, Portsmouth

VIOLAT, Jacksonville

REVELLE, Richmond

SCHIRM, Buffalo

KIERNAN, Columbia

REAGAN, New Orleans

THEBO, Waco

HELM, Columbus

Jack Bastian

BASTIAN, SAN ANTONIO

Born:
Unknown
Died:
Unknown

▷ Batted: N/A
▷ Threw: N/A
▷ Position: 1B
▷ Career BA: .225

Teams:
Albany Senators NYSL (1908)
Gloversville-Johnstown Jags NYSL (1908)
Elmira Colonels NYSL (1908)
San Antonio Bronchos TL (1909)
Reading Pretzels TRIS (1910)
Wilmington Chicks TRIS (1911)

Very little is known about Jack Bastian. He never made it to the major leagues, and he was a marginal first baseman even as a minor leaguer. In 1908 Bastian played in the New York State League for three different teams, and between all of them he batted a lowly .180. He fared better for the San Antonio Bronchos in the Texas League, hitting a respectable .248. He finished up in the Tri-State League, and packed it in after batting .225 in 1,384 at bats and 397 games over four minor league seasons. Why Jack Bastian was included in the historic T206 collection is frankly a mystery.

John K. Bastian

Bill Cranston

CRANSTON, MEMPHIS

Bill Cranston played for 15 seasons in the minors for many different teams. He was a second baseman with a pretty good glove and a fair bat. In 1908 and 1909 Cranston played in the Southern Association for Memphis, as pictured on his T206 card. His best year was 1910, when he batted .335 for the Denver Grizzlies of the Western League. He spent most of his career in the New York State League, playing for six different teams. His claim to fame is that in 1911, while playing for Wilkes-Barre, he was arrested, along with several teammates, for charging admission to a Sunday game which was illegal at the time. That team won the NYSL championship under Billy Clymer.

Born:
Unknown
Died:
Unknown

▷ Batted: N/A
▷ Threw: N/A
▷ Position: 2B
▷ Career BA: .275

William Cranston

Teams:
Wilmington Giants VNCL (1901)
Erie Sailors ISLG (1906)
Syracuse Stars NYSL (1907)
Memphis Egyptians SOUA (1908)
Memphis Turtles SOUA (1909)
Kansas City Blues AA (1910)
Denver Grizzlies WL (1910)
Wilkes-Barre Barons NYSL (1911)
Troy Trojans NYSL (1912–1913)
Binghamton Bingoes NYSL (1914, 1916)
Utica Utes NYSL (1915, 1916)
Scranton Miners NYSL (1916)

Paul Davidson

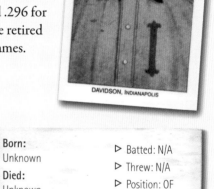

DAVIDSON, INDIANAPOLIS

Paul Davidson had a steady career in the minors, playing for nine different teams. An outfielder with a pretty good glove, Davidson also pitched in 1911 for the Rock Island Islanders and the Dubuque Hustlers, going 1–4. His 1908 Indianapolis Indians team was managed by Charlie Carr. Davidson's best season was 1910, when he batted .296 for Rock Island. After eight seasons in the minors, he retired in 1911 with 883 hits in 3,402 at bats and 911 games.

Teams:
Rockford Red Sox IIIL (1904)
Dubuque Shamrocks IIIL (1905)
Dubuque Dubs IIIL (1906)
Peoria Distillers IIIL (1907)
Indianapolis Indians AA (1908–1909)
Omaha Rourkes WL (1909)
Rock Island Islanders IIIL (1910–1911)
Dubuque Hustlers IIIL (1911)
Seattle Giants NWES (1911)

Born:
Unknown
Died:
Unknown

▷ Batted: N/A
▷ Threw: N/A
▷ Position: OF
▷ Career BA: .260

Paul Davidson

Tom Guiheen

GUIHEEN, PORTSMOUTH

Tom Guiheen had a 14-year career in the minors, but never made it past the B level. A lifetime .250 hitter, he bounced around the minors, spending most of his time in the New England League and the Virginia League. His best year was 1913, when he batted .340 for the Danbury Hatters. Guiheen was an average second baseman, with a career .935 fielding percentage. He also managed the Portsmouth Truckers in 1909 and the Danbury Hatters in 1914.

Born:
December 27, 1882
Vermont
Died:
Unknown

▷ Batted: N/A
▷ Threw: N/A
▷ Position: 2B
▷ Career BA: .250

Teams:

Bangor NENL (1901)
Dover NENL (1902)
Amsterdam-Gloversville-Johnstown NYSL (1902)
Brockton/New Bedford Whalers NENL (1903–1904)
Fall River Indians NENL (1905–1907)
Lynn Shoemakers NENL (1908)
Portsmouth Truckers VIRL (1908–1910; player/manager: 1909)
Petersburg Goobers VIRL (1910–1911)
Danbury Hatters NYNJ/ATLL (1913; player/manager: 1914)
Wellsville Rainmakers ISLG (1916)

Thomas Aloysius Guiheen

James Helm

HELM, COLUMBUS

James Ross Helm

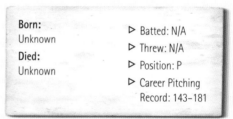

Born:
Unknown
Died:
Unknown

▷ Batted: N/A
▷ Threw: N/A
▷ Position: P
▷ Career Pitching
   Record: 143–181

Teams:

Monroe Hill Citys CSTL (1903–1904)
Macon Brigands SALL (1905–1907)
Montgomery Senators SOUA (1907, 1908)
Jacksonville Jays SALL (1908)
Little Rock Travelers SOUA (1908)
Columbus Foxes SALL (1909)
Chattanooga Lookouts SALL (1909)
Galveston Sand Crabs/Pirates TL (1911–1912, 1914)
Houston Buffaloes TL (1912)
Waco Navigators TL (1913)
Austin Senators TL (1914)

James Ross Helm pitched 12 seasons in the minors, mostly in the Southern Association, the South Atlantic League, and the Texas League. Helm went 18–13 for the Macon Brigands of the South Atlantic Leauge in 1907 and 11–4 for the Jacksonville Jays of the South Atlantic League in 1908, which probably led to his inclusion in the T206 set. When he advanced to the Southern Association in 1908, Helm went only 2–7 in 10 games. Once back in the South Atlantic League in 1909, Helm went 18–12, split between the Columbus Foxes and Chattanooga Lookouts. He went 35–72 in four seasons in the Texas League from 1911 to 1914 before retiring from baseball.

Gordon Hickman

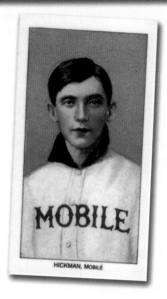

HICKMAN, MOBILE

Gordon Hickman

Born:
Unknown
Died:
Unknown

▷ Batted: N/A
▷ Threw: N/A
▷ Position: P
▷ Career Pitching
    Record: 90–78

Teams:

Monroe Hill Citys CSTL (1904)
Birmingham Barons SOUA (1906)
Shreveport Pirates SOUA (1906–1907)
Mobile Sea Gulls SOUA (1908–1910)
Montgomery Climbers SOUA (1910)
New Orleans Pelicans SOUA (1910)
Decatur Twins SEAL (manager: 1911)
Bessemer Pipemakers SEAL (manager: 1912)

Pitcher Gordon Hickman started his pro career in 1904 with the Monroe Hill Citys of the Cotton States League, going 24–11 that season. He played for five different teams in the A-level Southern Association for the balance of his playing career, going 66–67 over five seasons. In 1910, Hickman, along with the arms of Pat Paige and Otto Hess, supported "Shoeless Joe" Jackson's bat and won the New Orleans Pelicans their second SOUA pennant with an 87–53 record. He managed the Southeastern League's Decatur Twins (1911) and the Bessemer Pipemakers (1912) before retiring from baseball.

Ernie Howard

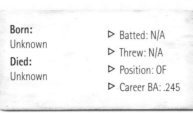

HOWARD, SAVANNAH

Ernie Howard played 14 seasons in the minors beginning in 1902. Howard played six seasons for the Savannah Indians in the South Atlantic League beginning in 1905, hitting .253 as an outfielder, and in 1909 he served as player/manager. His T206 card shows Howard in his Indians uniform. He moved up to the Texas League in 1911 and played for the Fort Worth Panthers until 1914 when he moved to the Austin Senators to finish the season. Howard split 1 more year between the Houston Buffaloes and the Beaumont Oilers of the Texas League in 1915, after which he retired as a .250 career hitter.

Teams:

Baton Rouge Cajuns/Redsticks CSTL (1902–1904)
Savannah Pathfinders/Indians SALL (1905–1910;
player/manager: 1909)
Fort Worth Panthers TL (1911–1914)
Austin Senators TL (1914)
Houston Buffaloes/Beaumont Oilers TL (1915)

Born:
Unknown
Died:
Unknown

▷ Batted: N/A
▷ Threw: N/A
▷ Position: OF
▷ Career BA: .250

Ernest E. Howard

John Kiernan

KIERNAN, COLUMBIA

Teams:

New Bedford Whalers NENL (1904, 1907)
Fall River Indians NENL (1905–1906)
Portsmouth Truckers VIRL (1907)
Columbia Gamecocks SALL (1908–1909)
Jacksonville Jays/Charleston Sea Gulls/Knoxville Appalachians SALL (1909)
Worcester Busters NENL (1909)
Waterbury Finnegans CTST (1910)
Fall River Spindles COLL (player/manager: 1914)
Haverhill Hillies NENL (manager: 1926–1928)

John Kiernan toiled eight seasons in the minors. From 1907 to 1909, he was truly a baseball gypsy, playing for six different teams in three different leagues. He spent most of his pro career in the New England League, playing for the New Bedford Whalers, the Fall River Indians, and the Worcester Busters, and finished his career managing the Haverhill Hillies in that league. Kiernan spent most of 1908 and 1909 in the South Atlantic League with the Columbia Gamecocks, hitting just .217 as an outfielder. He retired after the 1914 season as a .245 career hitter, but returned in 1926 to manage the Hillies.

Born:
Unknown
Died:
Unknown

▷ Batted: N/A
▷ Threw: N/A
▷ Position: OF
▷ Career BA: .245

John F. Kiernan

Frank King

Frank King played seven seasons in the minor leagues from 1904 to 1910, mostly with the Savannah Pathfinders/Indians of the South Atlantic League. Although he was a career .222 hitter, he fared better in Roanoke and Danville, batting .252 for the Roanoke Tigers in 1908 and .243 for the Danville Red Sox in 1909. Over his seven seasons in the South Atlantic League, the Virginia League, and the Carolina Association, he played in 611 games with 487 hits in 2,191 at bats. Frank King retired after the 1910 season.

KING, DANVILLE

Born:
Unknown
Died:
Unknown

▷ Batted: N/A
▷ Threw: N/A
▷ Position: OF
▷ Career BA: .222

Teams:
Savannah Pathfinders/Indians SALL (1904–1907)
Roanoke Tigers VIRL (1908)
Danville Red Sox VIRL (1909)
Winston-Salem Twins CARA (1910)

Frank J. King

James LaFitte

LAFITTE, MACON

Catcher James LaFitte played ball at the minor league level for eight seasons and eight different teams in the Southern Association, the South Atlantic League, the North Carolina State League, the Virginia League, and the Georgia-Alabama League. He is pictured in his Macon Peaches uniform on his T206 card. A lifetime .241 batter, his best year was 1914, when he played for the La Grange Terrapins and hit a robust .278. LaFitte played in some of the lesser C and D leagues for most of his career, but did play in the A league for the New Orleans Pelicans in 1910 and part of 1912.

Teams:
Macon Brigands SALL (1907)
Macon Peaches SALL (1909)
New Orleans Pelicans SOUA (1910, 1912)
Augusta Tourists/Orphans SALL (1911)
Roanoke Tigers VIRL (1912, 1913)
Greensboro Patriots NCSL (1913)
La Grange Terrapins GAAL (1914–1915)

Born:
Unknown
Died:
Unknown

▷ Batted: N/A
▷ Threw: N/A
▷ Position: C
▷ Career BA: .241

James A. LaFitte

Perry Lipe

LIPE, RICHMOND

Perry Hamilton Lipe

Born:
February 14, 1875
Unknown
Died:
January 25, 1955
Irving, IL

▷ Batted: N/A
▷ Threw: N/A
▷ Position: 3B
▷ Career BA: .219
▷ Managerial Record:
584–474

Teams:
Memphis Egyptians SOUA (1902)
Macon Highlanders SALL (1904)
Macon Brigands SALL (1905;
player/manager: 1906–1907)
Richmond Colts VIRL (player/manager: 1908–1909)
Macon Peaches SALL (player/manager: 1910–1911;
manager: 1913)
Savannah Indians SALL (1912)
Savannah Colts SALL (player/manager: 1913–1915)
Albany Babies SALL (player/manager: 1916)

Perry Lipe was a player/manager in the minors for about eight of his 16 total seasons. He was, in fact, a much better manager than player, either winning or always contending for South Atlantic League or Virginia League titles. In 1908, he led the Richmond Colts to the Virginia League championship and he won the South Atlantic League title in 1914 with the Savannah Colts. Lipe also had several second-place and third-place finishes. As a player, he had a .219 career average with very little power. As a manager he won 584 games, 110 more than he lost.

George Manion

MANION, COLUMBIA

George Manion dabbled in the lower minors, playing for the New England League, the Virginia League, the South Atlantic League, and the Central Association. Over his six seasons, he compiled a .196 batting average as well as an anemic .878 fielding percentage. He is pictured as a player for the Columbia Gamecocks on his T206 card, where he batted .173 in 1908. It is interesting that Manion was included in this collection as his batting averages from 1909 through 1911 were .211, .189, and .228, hardly memorable.

Born:
Unknown
Died:
Unknown

▷ Batted: N/A
▷ Threw: N/A
▷ Position: SS
▷ Career BA: .196

Teams:
Fall River Indians NENL (1906)
Norfolk Tars VIRL (1907)
Columbia Gamecocks SALL (1908–1909)
Jacksonville Jays SALL (1909–1910)
Muscatine Camels CENA (1911)
Monmouth Browns CENA (1911)

George Manion

Molly Miller

Charles "Molly" Miller played 11 seasons in the minors, mostly catching for teams like the Cedar Rapids Rabbits of the Illinois-Indiana-Iowa League and the Sioux City Packers of the Western League. From 1907 to 1909 he hit .264 for the Dallas Giants of the Texas League, the team on his T206 card. The A-rated Packers were the highest-level team Miller played for, and he hit .276 in two seasons for them between 1910 and 1911. He had his best year in 1910, when he hit .317 in 477 at bats with 10 home runs and 25 doubles, slugging a hefty .453. Miller retired in 1914 after playing one season for the Peterborough Petes in the Canadian League.

MILLER, DALLAS

Born:
Unknown
Died:
Unknown

▷ Batted: N/A
▷ Threw: N/A
▷ Position: C/P
▷ Career Pitching Record: 6–7
▷ Career BA: .256

Teams:
Cedar Rapids Rabbits IIIL (1902)
Portland Green Gages PNAL (1903)
Salt Lake City Elders PNAL (1903)
Evansville River Rats CENL (1904–1905)
Dallas Giants TL (1907–1909)
Sioux City Packers WL (1910–1911)
Youngstown Steelmen CENL (1912)
Peterborough Petes CANL (1914)

Charles B. Miller

Dom Mullaney

MULLANEY, JACKSONVILLE

Dom Mullaney played parts of 11 seasons in the minors anywhere from the low D leagues to the A leagues. He began his pro career in 1898 as manager of the Atlanta Colts in the Southern Association. A .269 lifetime hitter, his best year was 1905, when he batted .300 for the Montgomery Senators in the A-level South Atlantic League. As first baseman, he was a pretty good fielder, posting a .991 fielding percentage in 1906. Mullaney was player/manager for 9 of his years in the minors. He posted a 252–213 record over his four seasons as manager of the Jacksonville Jays, leading them to a second-place finish in 1907 and the league championship in 1908.

Born:
Unknown
Died:
Unknown

▷ Batted: N/A
▷ Threw: N/A
▷ Position: 1B
▷ Career BA: .269

Teams:
Atlanta Colts SOUA (manager: 1898)
Rock Island Islanders IIIL (1901)
Columbus Senators WA (1901)
Bloomington Blues/Bloomers IIIL (1902–1903)
Memphis Egyptians SOUA (1904)
Birmingham Barons SOUA (1904)
Savannah Pathfinders SALL (player/manager: 1904)
Montgomery Senators SOUA (1905)
Montgomery Senators SALL (player/manager: 1906)
Jacksonville Jays SALL (player/manager: 1907–1910)
Savannah Indians SALL (1911)
Yazoo City Zoos CSTL (player/manager: 1911–1912)
New Orleans Little Pets CSTL (manager: 1912)
Jacksonville Scouts FLOR (player/manager: 1921)

Dominick J. Mullaney

Billy Nattress

Billy Nattress had a pretty good run in the minors, playing primarily at the A level as a shortstop. His best year was his first, when he batted .282 for the Fort Wayne Railroaders in the Western Association in 1901. He also had some good years with the Buffalo Bisons in the Eastern League, where he batted .256 in 1907. He played eight of his career seasons with Buffalo. Defensively, Nattress was average or a little below average, but overall he had a solid 12-year career in the minors. When he moved from Buffalo to the Montreal Royals in 1910, he also moved from playing shortstop to second base, where he played for the rest of his pro career.

Teams:
Fort Wayne Railroaders WA (1901)
Columbus Senators AA (1902)
Buffalo Bisons EL (1902–1909)
Montreal Royals EL (1910–1912)
Syracuse Stars EL (1912)

Born:
1878
Unknown
Died:
December 28, 1956
Sunbury, PA

▷ Batted: N/A
▷ Threw: N/A
▷ Position: SS/2B
▷ Career BA: .242

William W. Nattress

Jimmy Phelan

PHELAN, PROVIDENCE

Born:
Unknown
Died:
Unknown

▷ Batted: N/A
▷ Threw: N/A
▷ Position: OF
▷ Career BA: .241

John "Jimmy" Phelan spent ten seasons in the minors. His T206 card pictures him as a member of the Providence Grays, where he played for four complete seasons and parts of two more as an outfielder. Phelan failed to top a .227 batting average in his last 4 years with the Grays and moved on to play 3 more years with the Utica Utes in the New York State League before retiring after the 1914 season. Overall, Phelan hit .241 in his pro career.

Teams:
Nashua NENL (1905)
Manchester Textiles NENL (1906)
Montreal Royals EL (1906–1907)
Providence Grays EL (1907–1911)
Toronto Maple Leafs EL (1908)
Utica Utes NYSL (1912–1914)

John F. Phelan

Archie Persons

In Archie Persons' first pro season in 1908 he had a .280 season as an outfielder with the Southern Association's Montgomery Senators. This earned him a place in the 1909 T206 collection. Persons never fulfilled his promise, however, and bounced around the Southern Association for two seasons in 1908 and 1909, split 1 year between two teams in the Texas League in 1911, and played his swan song in the Western Canada League in 1912. He did play against "Shoeless Joe" Jackson and the New Orleans Pelicans in 1909.

PERSONS, MONTGOMERY

Teams:
Montgomery Senators SOUA (1908)
Montgomery Climbers SOUA (1909)
Little Rock Travelers SOUA (1909)
Oklahoma City Indians TL (1911)
San Antonio Bronchos TL (1911)
Bassano Boosters WCAN (1912)

Born:
Unknown
Died:
Unknown

▷ Batted: N/A
▷ Threw: RH
▷ Position: OF
▷ Career BA: .279

Archie Persons

Phillip Poland

POLAND, BALTIMORE

Phillip Poland played ten seasons with a lifetime .284 batting average at the A-level and B-level of minor league baseball, so it's a mystery why he never got a chance to play in the big leagues. His best years were with the Trenton Tigers, when he batted .326 in 1913 and .324 in 1914. He also had good seasons in the tough Eastern League with the Providence Clamdiggers/Grays and the Baltimore Orioles. Poland's fielding records are incomplete, but from what is available, he was an average outfielder. He retired in 1914 after playing 1,152 minor league games with 4,322 at bats, 1,229 hits, and 8 homers.

Born: Unknown	▷ Batted: N/A
Died: Unknown	▷ Threw: N/A
	▷ Position: OF
	▷ Career BA: .284

Teams:
Providence Clamdiggers/Grays EL (1905–1908)
Haverhill Hustlers NENL (1908)
Baltimore Orioles EL (1909)
Troy Trojans NYSL (1910–1911)
Johnstown/Chester Johnnies TRIS (1912)
Trenton Tigers TRIS (1913–1914)

Phillip Poland

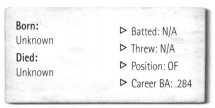

Ed Reagan

REAGAN, NEW ORLEANS

Edward L. Reagan

Born: Unknown	▷ Batted: N/A
Died: Unknown	▷ Threw: N/A
	▷ Position: SS/2B
	▷ Career BA: .227

Teams:
Cordele GASL (1906)
Monroe Municipals GULF/CSTL (1907–1908)
East Liverpool Potters OHPA (1909)
Savannah Indians SALL (1910)
New Orleans Pelicans SOUA (1910)
Meridian White Ribbons CSTL (1911)
Columbus Foxes SALL (1912)
Cordele Babies EMST (player/manager: 1913)
Cordele Ramblers GASL (player/manager: 1914)
Charleston Sea Gulls SALL (manager: 1915)
Griffin Lightfoots GAAL (manager: 1916)

For nine seasons, Ed Reagan toiled in the lower minors playing shortstop and second base for teams like the Monroe Municipals and Cordele Babies. He split 1910 between the Savannah Indians of the C-level South Atlantic League and the New Orleans Pelicans of the A-level Southern Association. Only 32 of his 2,562 career at bats were with New Orleans, since he only lasted 10 games at the highest level of professional baseball he ever reached. Reagan retired as a player after the 1914 season, hitting .227 over his career. He served as player/manager his last two seasons in Cordele, and then managed 2 more years after his playing days, most notably with the Charleston Sea Gulls of the South Atlantic League.

Dutch Revelle

REVELLE, RICHMOND

Ray Ryan

RYAN, ROANOKE

A catcher for 11 seasons in the minors, Ray Ryan made his mark on the game as a manager. His T206 card shows him during his Roanoke Tigers days, when he hit .213 in 1909. A mediocre hitter, Ryan ended up managing as well as catching for his Chillicothe, Norfolk, Wheeling, and Rocky Mount teams, leading the Rocky Mount Carolinians to first place in the league in 1915. After his playing career, Ryan managed in the Pennsylvania State Association and the New York–Pennsylvania League from 1934 to 1936. He managed the Palatka Azaleas of the Florida State League in 1948 before retiring from the game. He was president of the Appalachian League (1937, 1939), the Mountain State League (1937–1941), and the Virginia League (1939–1941).

Robert "Dutch" Revelle played eight seasons in the Virginia League, mostly with the Richmond Colts, as shown on his T206 card. His best years were 1908, when he went 26–12 for the Colts, and 1909, when he pitched an even better 29–11. Revelle pitched more than 300 innings in three separate seasons, one with the Portsmouth Truckers and two with the Colts. After playing 21 innings with the Portsmouth Pirates in 1913, he retired at the age of 31 with a career record of 110–94.

Ray Ryan

Teams:
Lancaster Lanks OHPA (1906)
Danville Red Sox VIRL (1907–1908)
Roanoke Tigers VIRL (1909)
Birmingham Barons SOUA (1910)
Chillicothe Infants OHSL (player/manager: 1912)
Springfield Reapers CENL (1912)
South Bend Benders CENL (1912)
Norfolk Tars VIRL (player/manager: 1913)
Wheeling Stogies ISLG (manager: 1913)
Richmond Colts VIRL (1914)
Rocky Mount Carolinians/Tar Heels VIRL (player/manager: 1915–1916; manager: 1917)
Syracuse Stars IL (1922)
Jeannette Reds PASA (manager: 1934)
Reading/Allentown Brooks NYPL (manager: 1935)
McKeesport Tubers PASA (manager: 1936)

Born:
1882
Virginia
Died:
Unknown

▷ Batted: N/A
▷ Threw: N/A
▷ Position: P
▷ Career Pitching Record: 110–94

Teams:
Portsmouth Truckers VIRL (1906–1907)
Richmond Colts VIRL (1907–1911)
Newport News Shipbuilders VIRL (1912)
Portsmouth Pirates VIRL (1913)

Robert H. Revelle

Born:
Unknown
Died:
August 9, 1958
Miami, FL

▷ Batted: N/A
▷ Threw: N/A
▷ Position: C
▷ Career BA: .217

George Schirm

SCHIRM, BUFFALO

George Schirm played nine seasons in the minors, including six seasons with the Buffalo Bisons in the Eastern League and the International League. He hit .267 in 1908 for the Bisons, his third pro season. His best year was 1912, when the Bisons moved to the International League. Schirm hit .313 that season in 352 at bats. He retired at 29 years old after playing for the Springfield Reapers in the Central League in 1914.

Born:
November 22, 1884
Unknown
Died:
Unknown

▷ Batted: N/A
▷ Threw: N/A
▷ Position: OF
▷ Career BA: .260

Teams:
Columbia Gamecocks SALL (1906)
Buffalo Bisons EL (1907–1911)
Buffalo Bisons IL (1912)
Oakland Oaks PCL (1913)
Springfield Reapers CENL (1914)

George W. Schirm

Charlie Seitz

Charlie Seitz played for seven different minor league teams at a variety of different levels, from the D-level Burlington Flint Hills to the Atlanta Crackers and Mobile Sea Gulls in the A-level Southern Association. He started his career as a pitcher, but moved to outfield for Norfolk after going a dismal 2–11 in 1905 for Burlington. A steady player and a .261 lifetime hitter, Seitz batted .326 in 1909 for the Norfolk Tars, which was his best year by far. He switched to playing second base in 1910, and that was his position for the balance of his career.

SEITZ, NORFOLK

Born:
August 14, 1884
Dayton, OH
Died:
Unknown

▷ Batted: N/A
▷ Threw: N/A
▷ Position: 2B/OF
▷ Career BA: .261

Teams:
Burlington Flint Hills ILPB (1905)
Norfolk Tars VIRL (1906–1909)
Atlanta Crackers SOUA (1910)
Mobile Sea Gulls SOUA (1910–1911)
San Antonio Bronchos TL (1912–1913)
Oakland Oaks PCL (1913)
Houston Buffaloes TL (1914–1916)

Charles W. Seitz

Harry Sentz (Lentz)

LENTZ, LITTLE ROCK

Harry Sentz played most of his 5-year career in the C-rated minor leagues. His best season was 1911, when he batted .295 for the East Liverpool Potters in the Ohio-Pennsylvania League, but this was one of the lower leagues. In the A league, he only managed to bat .238 for the Little Rock Travelers. Sentz was considered a good defensive outfielder with a strong arm.

Teams:
Fort Worth Panthers TL (1908)
Little Rock Travelers SOUA (1909)
Wheeling Stogies CENL (1910)
East Liverpool Potters OHPA (1910–1911))
Richmond Colts VIRL (1913)

Born:
Unknown
Died:
Unknown

▷ Batted: N/A
▷ Threw: N/A
▷ Position: OF
▷ Career BA: .271

Harry Sentz

Carlos Smith

SMITH, SHREVEPORT

A very good hitter and outfielder, Carlos Smith had a distinguished 12-year career playing for several minor league teams at different levels. In 1904 he was at bat an incredible 859 times, banging out 243 hits and batting .283 for the Seattle Siwashes in the A-rated Pacific Coast League. He had some other great seasons batting .322 for the Shreveport Pirates in 1909 and .401 for the Hattiesburg Woodpeckers in 1911. Smith was also a good defensive player, and even appeared as a pitcher on 13 occasions over his career. He managed several teams in the Cotton States League from 1911 to 1913.

Born:
Unknown
Died:
Unknown

▷ Batted: N/A
▷ Threw: N/A
▷ Position: OF
▷ Career BA: .296

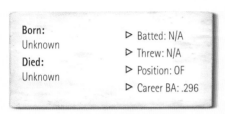

Carlos Smith

Teams:
Natchez Indians CSTL (1902)
New Orleans Pelicans SOUA (1902)
Portland Browns PCL (1903)
Seattle Siwashes PCL (1903–1904)
Birmingham Barons SOUA (1905–1908)
Indianapolis Indians AA (1909)
Shreveport Pirates TL (1909–1910)
Vicksburg Hill Billies CSTL (manager: 1911)
Hattiesburg Woodpeckers/Timberjacks CSTL (1911; player/manager: 1912)
Columbus Joy Riders CSTL (player/manager: 1912)
Meridan Metropolitans CSTL (player/manager: 1913)
Clarksdale Swamp Angels CSTL (manager: 1913)

Tony Thebo

Tony Thebo's professional career spanned 20 years, but it took 12 years just for him to get out of Texas. On his T206 card he is pictured as one of the Waco Navigators, where he hit .224 in 1909. Thebo bounced around three Texas leagues until 1913, hitting over .246 just three of those seasons. His best year was 1907, when he hit .254 with 24 doubles, 8 triples, and 9 home runs for the Temple Boll Weevils. Legend holds that he stole 90 bases 1 year in the Texas League.

Teams:
Paris Eisenfelder's Homeseekers TL (1902)
Natchez Indians CSTL (1903)
Corsicana Oil Citys TL (1903, 1904)
Beaumont Millionaires STEX (1904, 1905)
Brenham Orphans STEX (1905)
San Antonio Bronchos STEX (1905–1906, 1912)
Temple Boll Weevils TL (1907)
Shreveport Pirates TL (1908)
Waco Navigators TL (1909–1910)
Dallas Giants TL (1910–1911)
Galveston Sand Crabs/Pirates TL (1911, 1912)
Beaumont Oilers TL (1912)
Denison Katydids TXOK (1912)
Ardmore Giants TXOK (1913)
Flint Vehicles SMIL (1914)
Muskogee Mets WA (1915–1916)
Paris Athletics/Ardmore Foundlings WA (1917)
Clarksdale Cubs MSSL (1921)

THEBO, WACO

Born:
1882
Unknown
Died:
Unknown

▷ Batted: N/A
▷ Threw: N/A
▷ Position: OF
▷ Career BA: .233

Antonio V. Thebo

Woody Thornton

THORNTON, MOBILE

Born:
April 1, 1882
California, PA
Died:
December 11, 1956
Mobile, AL

▷ Batted: N/A
▷ Threw: RH
▷ Position: OF
▷ Career BA: .261

Teams:
Columbia Skyscrapers SALL (1904)
Augusta Tourists SALL (1904)
Montgomery Senators SOUA (1905–1906)
Gulfport Crabs CSTL (1906)
Mobile Sea Gulls CSTL/SOUA (1906–1909)
Greenwood Chauffeurs/Scouts CSTL
(player/manager: 1910–1911)
Jackson Drummers CSTL (1911)
Columbus Foxes SALL (1914)

Woody Thornton spent 9 years in the minors, playing for teams like the Columbia Skyscrapers and the Augusta Tourists of the South Atlantic League, the Montgomery Senators and the Mobile Sea Gulls of the Southern Association, and the Jackson Drummers and the Greenwood Chauffeurs of the Cotton State League. A .261 career hitter, Thornton hit .279 or better three times in his career, including a .316 season in 1911. He managed Greenwood for two seasons, winning the pennant in 1910, and in 1911 his 10 triples were good for first in the league.

Woody Austin Thornton

Juan Violat

VIOLAT, JACKSONVILLE

Although his personal information is spotty, we do know that Juan Violat was one of the first Cuban players ever to play the game in the United States. An outfielder with a good bat, Violat's best years were 1913, when he batted .349, and 1914, when he batted .420, for the D-league Long Branch Cubans. He had a steady bat playing in the C-rated South Atlantic League for the Jacksonville Jays and the Augusta Tourists, hitting .256 over his eight seasons in the league. Defensively, he was an average outfielder. Violat did play 40 games in 1911 for the Nashville Volunteers of the A-level Southern Association, batting .212. He also pitched 6 games for the Jacksonville Jays in 1908, going 3–3.

Born:
Cuba
Died:
Unknown

▷ Batted: N/A
▷ Threw: RH
▷ Position: OF
▷ Career BA: .276

Teams:
Jacksonville Jays SALL (1904–1909)
Augusta Tourists SALL (1909–1910)
Jacksonville Tarpons SALL (1911)
Nashville Volunteers SOUA (1911)
Long Branch Cubans NYNJ (1913)
Newark/Long Branch Cubans ATLL (1914)

Juan Violat

James Westlake

James Westlake wandered his way through eight pro seasons, catching for seven different teams in six different leagues. He started with the Paterson Intruders in the Hudson Valley League in 1904, and over the course of his pro career he played for the Virginia League, the Eastern Carolina League, the Carolina Association, the Appalachian League, and the Atlantic League. Westlake hit .265 with the Spartanburg Spartans in 1911, but never had another season above .239. While with the Danville Red Sox, as pictured on his T206 card, Westlake hit just .169 in 1909. Over his career, he batted .226 with 416 hits and 1 homer in 1,837 at bats and 429 games.

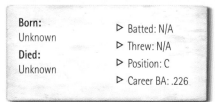

WESTLAKE, DANVILLE

Born:
Unknown
Died:
Unknown

▷ Batted: N/A
▷ Threw: N/A
▷ Position: C
▷ Career BA: .226

Teams:
Paterson Intruders HUDR (1904, 1906)
Lynchburg Shoemakers VIRL (1908)
Danville Red Sox VIRL (1909)
Wilson Tobacconists ECAR (1910)
Spartanburg Spartans CARA (1911)
Morristown Jobbers APPY (1912)
Paterson Silk Citys ATLL (1914)

James A. Westlake

WHITE, HOUSTON

Foley White

How can you not like someone who played for teams like the Millionaires, the Boll Weevils, and the Brownies? Foley White bounced around 11 different teams during his eight-season minor league career. He was a catcher who played C-level and D-level ball, mostly in the Texas League, the South Texas League, and the Texas-Oklahoma League. White did manage 24 at bats in the A-level Southern Association, batting a meager .143 for Mobile in 1908. He retired after the 1914 season, with a .243 batting average in 556 minor league games and 1,875 at bats.

Teams:
Beaumont Millionaires STEX (1905)
Brenham Orphans STEX (1905)
Temple Boll Weevils TL (1907)
Shreveport Pirates TL (1908)
Galveston Sand Crabs TL (1908)
Mobile Sea Gulls SOUA (1908)
Waco Navigators TL (1909–1910)
Brownsville Brownies SWTX (1910)
Dallas Giants TL (1910)
Jackson Drummers CSTL (1911)
Ardmore Giants TXOK (1913)
Ardmore Indians TXOK (1914)

Born:
Unknown
Died:
1955
Dallas, TX

▷ Batted: N/A
▷ Threw: N/A
▷ Position: C
▷ Career BA: .243

Foley B. White

6

THE COMMONS

COMMON MEN AND WOMEN are responsible for building this great nation, whether they were office workers, police officers, or construction workers. This holds true in any industry.

The game of baseball is no exception. The "commons" were (and still are) the majority of major league baseball players.

They came from a variety of backgrounds, but they all shared a love of the game, and each in his own way made a contribution. Some have long been forgotten; others remain in our memories. However, if it were not for the common players, we would not have a national pastime.

Meet the commons.

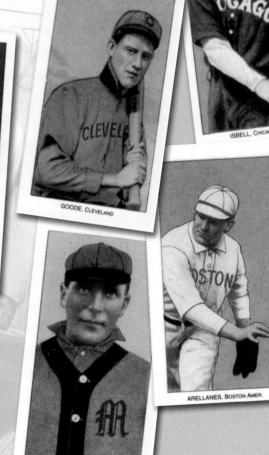

Fred Abbott

ABBOTT, TOLEDO

"Faithful Fred" Abbott was 28 years old when he came up to the majors after two seasons with the New Orleans Pelicans of the Southern Association. He had a short stint in the majors as a marginal hitter and mediocre catcher. Abbott got into a pretty good scrap on April 22, 1905, with Dan McGann of the Giants, which led to a bench-clearing brawl. After his brief tour in the majors, he went back to the minors and played in the American Association for the Columbus Senators in 1904 and the Toledo Mud Hens from 1906 to 1910. He finished up his pro career with the Los Angeles Angels of the Pacific Coast League in 1911. Abbott fared better in the minors, retiring at age 36 after batting .269 in 2,771 at bats over nine seasons.

Born:
October 22, 1874
Versailles, OH
Died:
June 11, 1935
Los Angeles, CA

▷ Batted: RH
▷ Threw: RH
▷ Position: C
▷ Career BA: .209

Teams:
Cleveland Naps AL (1903–1904)
Philadelphia Phillies NL (1905)

Harry Frederick Abbott

Born: Harry Frederick Winbigler

Bill Abstein

ABSTEIN, PITTSBURG

"Big Bill" Abstein was 23 when he got his first shot at the majors in 1906. He came up from Shreveport of the Southern Association, where he had batted .311 that year. Abstein saw just 20 at bats in 8 games before going back to the minors to play for the Providence Grays of the Eastern League. There he hit .279 in 1907 and .272 in 1908, and earned a trip back to the majors. The highlight of his short major league experience was playing in all 7 games of the 1909 World Series, helping the Pirates beat Ty Cobb's Tigers. After his tour with the Browns, he played seven more seasons in the minors, mostly with the Jersey City Skeeters in the Eastern League and the Memphis Chickasaws in the Southern Association. Abstein retired in 1916 after batting .273 in 1,501 games with 5,609 at bats over his minor league career. Bill Abstein was also considered one of the nation's best soccer players.

Teams:
Pittsburgh Pirates NL (1906, 1909)
St. Louis Browns AL (1910)

William Henry Abstein

Born:
February 2, 1883
St. Louis, MO
Died:
April 8, 1940
St. Louis, MO

▷ Batted: RH
▷ Threw: RH
▷ Position: 1B
▷ Career BA: .242

Whitey Alperman

ALPERMAN, BROOKLYN

Charles "Whitey" Alperman came up to the majors after four seasons with the Davenport River Rats of the Illinois-Indiana-Iowa League. Although he had a fairly unremarkable major league career, he did lead the National League with 16 triples in 1907. Alperman had a tendency to be hit by pitches; he was second in the league in that category in 1906 and third in 1907. His main claim to fame is that in 442 at bats in 1909 he walked only twice, which is the lowest single-season walk ratio in the 20th century for a player with more than 300 at bats. That year he batted .248, and ruined a no-hitter when he got a hit in the tenth inning on opening day. Alperman returned to the minors in 1910, playing for the Rochester Bronchos in the Eastern League. He then became player/manager of the Atlanta Crackers of the Southern Association in 1912. He retired in 1913 after batting .266 in 3,335 at bats over eight minor league seasons.

Born:
November 11, 1879
Etna, PA
Died:
December 25, 1942
Pittsburgh, PA

▷ Batted: RH
▷ Threw: RH
▷ Position: 2B
▷ Career BA: .237

Team:
Brooklyn Superbas NL (1906–1909)

Charles Augustus Alperman

ARELLANES, BOSTON AMER.

Frank Arellanes

Santa Clara University alumnus and West Coast native, Frank Arellanes was one of the first Latin American ballplayers and was a pretty good pitcher for a short time. In 1909 he went 16–12 for the Sox with a 2.18 ERA, and he led the league in saves with 8. That year he had the dubious distinction of replacing Cy Young in the rotation. After his tour with the Red Sox, he returned to the minors to pitch, mostly for the Sacramento Sacts in the Pacific Coast League. Although his major league career took place on the East Coast, his entire minor league career was on the West Coast, where he went 85–81 over 11 seasons. Arellanes pitched his final season in 1917 at age 35. He died the following year during the flu pandemic.

Team:
Boston Red Sox AL (1908–1910)

Frank Julian Arellanes

Born:
January 8, 1882
Santa Cruz, CA
Died:
December 13, 1918
San Jose, CA

▷ Batted: RH
▷ Threw: RH
▷ Position: P
▷ MLB Pitching Record: 24–22
▷ ERA: 2.28

ARMBRUSTER, ST. PAUL

Harry Armbruster

Harry "Army" Armbruster, also known as "Herman" and "Henry," was one of those players with very good minor league stats who only got one shot in the Bigs. After a few years with the Providence Grays in the Eastern League, he moved to the New England League. He split 1905 between the Manchester Textiles and the Lawrence Colts, and batted .339 to earn his berth in the majors. In his 91 MLB games, Armbruster batted .238 in 265 at bats, hit 2 homers, and swiped 13 bases. After leaving Connie Mack's A's, he went back to the minors to hit .322 for the Toledo Mud Hens in the American Association in 1907 and .302 for the Syracuse Stars in the New York State League in 1910. He played for the St. Paul Saints in the American Association in 1909, as pictured on his T206 card. Over a minor league career spanning 9 years, Armbruster batted .292 in 3,966 at bats.

Born:
March 20, 1882
Liverpool, OH
Died:
December 10, 1953
Cincinnati, OH

▷ Batted: LH
▷ Threw: LH
▷ Position: OF
▷ Career BA: .238

Team:
Philadelphia Athletics AL (1906)

Henry Gregory Armbruster

Harry Arndt

ARNDT, PROVIDENCE

Harry John Arndt

Harry Arndt's primary position was second base until he complained to his manager that he was afraid of being spiked on steal attempts. His manager promptly moved him to third base. In 1903 and 1904 Arndt played in the minors, hitting .309 for the Louisville Colonels of the American Association in 1904, which earned him a trip back to the big leagues. A .248 hitter, one of his best years was 1905, when he batted .243 with 101 hits. After his MLB days, he played six more seasons in the minors, primarily for the Providence Grays of the Eastern League. Arndt managed the South Bend Benders of the Central League in 1912 and the Ludington Mariners of the Michigan State League in 1913. After nine seasons in the minors, he retired in 1913 at age 34 with a career .275 batting average in the minors. He died of tuberculosis in 1921.

Teams:
Detroit Tigers AL (1902)
Baltimore Orioles AL (1902)
St. Louis Cardinals NL (1905–1907)

Born:
February 12, 1879
South Bend, IN
Died:
March 25, 1921
South Bend, IN

▷ Batted: RH
▷ Threw: RH
▷ Position: 2B/3B/OF
▷ Career BA: .248

Jap Barbeau

BARBEAU, ST. LOUIS NAT'L.

William "Jap" Barbeau was a utility third baseman for three different teams in his four major league seasons. In 1909 he made the National League's top ten in stolen bases (33), runs (83), walks (65), and hit by pitch (9). Other than that, he was basically a marginal player. He played for 13 seasons in the minors around his MLB seasons. After his stint in the big leagues, Barbeau played in the American Association, mostly for the Kansas City Blues and Milwaukee Brewers. He retired from the game after the 1919 season with a .265 batting average in 1,585 games and 5,540 minor league at bats.

Born:
June 10, 1882
New York, NY
Died:
September 10, 1969
Milwaukee, WI

▷ Batted: RH
▷ Threw: LH
▷ Position: 3B
▷ Career BA: .225

Teams:
Cleveland Naps AL (1905–1906)
Pittsburgh Pirates NL (1909)
St. Louis Cardinals NL (1909–1910)

William Joseph Barbeau

Cy Barger

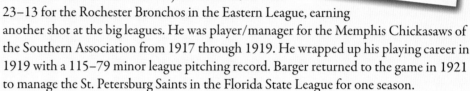

BARGER, ROCHESTER

Eros "Cy" Barger attended Transylvania University in Lexington, Kentucky, before his baseball days. Barger was a right-handed pitcher, utility infielder, and outfielder in the majors. He had no decisions in the American League, but won 15 games in 1910 and 11 games in 1911 for Brooklyn. He won a total of 19 games over 2 years with the Rebels. Barger played nine seasons in the minors around his three stints in the majors. In 1909, he went 23–13 for the Rochester Bronchos in the Eastern League, earning another shot at the big leagues. He was player/manager for the Memphis Chickasaws of the Southern Association from 1917 through 1919. He wrapped up his playing career in 1919 with a 115–79 minor league pitching record. Barger returned to the game in 1921 to manage the St. Petersburg Saints in the Florida State League for one season.

Born:
May 18, 1885
Jamestown, KY
Died:
September 23, 1964
Columbia, KY

▷ Batted: LH
▷ Threw: RH
▷ Position: P
▷ MLB Pitching Record:
   46–63
▷ ERA: 3.56
▷ K's: 297

Teams:
New York Highlanders AL (1906–1907)
Brooklyn Superbas/Dodgers NL (1910, 1911–1912)
Pittsburgh Rebels FL (1914–1915)

Eros Bolivar Barger

Shad Barry

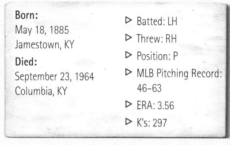

BARRY, MILWAUKEE

John "Shad" Barry was a decent journeyman ballplayer. After attending Niagara University, he bounced around the majors, playing for seven different teams over his 10-year career. His best years were 1905, when he batted .324 for the Reds with 495 at bats, and 1902, when he batted .287 with 543 at bats for the Phillies. He played for the Milwaukee Brewers of the American Association in 1909 and 1910. Barry then played for the Portland Beavers in the Pacific Coast League before moving to the Seattle Giants in the Northwestern League as player/manager in 1912. He played one last season for the Troy Trojans in the New York State League before retiring in 1913 at the age of 34 with a minor league career .244 batting average.

Born:
October 27, 1878
Newburgh, NY
Died:
November 27, 1936
Los Angeles, CA

▷ Batted: RH
▷ Threw: RH
▷ Position: OF/1B
▷ Career BA: .267

Teams:
Washington Senators NL (1899)
Boston Beaneaters NL (1900–1901)
Philadelphia Phillies NL (1901–1904)
Chicago Cubs NL (1904–1905)
Cincinnati Reds NL (1905–1906)
St. Louis Cardinals NL (1906–1908)
New York Giants NL (1908)

John C. Barry

Emil Batch

BATCH, ROCHESTER

A promising minor league outfielder, 24-year-old Emil Batch, also known as "Heinie" and "Ace," came up to the Superbas after batting .337 for Holyoke of the Connecticut State League. He split his time between the outfield and third base, but was only a marginal player. His best year was 1905, when he batted .252 with 568 at bats. His 5 home runs that year were good for seventh in the league. Unfortunately, he also made 57 errors in 145 games that year. Batch returned to the minors in 1908 to play 5 years for the Rochester Bronchos in the Eastern League. He then played for the Eastern Association's Bridgeport Crossmen and the New York State League's Binghamton Bingoes, finishing up with a .284 minor league batting average. He retired after the 1913 season at age 33 and became a telephone operator.

Born:
January 21, 1880
Brooklyn, NY
Died:
August 23, 1926
Brooklyn, NY

▷ Batted: RH
▷ Threw: RH
▷ Position: 3B/OF
▷ Career BA: .251

Team:
Brooklyn Superbas NL (1904–1907)

Emil Batch

Johnny Bates

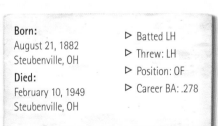

BATES, BOSTON NAT'L

A decent outfielder, Johnny Bates played both full-time and part-time for nine seasons in the majors. His best year was 1911, when he batted .292 and stole 33 bases. He also placed second in the league that year with 103 walks, and his on-base percentage of .415 was good for third in the league. Bates hit 6 homers in 1906 and 6 again in 1913, not bad for the dead-ball era. Considered a base-stealing threat, he swiped a total of 187 bases over his MLB career. After a short tour in the Federal League, he played four seasons in the minors for five teams in three different leagues. He retired in 1918 at age 35 with a .297 batting average in 1,225 minor league at bats.

Born:
August 21, 1882
Steubenville, OH
Died:
February 10, 1949
Steubenville, OH

▷ Batted LH
▷ Threw: LH
▷ Position: OF
▷ Career BA: .278

Teams:
Boston Beaneaters/Doves NL (1906–1909)
Philadelphia Phillies NL (1909–1910)
Cincinnati Reds NL (1911–1914)
Chicago Cubs NL (1914)
Baltimore Terrapins FL (1914)

John William Bates

Fred Beck

BECK, BOSTON NAT'L

Fred Beck was a pretty good power hitter during the dead-ball era. In 1910 he tied for the MLB lead in homers with 10. In 1914, while playing for Joe Tinker's Chicago team in the Federal League, he went deep another 11 times. At 24 years old, with a very good 1910 season under his belt, he became one of baseball's first holdouts during the winter of 1910 to 1911. He demanded more money for his performance, and was traded to Cincinnati. Around his time in the majors, Beck had a 16-year minor league career. He played his best years for Wichita in the Western League, batting .332 with 30 home runs in 1920, .324 with 35 homers in 1921, and .317 with 38 homers in 1924 at age 37. After 1,756 minor league games with 6,417 at bats, 166 home runs, and a .292 minor league career batting average, Beck retired in 1926.

Frederick Thomas Beck

Teams:
Boston Doves NL (1909–1910)
Cincinnati Reds NL (1911)
Philadelphia Phillies NL (1911)
Chicago Whales FL (1914–1915)

Born:
November 17, 1886
Havana, IL
Died:
March 12, 1962
Havana, IL

▷ Batted: LH
▷ Threw: LH
▷ Position: 1B/OF
▷ Career BA: .252

George Bell

BELL, BROOKLYN

George "Farmer" Bell was a hard-luck pitcher who played for some really lousy Brooklyn teams. Bell was 32 years old when he came up to the majors, after going 23–16 for the Tri-State League's Altoona Mountaineers in 1906. His MLB career 2.85 ERA indicates that Bell was actually a good pitcher. His best year was 1909, when he went 16–15 for a team that was 55–98. In 1910, Bell went 10–27 to lead the league in losses, but his ERA was an excellent 2.64. After his MLB days, he pitched in the minors for 5 more years, 3 of them for the Newark Indians of the International League. Bell retired in 1915 at age 40 with a seven-season minor league record of 56–42.

Born:
November 2, 1874
Greenwood, NY

Died:
December 25, 1941
New York, NY

▷ Batted: RH
▷ Threw: RH
▷ Position: P
▷ MLB Pitching Record: 43–79
▷ ERA: 2.85

Team:
Brooklyn Superbas/Dodgers NL (1907–1911)

George Glenn Bell

BELL, BROOKLYN

Heinie Berger

BERGER, CLEVELAND

Charles Carl Berger

Born:
January 7, 1882
LaSalle, IL

Died:
February 10, 1954
Lakewood, OH

▷ Batted: N/A
▷ Threw: RH
▷ Position: P
▷ MLB Pitching Record: 32–29
▷ ERA: 2.60

Team:
Cleveland Naps AL (1907–1910)

After pitching four seasons in the minors, Charles "Heinie" Berger got his shot at the majors in 1907. The 25-year-old rookie came up to the Naps from the Columbus Senators of the American Association, where he went 25–14 in 1905 and 28–13 in 1906. A master of the spitter, he led American League pitchers in strikeout ratio, with an average of 5.90 K's per nine innings pitched in 1909. Berger had trouble with control in the majors, however, and ended up leading the league in wild pitches in 1909. He went 13–8 in 1908, probably his best year in the majors. After his MLB days, he returned to pitch another year for Columbus before moving to the Mobile Sea Gulls and the Nashville Volunteers in the Southern Association. He retired in 1915 after going 136–98 in nine minor league seasons.

Jack Bliss

BLISS, ST. LOUIS NAT'L

After attending the University of California, 21-year-old Jack Bliss began his pro career in 1903 with the Oakland Reliance of the California State League. He then moved up to the A level to catch for the Oakland Oaks of the Pacific Coast League before hitting the big time in 1908. During his 5-year tour with the Cardinals, Bliss was the backup catcher for player/manager, catcher, and future Hall of Famer Roger Bresnahan. He was a pretty good defensive player but a poor hitter, and was finally sold by the Cards to the Sacramento Sacts of the Pacific Coast League, where he played the 1913 season. Bliss then moved on to play the 1914 season with the Venice Tigers in that same league. He retired after the 1914 season with a .223 minor league batting average.

Born:
January 9, 1882
Vancouver, WA

Died:
October 23, 1968
Temple City, CA

▷ Batted: RH
▷ Threw: RH
▷ Position: C
▷ Career BA: .219

Team:
St. Louis Cardinals NL (1908–1912)

John Joseph Albert Bliss

Dave Brain

English-born Dave Brain came up to the majors from the Buffalo Bisons of the Eastern League. In 1903 he stole 21 bases for the Cards and hit 15 triples, but his poor fielding made him just a journeyman ballplayer. He had a decent bat, though, and led the league in home runs in 1907. Actually, Brain set league records when he hit 3 triples in a game twice in one season (1905). After his tour with the Giants, Brain returned to Buffalo for two seasons, retiring in 1910 with a .270 minor league batting average.

BRAIN, BUFFALO

Born:
January 24, 1879
Lugwardine, Hereford,
England

Died:
May 25, 1959
Los Angeles, CA

▷ Batted: RH
▷ Threw: RH
▷ Position: SS/3B
▷ Career BA: .252

Teams:
Chicago White Sox AL (1901)
St. Louis Cardinals NL (1903–1905)
Pittsburgh Pirates NL (1905)
Boston Beaneaters/Doves NL (1906–1907)
Cincinnati Reds NL (1908)
New York Giants NL (1908)

David Leonard Brain

Roy Brashear

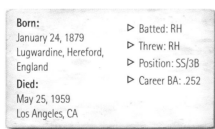

BRASHEAR, KANSAS CITY

Born:
January 3, 1874
Ashtabula, OH

Died:
April 20, 1951
Los Angeles, CA

▷ Batted: RH
▷ Threw: RH
▷ Position: 1B/2B
▷ Career BA: .268

Teams:
St. Louis Cardinals, NL (1902)
Philadelphia Phillies NL (1903)

Roy Parks Brashear

Roy Brashear had a short 2-year stint in the majors. His brother, Norman "Kitty" Brashear, had an even shorter career, with 2 at bats for Louisville in 1899. He came up from the Western League's Minneapolis Millers, where he batted .302 in 463 at bats in 1901. Considered average defensively, he had a pretty good year in 1902, batting .276 in 388 at bats and stealing 9 bases. After his tour with Philly, he played second base in the minors until 1914. He played in the American Association through 1909 for the Louisville Colonels and the Kansas City Blues. He then moved to the Pacific Coast League, playing for the Vernon Tigers, the Venice Tigers, the Portland Beavers, and the Los Angeles Angels. Over his 13 minor league seasons, Brashear batted .273 with 69 homers in 7,130 at bats in 1,972 games. He later umpired in the Pacific Coast League and managed in the West Texas League.

Al Burch

Al Burch was 22 when he came up to St. Louis after playing second base and shortstop in the minors for 2 years. He played the outfield so well in his rookie season for the Cards that he remained in that position for the balance of his MLB career. In 1909 he batted .271 with 601 at bats for Brooklyn and had 163 hits, placing second in the league in singles that year. However, he only had a total of 103 RBI over the course of his six seasons in the majors. After his MLB days, Burch finished up with five seasons in the minors, mostly playing for the Louisville Colonels in the American Association. After seven minor league seasons, Burch retired from the game in 1916 at age 32 with a career .265 minor league batting average. After his playing days, he worked as a chauffeur.

Born:
October 7, 1883
Albany, NY
Died:
October 5, 1926
Brooklyn, NY

▷ Batted: LH
▷ Threw: RH
▷ Position: OF
▷ Career BA: .254

Teams:
St. Louis Cardinals NL (1906–1907)
Brooklyn Superbas/Dodgers NL (1907–1911)

Albert William Burch

Fred Burchell

As a 23-year-old rookie, Fred Burchell pitched only 44 innings in 6 games for the Phillies before returning to the minors. There he pitched five seasons, going 92–71 for the Baltimore Orioles in the Eastern League before getting a second shot in the big leagues with Boston. As part of the 1908 Boston roster that included Cy Young and Eddie Cicotte, he won 10 games and had a 2.96 ERA. The next year he won 3 games and was out of major league baseball. Burchell went on to pitch in the Eastern League for the Buffalo Bisons and the Montreal Royals, and in 1912 he became player/manager of the Syracuse Stars in the New York State League. His playing days ended in 1914, but he came back in 1926 to manage the Newark Bears in the International League. He returned one last time in 1930 to manage the St. Thomas Blue Sox of the Ontario League. Burchell's 12-season minor league pitching record was 117–103.

Teams:
Philadelphia Phillies NL (1903)
Boston Americans/Red Sox AL (1907–1909)

Born:
July 14, 1879
Perth Amboy, NJ
Died:
November 20, 1951
Jordan, NY

▷ Batted: RH
▷ Threw: LH
▷ Position: P
▷ MLB Pitching Record: 13–15
▷ ERA: 2.93

Frederick Duff Burchell

Jimmy Burke

Jimmy Burke was a pretty good infielder with a marginal bat. His best year offensively was 1903, when he batted .285 with 431 at bats. In 1905 as player/manager of the Cards, he posted a 34–56 record. He played and managed in the minors from 1906 through 1913 for the American Association's Kansas City Blues, the Louisville Colonels, and the Indianapolis Indians, as well as the Central League's Fort Wayne Billikens. Over his six seasons as a minor league player, he posted a .258 batting average. Burke returned to the majors to coach for the Tigers from 1914 to 1917. He then managed the Browns from 1918 to 1920, losing all three seasons (172–180). Burke managed the Toledo Mud Hens in the American Association in 1924 and 1925. He later coached the 1929 Cubs and the 1932 World Series champion Yankees under Joe McCarthy.

Born:
October 12, 1874
St. Louis, MO

Died:
March 26, 1942
St. Louis, MO

▷ Batted: RH
▷ Threw: RH
▷ Position: 3B
▷ Career BA: .244
▷ Managerial Record: 206–236

Teams:
Cleveland Spiders NL (1898)
St. Louis Perfectos/Cardinals NL (1899, 1903–1904; player/manager: 1905)
Milwaukee Brewers AL (1901)
Chicago White Sox AL (1901)
Pittsburgh Pirates NL (1901–1902)
St. Louis Browns AL (manager: 1918–1920)

James Timothy Burke

John Butler

John Butler came up to the majors out of Fordham University to play just 1 game for the Brewers in 1901. A catcher who was weak offensively and defensively, he played four seasons in the big leagues with three different teams. He had a total of 119 at bats with an on-base percentage of .231 and a batting average of .134, which are not great numbers. Around his three MLB tours, Butler played ten seasons in the minors, mostly for the Kansas City Blues of the American Association, and then the Jersey City Skeeters and the Rochester Bronchos of the Eastern League. He retired at 31 after batting .247 in 2,478 minor league at bats. After his playing career ended, he did some coaching with the White Sox.

Born:
July 26, 1879
Boston, MA

Died:
February 2, 1950
Boston, MA

▷ Batted: RH
▷ Threw: RH
▷ Position: C
▷ Career BA: .134

Teams:
Milwaukee Brewers AL (1901)
St. Louis Cardinals NL (1904)
Brooklyn Superbas NL (1906–1907)

John Albert Butler

Bobby Byrne

A fine all-around player, Bobby Byrne was an excellent gloveman as well as a solid leadoff hitter. Byrne was acquired by the Pirates from the Cards in August 1909, and contributed to their run down the stretch all the way to the World Series championship. In 1910 he batted .296 and led the NL in hits (178) and doubles (43). He later played on the 1917 White Sox World Series championship team. After his MLB days, Byrne managed the Miami Indians of the Southwestern League in 1921 and the Saginaw Aces of the Michigan-Ontario League in 1922. After retiring from the game, he worked for the city of St. Louis, a steel company, and also owned a bowling alley. A New Year's Eve baby, he passed away on his 80th birthday.

Robert Matthew Byrne

Born:
December 31, 1884
St. Louis, MO

Died:
December 31, 1964
Wayne, PA

Batted: RH
Threw: RH
Position: 3B
Career BA: .254

Teams:
St. Louis Cardinals NL (1907–1909)
Pittsburgh Pirates NL (1909–1913)
Philadelphia Phillies NL (1913–1917)
Chicago White Sox AL (1917)

Billy Campbell

Billy Campbell got his ticket to the majors after pitching three seasons in the minors and going 26–14 for the American Association's Louisville Colonels in 1904. A 31-year-old rookie, he pitched only 2 games for the Cards, going 1–1 with a horrible 7.41 ERA. He was a pretty mediocre pitcher, but he did manage to win 12 games for the Reds in 1908, with a 2.60 ERA in 221 innings pitched. After his short time in the majors, he pitched for the Kansas City Blues of the American Association and the Mobile Sea Gulls of the Southern Association. Campbell retired in 1913 at age 39 after putting together a 135–99 record during his ten seasons in the minors.

Teams:
St. Louis Cardinals NL (1905)
Cincinnati Reds NL (1907–1909)

William James Campbell

Born:
November 5, 1873
Pittsburgh, PA
Died:
October 6, 1957
Cincinnati, OH

▷ Batted: LH
▷ Threw: LH
▷ Position: P
▷ MLB Pitching Record: 23–25
▷ ERA: 2.80

Charlie Carr

Charles Carbitt Carr

Born:
December 27, 1876
Coatesville, PA
Died:
November 25, 1932
Memphis, TN

▷ Batted: RH
▷ Threw: RH
▷ Position: 1B
▷ Career BA: .252

Teams:
Washington Senators NL (1898)
Philadelphia Athletics AL (1901)
Detroit Tigers AL (1903–1904)
Cleveland Indians AL (1904–1905)
Cincinnati Reds NL (1906)
Indianapolis Hoosiers FL (1914)

Charlie Carr was known more for his role as manager of the Indianapolis Indians in the American Association than for his playing skills in the major leagues. Dependable at first base, Carr played part-time for several different teams. His best year was 1903, when he batted .281 with 154 hits. After his tour with the Reds, Carr became player/manager of the Indianapolis Indians through the 1910 season. In 1908 he batted .301 while playing first base, leading the Indians to a first-place finish. Carr managed the Utica Utes of the New York State League in 1911 and the Kansas City Blues of the American Association in 1912 and 1913. He then returned to the majors in 1914. He finished up in the Federal League, batting a solid .293 at the age of 37. Carr made a comeback in 1919 to play for the Providence Grays in the Eastern League when he was 42. Over his nine minor league seasons he batted .289 in 4,119 at bats.

Scoops Carey

George "Scoops" Carey was a first baseman out of West Virginia University who played a total of four seasons in the majors over a period of 8 years. Carey's best year offensively was 1902, when he batted .314 for the Senators. He also placed in the American League top ten in doubles and triples that year. Not known for his bat, he earned his nickname because of his excellent glove work, ending his MLB tour with a .986 career fielding percentage. Around his major league tours, he played ten seasons in the minors, batting .276 in 3,401 minor league at bats. Carey managed the Eastern League Buffalo Bisons in 1901. After his stint with the Senators, he went on to play in the minors through 1911, mostly for the Memphis Egyptians in the Southern Association.

Teams:
Baltimore Orioles NL (1895)
Louisville Colonels NL (1898)
Washington Senators AL (1902–1903)

George C. Carey

Born:
December 4, 1870
Pittsburgh, PA
Died:
December 17, 1916
East Liverpool, OH

▷ Batted: RH
▷ Threw: RH
▷ Position: 1B
▷ Career BA: .271

CASEY, MONTREAL

Doc Casey

James "Doc" Casey played college ball for Maryland Agricultural College before starting his pro career when he was 28 years old. He was a pretty good third baseman who spent 10 years in the majors with four different teams. His best year was 1902, when he batted .273 for the Tigers with 142 hits and 3 homers in 520 at bats. After playing in a total of 1,114 major league games, he went on to manage and play for the Montreal Royals of the Eastern League in 1908 and 1909. Casey then became player/manager of the Fort Wayne Brakies in the Central League for one season, and retired in 1911 at age 41. He batted .247 in 1,286 at bats over his three seasons in the minors.

Born:
March 15, 1870
Lawrence, MA
Died:
December 31, 1936
Detroit, MI

▷ Batted: Switch
▷ Threw: RH
▷ Position: 3B
▷ Career BA: .258

Teams:
Washington Senators NL (1898–1899)
Brooklyn Superbas NL (1899–1900, 1906–1907)
Detroit Tigers AL (1901–1902)
Chicago Cubs NL (1903–1905)

James Patrick Casey

Pete Cassidy

CASSIDY, BALTIMORE

Although he only spent a couple of years in the majors, Pete Cassidy had a pretty solid minor league career. Cassidy's best year in the Bigs was 1899, when he batted .315 as a part-time player for the Senators. Primarily a first baseman, he was versatile, and also played shortstop and third base during his stint in the majors. After his MLB days, Cassidy went on to play at first base for nine more seasons in the minors, mostly in the Eastern League for the Providence Grays, the Jersey City Skeeters (under Mickey Doolin), and the Baltimore Orioles. Cassidy swiped 45 bases for Jersey City in 1903 while batting .311 in 457 at bats. He retired from the game after the 1909 season with a .288 batting average and 12 home runs in 3,713 minor league at bats.

Teams:
Louisville Colonels NL (1896)
Brooklyn Dodgers NL (1899)
Washington Senators NL (1899)

Born:
April 8, 1873
Wilmington, DE
Died:
July 9, 1929
Wilmington, DE

▷ Batted: RH
▷ Threw: RH
▷ Position: 1B
▷ Career BA: .257

Peter Francis Cassidy

Bill Chappelle

CHAPPELLE, ROCHESTER

"Big Bill" Chappelle had a short stint in the big leagues, playing 2 years in the National League and 1 year for the Brooklyn Tip-Tops of the Federal League. He closed out his MLB career in 1914, going 7–7 with a 2.38 ERA in 177.2 innings pitched. Before and between his major league tours, he played ten seasons in the minors. Chappelle played mostly A-level ball for the likes of the Des Moines Underwriters of the Western League, the Rochester Bronchos of the Eastern League, and the Memphis Egyptians, the Mobile Sea Gulls, and the Chattanooga Lookouts of the Southern Association. He checked out of the minors after the 1913 season with a minor league career record of 115–108 in 292 games and 634.2 innings pitched.

William Hogan Chappelle

Born:
March 22, 1881
Waterloo, NY
Died:
December 31, 1944
Mineola, NY

▷ Batted: RH
▷ Threw: RH
▷ Position: P
▷ MLB Pitching Record: 7–7
▷ ERA: 2.38

Teams:
Boston Doves NL (1908–1909)
Cincinnati Reds NL (1909)
Brooklyn Tip-Tops FL (1914)

Chappy Charles

CHARLES, ST. LOUIS NAT'L

Born:
March 25, 1881
Phillipsburg, NJ
Died:
August 4, 1959
Bethlehem, PA

▷ Batted: RH
▷ Threw: RH
▷ Position: 2B/SS/3B
▷ Career BA: .219

Raymond "Chappy" Charles came up to the big leagues from the Tri-State League's Williamsport Millionaires, where he hit .280 in 400 at bats in 1907. Charles was a weak-hitting utility infielder during his tours with the Reds and the Cards. On the plus side, he played shortstop and second and third base. His best year offensively was 1909, when he batted .236 for the Reds. After his brief stint in the majors, Charles returned to the minors, playing for the Milwaukee Brewers of the American Association from 1910 to 1912 and the San Francisco Seals of the Pacific Coast League from 1913 to 1915. He retired from the game at age 34 after batting .246 in the minor leagues.

Teams:
St. Louis Cardinals NL (1908–1909)
Cincinnati Reds NL (1909–1910)

Raymond Charles

Born: Charles Shub Achenbach

Bill Clancy

After four seasons in the minors, Bill Clancy got his chance in the majors when he was 26 years old after batting .317 in 1903 and .310 in 1904 for the Montreal Royals in the Eastern League. Unfortunately, Clancy was not able to perform at that level in the big leagues. A part-time first baseman for the Pirates, he batted .229 with 227 at bats, 52 hits, and 34 RBI in 1905. Certainly not Hall of Fame statistics, but he still made it to the big dance. After his MLB career, he went back to the Eastern League for six seasons, playing at first base for the Rochester Bronchos, the Buffalo Bisons, and the Baltimore Orioles. Clancy wrapped up his pro career after two seasons in the Central League with the Fort Wayne Brakies, retiring in 1912 at age 33 after batting .280 with 38 homers in 4,861 at bats over his 11 years in the minors.

Team:
Pittsburgh Pirates NL (1905)

William Edward Clancy

CLANCY, BUFFALO

Born:
April 12, 1879
Redfield, NY
Died:
February 10, 1948
Oriskany, NY

▷ Batted: LH
▷ Threw: RH
▷ Position: 1B
▷ Career BA: .229

Josh Clarke

CLARK, COLUMBUS

Josh "Pepper" Clarke, brother of the great Hall of Famer Fred Clarke, was a backup outfielder who did not have his brother's talent. He managed to bat .242 in 492 at bats in 1908 for the Naps, but did not play much in his other four MLB seasons. In 1908 he swiped 37 bases, good for fifth in the league, and he was fourth in the league in bases on balls with 76. Clarke was up and down in the minors throughout his career, playing for the Des Moines Undertakers and the Sioux City Packers in the Western League and the St. Paul Saints, the Toledo Mud Hens, the Columbus Senators, and the Kansas City Blues in the American Association. He was Sioux City's player/manager from 1913 to 1915. Over his 14 seasons as a minor league player, he batted .289 in 5,863 at bats. After his playing days ended in 1915, Clarke managed the Lincoln Links in the Western League in 1924 and 1925. He came back in 1936 when he was 57 to manage the Omaha Robin Hoods/Rock Island Islanders in the Western League.

Teams:
Louisville Colonels NL (1898)
St. Louis Cardinals NL (1905)
Cleveland Naps AL (1908–1909)
Boston Rustlers NL (1911)

Born:
March 8, 1879
Winfield, KS
Died:
July 2, 1962
Ventura, CA

▷ Batted: LH
▷ Threw: RH
▷ Position: OF
▷ Career BA: .239

Joshua Baldwin Clarke

Cad Coles

By the time Cad Coles had his shot in the majors, he was 28 years old and already had 7 years of minor league experience. He was a promising young outfielder when he played for the Augusta Tourists in the South Atlantic League from 1908 to 1911, batting .268 in 1909 and .270 in 1911. The Clemson University alumnus then hit .306 in 1912 for the Binghamton Bingoes and .357 in 1913 for the Elmira Colonels, both of the New York State League. That earned Coles his berth in the renegade Federal League in 1914. During his tour with the Packers,

COLES, AUGUSTA

he batted .253 with 49 hits and 25 RBI in 194 at bats. He then returned to the minors for 2 years, finally packing it in after the 1916 season when he was 30 years old. Over his nine minor league seasons, Coles batted .276 in 3,651 at bats.

Born:	▷ Batted: LH
January 17, 1886	▷ Threw: RH
Rock Hill, SC	▷ Position: OF
Died:	▷ **V**Career BA: .253
June 30, 1942	
Miami, FL	

Team:
Kansas City Packers FL (1914)

Cadwallader Coles

Bunk Congalton

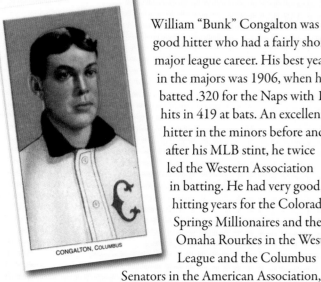

CONGALTON, COLUMBUS

William "Bunk" Congalton was a good hitter who had a fairly short major league career. His best year in the majors was 1906, when he batted .320 for the Naps with 134 hits in 419 at bats. An excellent hitter in the minors before and after his MLB stint, he twice led the Western Association in batting. He had very good hitting years for the Colorado Springs Millionaires and the Omaha Rourkes in the Western League and the Columbus Senators in the American Association, where he played in 1905 and again from 1908 to 1912. Congalton batted .300 or better in nine of his 12 minor league seasons,

retiring in 1914 with a minor league career batting average of .315 in 6,565 at bats. He died in 1937 after suffering a heart attack at an Indians' game while watching Bob Feller pitch.

Teams:
Chicago Orphans NL (1902)
Cleveland Naps AL (1905–1907)
Boston Americans AL (1907)

Born:	Batted: LH
January 24, 1875	Threw: LH
Guelph, Ontario, Canada	Position: RF
Died:	Career BA: .290
August 16, 1937	
Cleveland, OH	

William Millar Congalton

Wid Conroy

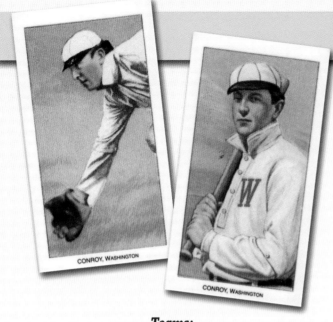

CONROY, WASHINGTON

CONROY, WASHINGTON

William "Wid" Conroy was the starting shortstop on the 1902 World Series champion Pirates team, and had a pretty good career playing several infield positions. A fair hitter, his best season was 1905, when he batted .273 for the Highlanders. Conroy ranked second in the league with his 41 stolen bases in 1907. He was excellent defensively at both shortstop and third base. After his major league career, he played for the Rochester Hustlers in the International League and was then player/manager for the Elmira Colonels in the New York State League from 1913 through 1916. Conroy retired in 1917 with a career .261 batting average over his six minor league seasons. He later coached for the Phillies.

Teams:
Milwaukee Brewers AL (1901)
Pittsburgh Pirates NL (1902)
New York Highlanders AL (1903–1908)
Washington Senators AL (1909–1911)

William Edward Conroy

Born:	Batted: RH
April 5, 1877	Threw: RH
Philadelphia, PA	Position: 3B/SS/OF
Died:	Career BA: .248
December 6, 1959	
Mt. Holly, NJ	

Frank Delahanty

One of the five Delahanty brothers who played professional ball, Frank "Pudgie" Delahanty unfortunately was not one of the better ones. Although his major league debut was in 1905, the same year as Ty Cobb, their careers could not have been more different. Delahanty started in left field for the Highlanders in 1906, but was a weak hitter, batting just a paltry .238. There was a gap of 6 years between his days in the American League and his return in 1914 to play in the new Federal League. During that time he played in the American Association for the Louisville Colonels, the St. Paul Saints, the Indianapolis Indians, and the Minneapolis Millers. Delahanty wrapped up his ten minor league seasons in 1913 with a career .252 batting average in 4,246 at bats. He retired from the game in 1915 after his tour with the Pittsburgh Rebels.

DELAHANTY, LOUISVILLE

Teams:
New York Highlanders AL (1905–1906, 1908)
Cleveland Naps AL (1907)
Buffalo Buffeds FL (1914)
Pittsburgh Rebels FL (1914–1915)

Frank George Delahanty

Born:	▷ Batted: RH
December 29, 1882	▷ Threw: RH
Cleveland, OH	▷ Position: OF
Died:	▷ Career BA: .226
July 22, 1966	
Cleveland, OH	

Jim Delahanty

DELEHANTY, WASHINGTON

Teams:
Chicago Orphans NL (1901)
New York Giants NL (1902)
Boston Beaneaters NL (1904–1905)
Cincinnati Reds NL (1906)
St. Louis Browns AL (1907)
Washington Senators AL (1907–1909)
Detroit Tigers AL (1909–1912)
Brooklyn Tip-Tops FL (1914–1915)

Another of the five baseball-playing Delahanty brothers, Jim Delahanty started his major league career at age 22 for the Chicago Orphans. He was a good second baseman whose best year was 1911, when he batted .339 for the Tigers. He participated in the 1909 World Series, batting .346 over the 7 games against the Pirates. Over his 13-year career, Delahanty played for eight different teams and banged out 1,159 hits and 19 homers over that span. Between his MLB tours, he played for the Little Rock Travelers in the Southern Association and the Minneapolis Millers in the American Association. After a 2-year stint in the Federal League, he wrapped up his major league career at age 36, but went on to play for 1 more year for the Beaumont Oilers in the Texas League. He batted .337 over his six seasons in the minors.

Born:
June 20, 1879
Cleveland, OH

Died:
October 17, 1953
Cleveland, OH

▷ Batted: RH
▷ Threw: RH
▷ Position: 2B
▷ Career BA: .283

James Christopher Delahanty

Ray Demmitt

DEMMITT, N.Y. AMERICAN

DEMMITT, ST. LOUIS AMERICAN

Ray Demmitt was a marginal outfielder who played for seven seasons in the majors. His best year was 1918, when he batted .281 with 114 hits. He had a fairly uneventful career but was considered a reliable outfielder and a good team player. Before and between his major league tours, he put together ten good seasons in the minors, batting .286 in 4,318 at bats. He mostly played in the tough Eastern League for the Baltimore Orioles, the Newark Indians, and the Montreal Royals. After a 2-year stint with the Columbus Senators in the American Association, where he batted .319 in 1917, Demmitt was called up to the majors again to play for the Browns for three seasons. He retired in 1920 to do farm work.

Teams:
New York Highlanders AL (1909)
St. Louis Browns AL (1910, 1917–1919)
Detroit Tigers AL (1914)
Chicago White Sox AL (1914–1915)

Born:
February 2, 1884
Illiopolis, IL

Died:
February 19, 1956
Glen Ellyn, IL

▷ Batted: LH
▷ Threw: RH
▷ Position: OF
▷ Career BA: .257

Charles Raymond Demmitt

Rube Dessau

DESSAU, BALTIMORE

Teams:
Boston Doves NL (1907)
Brooklyn Superbas NL (1910)

Born:
March 29, 1883
New Galilee, PA
Died:
May 6, 1952
York, PA

▷ Batted: Switch
▷ Threw: RH
▷ Position: P
▷ MLB Pitching Record:
2–4
▷ ERA: 6.53

Pitcher Frank "Rube" Dessau came up to Boston and Brooklyn for a "cup of coffee." His 6.53 ERA pretty much tells the story. Dessau managed to strike out a total of 25 batters over the 21 games that he appeared in, but he did not pitch effectively in the majors. Between his MLB tours, he pitched for the Baltimore Orioles of the Eastern League, going 15–13 in 1908 and 18–17 in 1909. He also went 21–11 for the Elmira Colonels of the New York State League in 1915. Dessau managed in the minors from 1923 through 1933, winning the New York–Pennsylvania League championship with the York White Roses in 1925 and the Illinois-Indiana-Iowa League championship with the Decatur Commodores in 1928. In all, he spent 22 years in the minors, finishing up with a 104–99 pitching record and a 703–548 managerial record.

Frank Rolland Dessau

Josh Devore

DEVORE, NEW YORK NAT'L

Josh Devore was only 20 years old went he got his shot at the majors, after batting .290 for the Newark Indians in 1908. Devore was a pretty good utility outfielder over his 7 years in the majors. He batted .304 for the Giants in 1910 and .280 in 1911. For the rest of his MLB career, he was mostly a bench player, but he did play on the Giants' 1911 and 1912 pennant-winning teams and the Braves' 1914 World Series championship team. As a fielder, Devore's best year was 1911, when he had 241 putouts in 149 games. After his tour with the Braves, he continued on in the minors through 1924. He was player/manager of the Grand Rapids Joshers in the Central League in 1920 and 1921 and the Grand Rapids Homoners in the Michigan-Ontario League in 1924. He then retired, with a .290 batting average over his nine minor league seasons.

Born:
November 13, 1887
Murray City, OH
Died:
October 6, 1954
Chillicothe, OH

▷ Batted: LH
▷ Threw: LH
▷ Position: OF
▷ Career BA: .277

Teams:
New York Giants NL (1908–1913)
Cincinnati Reds NL (1913)
Philadelphia Phillies NL (1913–1914)
Boston Braves NL (1914)

Joshua M. Devore

Gus Dorner

Gus Dorner went 18–10 in 1904 for the Columbus Senators in the American Association and 29–8 for them in 1905 to lead the AA in wins. However, his major league career was a different story. He had a season to forget in 1906, leading the league with 26 losses in 36 games and 33 starts for the Beaneaters. He also led the National League in hit batsmen that season and finished second in earned runs allowed and fifth in hits and walks allowed. Dorner's best MLB season was 1907, when he went 12–16 for the Doves with a 3.12 ERA. He finished his career with a 36–69 record in 131 games and a 3.37 ERA, not a memorable MLB career. He fared better in the minors, where he played until 1911, posting a 79–54 record over six seasons. After an ineffective season with the Kansas City Blues, Dorner went 12–6 for the Wilkes-Barre Barons of the New York State League in 1910. He managed the Chambersburg Maroons in the Blue Ridge League in 1915 before retiring.

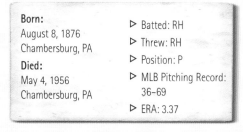

DORNER, KANSAS CITY

Born:
August 8, 1876
Chambersburg, PA
Died:
May 4, 1956
Chambersburg, PA

▷ Batted: RH
▷ Threw: RH
▷ Position: P
▷ MLB Pitching Record:
36–69
▷ ERA: 3.37

Teams:
Cleveland Bronchos/Naps AL (1902–1903)
Cincinnati Reds NL (1906)
Boston Beaneaters/Doves NL (1906–1909)

Augustus Dorner

Tom Downey

One of the game's better defensive players, Tom Downey played all four infield positions in his seven seasons, and he even snuck in one game behind the plate in 1909 and one in the outfield in 1911. Downey played the majority of his games at shortstop, however, especially early in his career, switching to the other side of second base when he went to the Federal League in 1914. His versatility, not his bat, was his ticket to a big league career, although he managed three seasons of .261 or better for the Reds and the Phillies from 1910 to 1912. Around his MLB days, Downey played ten seasons of minor league ball, retiring in 1919 with a .240 career batting average, which interestingly enough is the same as his major league batting average.

DOWNEY, CINCINNATI

DOWNEY, CINCINNATI

Teams:
Cincinnati Reds NL (1909–1911)
Philadelphia Phillies NL (1912)
Chicago Cubs NL (1912)
Buffalo Buffeds/Blues FL (1914–1915)

Thomas Edward Downey

Born:
January 1, 1884
Lewiston, ME
Died:
August 3, 1961
Passaic, NJ

▷ Batted: RH
▷ Threw: RH
▷ Position: IF
▷ Career BA: .240

Joe Dunn

Joe Dunn was 23 years old when he came up to the majors from the Evansville River Rats of the Central League. Starting in 1908, Dunn played two seasons for Brooklyn, backing up catcher Bill Bergen. He totaled 89 at bats for his career, hitting .169 with just 4 doubles and 7 RBI. He then played for the Mobile Sea Gulls and Atlanta Crackers of the Southern Association for five seasons before becoming a player/manager in 1915. As a player, Dunn batted only .200 over his minor league career. However, he developed a solid career as a minor league manager for 16 seasons in seven stops and collected three league championships, two with the Bloomington Bloomers of the Illinois-Indiana-Iowa League in 1919 and 1920 and another with the Springfield Blue Sox of the Central League in 1930. Dunn managed in the minors until 1931, retiring at age 46.

Team:
Brooklyn Superbas NL (1908–1909)

DUNN, BROOKLYN

Joseph Edward Dunn

Born:
March 11, 1885
Springfield, OH
Died:
March 19, 1944
Springfield, OH

▷ Batted: RH
▷ Threw: RH
▷ Position: C
▷ Career BA: .169

Jimmy Dygert

DYGERT, PHILA. AMER.

"Sunny Jim" Dygert was one of the early masters of the spitball in the era when it was legal and accepted. Dygert's best season was 1907, when he went 21–8 with a 2.34 ERA. Controlling his spitball was as difficult as hitting it, however, and he also walked 85 hitters that year. The following season he led the league with 97 walks, going just 11–15 with a 2.87 ERA. After his tour with the A's, he played three more seasons in the minors. Pitching in an exhibition game for the New Orleans Pelicans against Cleveland at Pelican Park in 1913, Dygert threw a complete game one-hitter against Cleveland's major league lineup, including Joe Jackson and Nap Lajoie, who between them collected 5,016 major league hits.

Born:
July 5, 1884
Utica, NY
Died:
February 8, 1936
New Orleans, LA

▷ Batted: RH
▷ Threw: RH
▷ Position: P
▷ MLB Pitching Record: 57–49
▷ ERA: 2.65

Team:
Philadelphia Athletics AL (1905–1910)

James Henry Dygert

Dick Egan

EGAN, CINCINNATI

Dick Egan spent six seasons in the minors before joining the Reds in 1908 when he was 24 years old. The prime of his career came between 1909 and 1912, when he was the Reds' starting second baseman. These were the only seasons of his 9-year career in which he saw more than 350 at bats. During those seasons he swiped 141 of his 167 career stolen bases, finishing in the top ten in the league in 3 of those years. He was often the other end of a double steal, along with teammate Bob Bescher, who led the league in stolen bases each of those four seasons. Egan was also adept at moving runners along with the sacrifice bunt. He finished third in the league in sacrifices in 1910 and fourth in 1912. After his tour with the Braves, he went back to the minors for one more season, and then retired in 1918 at age 34 with a minor league career .253 batting average.

Born:
June 23, 1884
Portland, OR
Died:
July 7, 1947
Oakland, CA

▷ Batted: RH
▷ Threw: RH
▷ Position: 2B
▷ Career BA: .249

Teams:
Cincinnati Reds NL (1908–1913)
Brooklyn Robins NL (1914–1915)
Boston Braves NL (1915–1916)

Richard Joseph Egan

Roy Ellam

ELLAM, NASHVILLE

Roy "Slippery" Ellam, also known as "Whitey," collected a mere 98 at bats over his two seasons in the majors that came 9 years apart at the ages of 23 and 32. His at bats were less than productive, since he hit just .143 with only 4 extra base hits and 6 RBI. In 1909 he hit his only major league home run. Ellam finished his career with 14 major league hits, 13 errors at shortstop, and two nicknames. Between his major league stints, he played in the Southern Association for the Birmingham Barons. He became player/manager for the Nashville Volunteers in that same league in 1916 and, except for his brief tour with the Pirates, he continued to manage in the minors for 12 seasons, retiring in 1930 with a 17-season career .231 minor league batting average.

Born:
February 8, 1886
West Conshohocken, PA
Died:
October 28, 1948
Conshohocken, PA

▷ Batted: RH
▷ Threw: RH
▷ Position: SS
▷ Career BA: .143

Teams:
Cincinnati Reds NL (1909)
Pittsburgh Pirates NL (1918)

Roy Ellam

Cecil Ferguson

FERGUSON, BOSTON NAT'L

Born:
August 19, 1886
Ellsworth, IN
Died:
September 5, 1943
Montverde, FL

▷ Batted: RH
▷ Threw: RH
▷ Position: P
▷ MLB Pitching Record:
  29–46
▷ ERA: 3.34

Teams:
New York Giants NL (1906–1907)
Boston Doves/Rustlers NL (1908–1911)

Cecil B. Ferguson

Indiana native Cecil "George" Ferguson had a respectable 11–11 season with the Boston Braves in 1908 with a 2.47 ERA, but then he injured his arm, effectively snuffing out a promising career. The following season Ferguson had 30 starts and appeared in 36 games, going 5–23 with a 3.73 ERA. He led the National League in losses that year, and finished second-worst in earned runs allowed. He pitched just 147 innings after that season and was out of the majors 2 years later. Ferguson did try the minors but without success. He pitched a 1–6 season for the Venice Tigers in the Pacific Coast League and then left baseball after the 1913 season when he was 29 years old.

Lou Fiene

Lou "Big Finn" Fiene was a member of the White Sox World Series championship team in 1906, his rookie year, although he did not contribute in the Series. After sporadic tries with the Sox from 1906 to 1908, Fiene finally got his "full shot" in 1909, making 13 appearances, including six starts. He went 2–5 over 72 innings pitched, however, and posted a 4.12 ERA, so that was his final season in the majors. After his MLB career, he went back to the American Association to pitch for the Minneapolis Millers, the Kansas City Blues, and the Milwaukee Brewers. Fiene had his best years with Minneapolis, going 20–13 in 1908, 15–6 in 1910, and 13–10 in 1914. He retired in 1915 after nine seasons in the minors with an overall 73–59 record.

FIENE, CHICAGO AMER.

FIENE, CHICAGO AMER.

Team:
Chicago White Sox AL (1906–1909)

Louis Henry Fiene

Born:
December 29, 1884
Fort Dodge, IA
Died:
December 22, 1964
Chicago, IL

▷ Batted: RH
▷ Threw: RH
▷ Position: P
▷ MLB Pitching Record:
  3–8
▷ ERA: 3.85

Steamer Flanagan

FLANAGAN, BUFFALO

James "Steamer" Flanagan may have had an early 1900s baseball name right out of central casting, but he wasn't destined to play a big role in baseball history. He saw just 25 career at bats in 7 games, but he did well with them, hitting .280 with a double, a triple, and 3 RBI, as well as 3 stolen bases. It is likely, however, that when he told tales of his baseball career to his children and grandchildren, he talked about playing those 7 games with Honus Wagner. Around his brief MLB career, he played in the outfield for ten seasons in the minor leagues, including stints with the Rochester Bronchos and the Buffalo Bisons of the Eastern League and the Toledo Mud Hens of the American Association. Flanagan retired in 1913 with a minor league career .272 batting average.

Team:
Pittsburgh Pirates NL (1905)

James Paul Flanagan

Born:
April 20, 1881
Kingston, PA
Died:
April 21, 1947
Wilkes-Barre, PA

▷ Batted: LH
▷ Threw: LH
▷ Position: OF
▷ Career BA: .280

Ed Foster

FOSTER, CHARLESTON

Edward Lee Foster

Born:
1880
Georgia
Died:
March 1, 1929
Montgomery, AL

▷ Batted: RH
▷ Threw: RH
▷ Position: P
▷ MLB Pitching Record: 1–0
▷ ERA: 2.14

Team:
Cleveland Naps AL (1908)

Ed "Slim" Foster made six appearances for Nap Lajoie's Cleveland team in the back half of 1908 as a rash of injuries took out the Naps' star pitchers Addie Joss, Glenn Liebhardt, and Heinie Berger. Foster made only one start, but collected a major league win, pitching 21 innings and posting a 2.14 ERA. That year, he also pitched for the Jacksonville Jays in the South Atlantic League, going 13–2 for them. After his tour with the Naps, Foster went back to the minors, playing three seasons for the New Haven Murlins in the Connecticut State League and two seasons each for the Charleston Sea Gulls and the Macon Peaches in the South Atlantic League. He finished up in 1923 after five seasons with the St. Paul Saints in the American Association with a 135–114 minor league record.

Jerry Freeman

Jerry "Buck" Freeman played eight seasons in the minors, mostly in the American Association, where he batted .362 for the Minneapolis Millers in 1907 before going up to the majors. He was one of the best of a bad lot of Senators' hitters in his 1908 rookie season, leading the team with 45 RBI, 134 hits, and .304 on-base percentage. In 154 games Freeman hit .252 in 531 at bats, with 1 homer and 6 swipes. One of his 134 hits in 1908 came off a 40-year-old Cy Young, breaking up Young's bid for his third career no-hitter, although he collected that later in the season. Freeman's career with the Senators ended when Washington bought Bob Unglaub from the Red Sox. After his tour with the Senators, Freeman played three more seasons in the American Association for the Toledo Mud Hens and the Indianapolis Indians before retiring in 1911 with a career .280 minor league batting average.

Team:
Washington Senators AL (1908–1909)

Frank Ellsworth Freeman

Born:
December 26, 1879
Placerville, CA
Died:
September 30, 1952
Los Angeles, CA

▷ Batted: LH
▷ Threw: RH
▷ Position: 1B
▷ Career BA: .245

John Frill

John Frill was a minor league pitcher until the age of 31, when the Yankees tapped him to shore up their pitching staff in the 1910 pennant race. The Yanks called him up for good reason. He posted a 13–10 season in 1908 and then a 16–13 season in 1909 for the Newark Indians of the Eastern League. In the majors, he won 2 games, 1 by shutout, and finished out 3 other games despite a bloated 4.47 ERA. The Yankees finished second that year, and Frill returned to the minors in 1912 after only 19 more innings split between the Browns and the Reds. He finished 1912 in the minors with a 17–8 record split between the Jersey City Skeeters and the Buffalo Bisons in the International League. Around his brief MLB stints, he put together a 10-year minor league pitching career, retiring in 1915 with a 109–110 record.

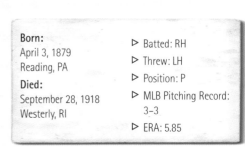

FRILL, N.Y. AMER.

Teams:
New York Highlanders AL (1910)
St. Louis Browns AL (1912)
Cincinnati Reds NL (1912)

Born:
April 3, 1879
Reading, PA
Died:
September 28, 1918
Westerly, RI

▷ Batted: RH
▷ Threw: LH
▷ Position: P
▷ MLB Pitching Record: 3–3
▷ ERA: 5.85

John Edmond Frill

Charlie Fritz

Charlie Fritz toiled 11 years in the minors, paying his dues for just 1 game and three innings pitched in the majors with the Athletics in 1907. In that outing he gave up 1 run on 3 walks without a hit and had 1 strikeout. He was not involved in the decision. Fritz played for the Greenville Grays, the Vicksburg Hill Billies, and the Mobile Sea Gulls in the Cotton States League and the Columbia Gamecocks in the South Atlantic League before advancing to the A-level Southern Association. There he played 8 years between the Shreveport Pirates, the New Orleans Pelicans, and the Memphis Turtles, winning 17 games for Memphis in 1910. After going 2–7 for the Waco Navigators in the Texas League in 1913, Fritz retired from baseball with a 115–145 record compiled over his 11 minor league seasons.

FRITZ, NEW ORLEANS

Born:
June 13, 1882
Mobile, AL
Died:
July 30, 1943
Mobile, AL

▷ Batted: N/A
▷ Threw: LH
▷ Position: P
▷ MLB Pitching Record: 0–0

Team:
Philadelphia Athletics AL (1907)

Charles Cornelius Fritz

Art Fromme

FROMME, CINCINNATI

Art Fromme left two teams regretting trades that he was involved in; one team regretted trading him away and the other team regretted trading for him. After two 5–13 seasons in St. Louis, Fromme was traded to the Reds, where he went 19–13 with a 1.90 ERA in 1909, the sixth-best ERA in the league. After he lost almost all of 1910 to illness, he went just 29–33 for Cincinnati over the next two-plus seasons, with a 3.08 ERA in 553 innings pitched. Fromme was traded to the Giants in May 1913 for three players and $20,000, and went 11–6 for John McGraw the rest of the way. But his 4.01 ERA that season for the Giants was such a disappointment that McGraw benched him for the 1913 World Series. He pitched just 150.1 innings for the Giants over the next 2 years before moving on to the Pacific Coast League's Vernon Tigers, where he went 93–66 over seven seasons, finally retiring in 1921.

Teams:
St. Louis Cardinals NL (1906–1908)
Cincinnati Reds NL (1909–1913)
New York Giants NL (1913–1915)

Born:
September 3, 1883
Quincy, IL
Died:
August 24, 1956
Los Angeles, CA

▷ Batted: RH
▷ Threw: RH
▷ Position: P
▷ MLB Pitching Record: 80–90
▷ ERA: 2.90

Arthur Henry Fromme

Bob Ganley

GANLEY, WASHINGTON

Bob Ganley played just five seasons in the majors, but reached the heights and depths of the standings. Breaking into the majors at 30 years old, he played for two Pirates teams that won 96 games in 1905 and 93 games in 1906. He was then sold to a Washington team that won a total of 109 games over the next two seasons. Ganley finished fourth in the American League in hits and stolen bases in 1907. In May 1909, the Philadelphia A's claimed him off waivers and won 95 games that year. A skilled situational hitter in the dead-ball era, he finished sixth or better in his league in sacrifices in four of his five seasons. After leaving the A's, he played and managed in the minors through the 1914 season, finishing with a .280 career batting average over his seven minor league seasons.

Born:
April 23, 1875
Lowell, MA
Died:
October 9, 1945
Lowell, MA

▷ Batted: LH
▷ Threw: LH
▷ Position: OF
▷ Career BA: .254

Teams:
Pittsburgh Pirates NL (1905–1906)
Washington Senators AL (1907–1909)
Philadelphia Athletics AL (1909)

Robert Stephen Ganley

Harry Gaspar

Harry Gaspar had a pretty short career with the Reds, yet it was fairly productive. In 1909 he compiled a nifty 19–11 record, with an outstanding 2.01 ERA. The next 2 years he won 15 and 11 games, respectively, but won only 1 game in 1912, which was his final campaign. He had 7 saves in 1910, good for first in the league, but he also led the league with 15 hit batsmen that year. Gaspar wound up 2 games under .500, but there have been a lot worse. After his major league days, he pitched for the Sioux City Indians in the Western League in 1914 and was their player/manager in 1915 and 1916. He then retired, with a 94–54 pitching record compiled over seven minor league seasons.

Born:
April 28, 1883
Kingsley, IA
Died:
May 14, 1940
Orange, CA

▷ Batted: RH
▷ Threw: RH
▷ Position: P
▷ MLB Pitching Record: 46–48
▷ ERA: 2.69

Team:
Cincinnati Reds NL (1909–1912)

Harry Lambert Gaspar

Rube Geyer

Jacob "Rube" Geyer pitched four seasons in the minors before cashing his ticket to the major leagues. Playing for the Columbus Senators in the American Association, he went 12–10 in 1907, 20–20 in 1908, and 20–17 in 1909, earning him a berth in the majors with the Cards. He didn't live up to his promise in St. Louis, however, although he did have one winning season in 1911, when he went 9–6. Overall Geyer finished 9 games below .500, and was just not effective in the big leagues. In 1914 he returned to pitch one last but unsuccessful season in the minors, going 9–18 for the Oakland Oaks in the Pacific Coast League. He retired after the 1914 season with a 76–81 minor league pitching record.

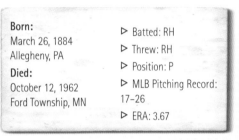

Born:
March 26, 1884
Allegheny, PA
Died:
October 12, 1962
Ford Township, MN

▷ Batted: RH
▷ Threw: RH
▷ Position: P
▷ MLB Pitching Record: 17–26
▷ ERA: 3.67

Team:
St. Louis Cardinals NL (1910–1913)

Jacob Bowman Geyer

Billy Gilbert

A pretty good fielder with a fairly mediocre bat, Billy Gilbert stayed in the majors for eight seasons. A solid second baseman with very good range, he had several seasons when he batted from .245 to .255, and as a rookie he batted .270. Overall, Gilbert's most productive years were his four seasons with the Giants. He batted .313 in the 1905 World Series, helping the Giants nail the series that year. He had a steady, yet unheralded career in the majors, after which he dabbled in the minors as a player until 1910. He was player/manager of the Central League's Erie Sailors in 1911 and 1912. Gilbert also managed in the A-level Eastern and Western Leagues for the Waterbury Brasscos, the Denver Bears, and the Pittsfield Hillies from 1921 to 1924.

Born:
June 21, 1876
Tullytown, PA
Died:
August 8, 1927
New York, NY

▷ Batted: RH
▷ Threw: RH
▷ Position: 2B
▷ Career BA: .247

Teams:
Milwaukee Brewers AL (1901)
Baltimore Orioles AL (1902)
New York Giants NL (1903–1906)
St. Louis Cardinals NL (1908–1909)

William Oliver Gilbert

Wilbur Good

GOODE, CLEVELAND

A pretty good outfielder for several different teams, Wilbur "Lefty" Good appeared in 5 games as a pitcher in 1905 for the New York Highlanders with no wins and 2 losses. He had his best years with the Cubs, batting .272 in 1914 and always hovering around the .260 mark. He was an above-average outfielder whose fielding percentage was in the high 90s. Before and after his major league career, he had some excellent minor league years as both player and manager. As a player through the 1931 season, Good posted a minor league career .334 batting average in 8,227 at bats. He managed until 1949 in the minors, winning league championships in the American Association with the Kansas City Blues in 1923 and the Mid-Atlantic League with the Johnstown Johnnies in 1930.

Born:
September 28, 1885
Punxsutawney, PA
Died:
December 30, 1963
Brooksville, FL

▷ Batted: LH
▷ Threw: LH
▷ Position: OF
▷ Career BA: .258

Teams:
New York Highlanders AL (1905)
Cleveland Naps AL (1908–1909)
Boston Doves/Rustlers NL (1910–1911)
Chicago Cubs NL (1911–1915)
Philadelphia Phillies NL (1916)
Chicago White Sox AL (1918)

Wilbur David Good

Peaches Graham

GRAHAM, BOSTON NAT'L

A versatile player, George "Peaches" Graham was predominantly a catcher, but also played first, second, and third base, shortstop, and outfield during his seven major league seasons. He even pitched 1 game for Chicago in 1903, giving up 3 runs in five innings. Graham's most productive season offensively was 1910, when he batted .282 with 82 hits. In his final season in the majors, he gave up 9 stolen bases in a game against the Giants. Between the Cubs and the Doves, Graham played for the Minneapolis Millers in the American Association. After his MLB days, he continued on in the minors through 1916, wrapping up with a .253 batting average in 3,949 minor league at bats over 12 seasons. His son, John "Jack" Graham, played with the Dodgers, the Giants, and the Browns from 1946 to 1949.

Teams:
Cleveland Bronchos AL (1902)
Chicago Cubs NL (1903, 1911)
Boston Doves/Rustlers NL (1908–1911)
Philadelphia Phillies NL (1912)

Born:
March 23, 1877
Aledo, IL
Died:
July 25, 1939
Long Beach, CA

▷ Batted: RH
▷ Threw: RH
▷ Position: C
▷ Career BA: .265

George Frederick Graham

Bill Grahame

GRAHAM, ST. LOUIS AMER.

Bill Grahame had a fairly short, unsuccessful pro career. Coming out of the Southern Association's Shreveport Pirates, where he had a 15–19 record, he joined St. Louis in 1908 at age 23. Grahame stuck around for three uneventful seasons; his best was 1908, when he sported a 6–7 record. The next year he lost 14 games, followed by a 0–8 record in 1910, which sent him back to the minors. He compiled a 1–7 record with the Southern Association's Chattanooga Lookouts in 1910 and then drifted out of baseball. Grahame resurfaced in 1913, pitching in the D-level Appalachian League for the Rome, Georgia, Romans. With his 5–3 record that year, he was able to finish his lackluster career on a winning note.

Born:
July 22, 1884
Owosso, MI
Died:
February 15, 1936
Holt, MI

▷ Batted: N/A
▷ Threw: LH
▷ Position: P
▷ MLB Pitching Record: 14–29
▷ ERA: 2.90

Team:
St. Louis Browns AL (1908–1910)

William James Grahame

Ed Gremminger

GREMINGER, MONTGOMERY

Ed "Battleship" Gremminger played 4 years in the majors, and was among the National League leaders in doubles in 1902, his "second" rookie season. His first rookie season was 1895, when the third baseman played 20 games for Cleveland. After a 6-year hiatus, he resurfaced in the majors in 1902. He had a few decent seasons in Boston, batting .257 in 1902 and .264 in 1903. After a short 83-game tour with the Tigers, he returned to the minors for 9 more years, playing A-level ball in the American and Southern Associations. Gremminger was player/manager for the Montgomery Senators in the Southern Association, leading the team to a fourth-place finish in 1908 and a third-place finish in 1909. After managing the Canton Statesmen of the Central League in 1912, he pretty much disappeared from the annals of baseball. He finished up with a .271 batting average over ten minor league seasons and 4,521 at bats.

Teams:
Cleveland Spiders NL (1895)
Boston Beaneaters NL (1902–1903)
Detroit Tigers AL (1904)

Lorenzo Edward Gremminger

Born:
March 30, 1874
Canton, OH
Died:
May 26, 1942
Canton, OH

▷ Batted: RH
▷ Threw: RH
▷ Position: 3B
▷ Career BA: .251

Moose Grimshaw

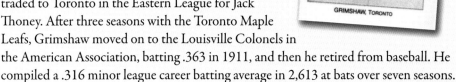

GRIMSHAW, TORONTO

Myron "Moose" Grimshaw patrolled first base for the Boston Americans of the American League for three seasons, beginning in 1905. Although he hit 4 home runs in his rookie season, good for ninth in the league, his best year was 1906, when he hit .290 in 428 at bats with 16 doubles, 12 triples, and 48 RBI. The 12 triples placed him fifth in the AL that season, and he did all that despite suffering a broken wrist in May of that year. In 1907 he and Larry Schlafly were traded to Toronto in the Eastern League for Jack Thoney. After three seasons with the Toronto Maple Leafs, Grimshaw moved on to the Louisville Colonels in the American Association, batting .363 in 1911, and then he retired from baseball. He compiled a .316 minor league career batting average in 2,613 at bats over seven seasons.

Team:
Boston Americans AL (1905–1907)

Myron Frederick Grimshaw

Born:
November 30, 1875
St. Johnsville, NY
Died:
December 11, 1936
Canajoharie, NY

▷ Batted: Switch
▷ Threw: RH
▷ Position: 1B
▷ Career BA: .256

Bob Groom

GROOM, WASHINGTON

Bob Groom burst into the major leagues at the age of 23 after going 29–15 for the Western League Portland Beavers in 1908. Groom had some interesting highlights and lowlights in his 10-year major league career. The highlights were his no-hitter against the White Sox on May 6, 1917, and the fact that he won 24 games in 1912. The lowlights were his 26 losses against only 7 wins in 1909, and his 17 losses in both 1910 and 1911. He ended up 31 games below .500, losing 150 games. After his playing days were over, Groom ran a family coal mining business in Belleville and managed various amateur teams in Illinois. He was inducted into the Hilgard Hall of Fame in 2008 for his role in founding the Hilgards, Belleville's first tournament team.

Born:
September 12, 1884
Belleville, IL
Died:
February 19, 1948
Belleville, IL

▷ Batted: RH
▷ Threw: RH
▷ Position: P
▷ MLB Pitching Record: 119–150
▷ ERA: 3.10

Teams:
Washington Senators AL (1909–1913)
St. Louis Terriers FL (1914–1915)
St. Louis Browns AL (1916–1917)
Cleveland Indians AL (1918)

Robert Groom

Ed Hahn

HAHN, CHICAGO AMER.

William Edgar Hahn

Born:
August 27, 1875
Nevada, OH
Died:
November 29, 1942
Des Moines, IA

▷ Batted: LH
▷ Threw: RH
▷ Position: OF
▷ Career BA: .237

Ed Hahn was an outfielder who had a couple of productive seasons for the Highlanders and was even more successful for the White Sox. He was not a great hitter, but he had a decent 6-year career in the big leagues because of his fielding abilities. Hahn had 709 career putouts in 790 chances, considered a good record in that era. He played in the post season in 1906, batting .273 in 25 at bats, and helping the Sox win the Series that year. In 1907 he led the American League in plate appearances, with 698, to go along with his .255 batting average. After his MLB days, Hahn returned to the minors as player/manager of the Mansfield Brownies in the Ohio-Pennsylvania League in 1911. He then played five seasons for the Des Moines Boosters in the Western League and retired in 1916 at age 40 after hitting .292 in 4,356 at bats in his nine minor league seasons.

Teams:
New York Highlanders AL (1905–1906)
Chicago White Sox AL (1906–1910)

Bob Hall

A very weak hitter and below-average fielder, it is frankly surprising that Bob Hall lasted 2 years in the pros. He played for three teams in those 2 years, and never hit higher than .238. Most likely he lasted that long because he played almost every position in the infield and outfield, but even there he had a lowly .892 fielding percentage. In 1905 the Giants loaned Hall to the Superbas in April, getting him back in November. After his brief stint in the majors, he played six seasons of A-level ball in the minors, mostly for the Baltimore Orioles of the Eastern League. After the 1911 season, Hall retired at 32 years old after hitting .240 in 3,112 at bats over eight minor league seasons.

HALL, BALTIMORE

Born:
December 20, 1878
Baltimore, MD
Died:
December 1, 1950
Wellesley, MA

▷ Batted: N/A
▷ Threw: R
▷ Position: 1B/2B/3B/ SS/OF
▷ Career BA: .203

Teams:
Philadelphia Phillies NL (1904)
New York Giants NL (1905)
Brooklyn Superbas NL (1905)

Robert Prill Hall

Jack Hannifin

Jack Hannifin only batted over .238 twice in his pro career, including hitting .272 for the New Haven Blues in the Connecticut State League in 1906. That season probably earned him his 3 years in the majors. He bounced through the majors for three seasons, playing for three different teams along the way. A utility infielder and sometimes an outfielder, Hannifin was a .214 career hitter for the A's (for 1 at bat in 1906), the Giants, and the Doves, but never collected more than 260 at bats in a season. Hannifin played eight seasons in the minors, four of which came after his last major league game. In 1909 and 1910 he played for the Jersey City Skeeters in the Eastern League, hitting .210. He retired in 1912 after batting .226 in 3,418 at bats over eight minor league seasons.

HANNIFAN, JERSEY CITY

Born:
February 25, 1883
Holyoke, MA
Died:
October 27, 1945
Northampton, MA

▷ Batted: RH
▷ Threw: RH
▷ Position: 3B/SS
▷ Career BA: .214

Teams:
Philadelphia Athletics AL (1906)
New York Giants NL (1906–1908)
Boston Doves NL (1908)

John Joseph Hannifin

Jimmy Hart

Jimmy "Hub" Hart had 127 at bats in the big leagues as a backup catcher with the Chicago White Sox from 1905 to 1907. He hit .213 in the majors, driving in 11 runs and scoring 10. Hart also has 1 double and 1 stolen base to his credit in his 57 career games played. He played six seasons in the minors, including one season in the outfield. Hart hit .252 in the minors over a career that included three seasons with the Montgomery Senators/Climbers in the Southern Association, as pictured on his T206 card. His best minor league seasons were 1909, when he hit .307 for Montgomery, and 1911, when he batted .272 for the Utica Utes in the New York State League. Hart finished up with the Sacramento Sacts of the Pacific Coast League in 1912, and then retired from the game when he was 34 years old.

Born:
February 2, 1878
Everett, MA
Died:
October 10, 1960
Fort Wayne, IN

▷ Batted: LH
▷ Threw: RH
▷ Position: C
▷ Career BA: .213

Team:
Chicago White Sox AL (1905–1907)

James Henry Hart

Bill Hart

Bill Hart carved out an 8-year career in the majors from 1886 to 1901, despite losing 120 games with just a .355 winning percentage. He led the league with 29 losses in 1896, allowing a league-worst 191 earned runs. He lost 27 games the following year, going 21–56 over those two seasons. Overall Hart posted a 66–120 MLB career record with a 4.65 ERA. His last major league season was 1901, but he pitched in the minors for eight more seasons, winning 83 games against 80 losses. Hart pitched in the Western League as player/manager for the Peoria Distillers in 1902 and in the American Association for the Columbus Senators and the Indianapolis Indians through 1906. He moved on to the Southern Association to play for the Little Rock Travelers for three seasons and then for the Chattanooga Lookouts. He retired in 1910 when he was 44 years old.

Born:
July 19, 1865
Louisville, KY
Died:
September 19, 1936
Cincinnati, OH

▷ Batted: N/A
▷ Threw: RH
▷ Position: P
▷ MLB Pitching Record: 66–120
▷ ERA: 4.65

Teams:
Philadelphia Athletics AA (1886–1887)
Brooklyn Grooms NL (1892)
Pittsburgh Pirates NL (1895, 1898)
St. Louis Browns NL (1896–1897)
Cleveland Blues AL (1901)

William Franklin Hart

Jack Hayden

In his 11 minor league seasons, Jack Hayden amassed a more than respectable .288 career average. He played mostly for the Baltimore Orioles in the Eastern League and the Indianapolis Indians in the American Association. His minor league career included three seasons of .300 or better and two seasons with 6 or more homers. All of that only earned him 578 at bats in the majors, which he collected in three seasons with three separate teams over 7 years. Hayden hit .265 for the A's in 211 at bats in 1901 and didn't reappear in the majors until 1906, when he hit .248 for Boston in 322 at bats. He got one last look at the show in 1908, hitting .200 in 45 at bats for the Cubs. After his playing days, Hayden managed the Louisville Colonels in the American Association for four seasons.

Born:
October 21, 1880
Bryn Mawr, PA
Died:
August 3, 1942
Haverford, PA

▷ Batted: LH
▷ Threw: LH
▷ Position: OF
▷ Career BA: .251

Teams:
Philadelphia Athletics AL (1901)
Boston Americans AL (1906)
Chicago Cubs NL (1908)

John Francis Hayden

Charlie Hemphill

Charlie "Eagle Eye" Hemphill was the first right fielder in Boston Red Sox franchise history. A solid gutsy player, he played for six different teams during his 11-year MLB career. In 1902, his best year offensively, he batted .308 between St. Louis and Cleveland. Hemphill had another good year in 1908, batting .297 for New York and stealing 42 bases. He managed to bang out 1,230 hits over his MLB career and had 421 RBI. A strong defensive player, he had 320 putouts for St. Louis in 1907. Hemphill managed the Atlanta Crackers of the Southern Association in 1912 and continued to play outfield in the minors through 1915, finishing with a .308 batting average for his five minor league seasons. One of his brothers, Frank Hemphill, also played outfield in the majors for the White Sox and the Senators.

Teams:
St. Louis Perfectos NL (1899)
Cleveland Spiders NL (1899)
Boston Americans AL (1901)
Cleveland Bronchos AL (1902)
St. Louis Browns AL (1902–1907)
New York Highlanders AL (1908–1911)

Charles Judson Hemphill

Born:
April 20, 1876
Greenville, MI
Died:
June 22, 1953
Detroit, MI

▷ Batted: LH
▷ Threw: LH
▷ Position: OF
▷ Career BA: .271

Buck Herzog

HERZOG, BOSTON NAT'L

HERZOG, N.Y. NAT'L

Charles "Buck" Herzog had a long steady career playing just about every infield position at one time or another. A pretty good batsman who always hovered around the .260 mark, Herzog's most productive season was 1914, when he batted .281. He was a dependable player and a great clubhouse guy. Herzog was player/manager of the Reds from 1914 to 1916, and in 1919 he led the league in hit-by-pitch with 14. After his stint with the Cubs, he played one season in the minors and then came back to manage the Easton Farmers in the Eastern Shore League in 1925 and 1926. He worked for the B&O Railroad after leaving the game.

Teams:
New York Giants NL (1908–1909, 1911–1913, 1916–1917)
Boston Doves/Rustlers/Braves NL (1910–1911, 1918–1919)
Cincinnati Reds NL (player/manager: 1914–1916)
Chicago Cubs NL (1919–1920)

Born:
July 9, 1885
Baltimore, MD
Died:
September 4, 1953
Baltimore, MD

▷ Batted: RH
▷ Threw: RH
▷ Position: 2B/3B/SS/1B
▷ Career BA: .259
▷ Managerial Record: 165–226

Charles Lincoln Herzog

Harry Hinchman

HINCHMAN, TOLEDO

Born:
August 4, 1878
Philadelphia, PA

Died:
January 19, 1933
Toledo, OH

▷ Batted: Switch
▷ Threw: RH
▷ Position: 2B
▷ Career BA: .216

Harry Hinchman, Bill Hinchman's big brother, also started his pro career with the New York State League's Ilion club. After six seasons in the NYSL, he finally got his shot at the majors at age 28. He played just 15 games for the Naps in 1907, batting .216 in 51 at bats. He was weak defensively at second base and left the Naps in 1908 to play five seasons for the Toledo Mud Hens in the American Association, batting .307 in 1911. He continued to play in the minors until 1921, batting .260 over his 19 seasons. Hinchman went on to manage in the New York–Pennsylvania League, the Eastern League, and the International League for nine seasons until he retired in 1932. As a manager with the New York–Pennsylvania League's Williamsport Grays, he posted four consecutive winning seasons from 1923 to 1926. The Grays were league champions in 1923 (82–42) and 1924 (87–46), they tied for first place in 1925 (77–55), and placed fourth in 1926.

Team:
Cleveland Naps AL (1907)

Harry Sibley Hinchman

Izzy Hoffman

HOFFMAN, PROVIDENCE

Outfielder Harry "Izzy" Hoffman started his 15 years in the minors in 1904, hitting .217 for the Eastern League's Montreal Royals. In 1905 he tried pitching for the Holyoke Paperweights of the Connecticut State League, and went 2–0. Those pro adventures came as Izzy was 29 and 30 years old. He took up pro ball late, but made it to the majors in 1904, going 3 for 30 (.100) with 1 double and 1 RBI for the Washington Senators. In 1907 he returned to the majors for 92 at bats with the Boston Doves, hitting .279 with 3 doubles, 3 RBI, and 2 stolen bases. After his tour in Boston, Hoffman returned to the minors and played for the Eastern League's Providence Grays and the Oakland Oaks in the Pacific Coast League. He then played and managed in the minors for five different teams in five different leagues, retiring after hitting .294 for Ridgeway of the Interstate League in 1916. After 6 years off, Hoffman returned at age 48 for one last season, playing 22 games for the Montreal Royals in the Eastern Canada League, hitting .344 in 64 at bats.

Born:
January 5, 1875
Bridgeport, NJ

Died:
November 13, 1942
Philadelphia, PA

▷ Batted: LH
▷ Threw: LH
▷ Position: OF
▷ Career BA: .233

Teams:
Washington Senators AL (1904)
Boston Doves NL (1907)

Harry C. Hoffman

Buck Hooker

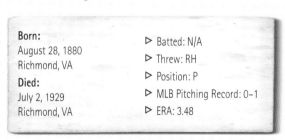

HOOKER, LYNCHBURG

William "Buck" Hooker pitched just 10.1 innings for the Cincinnati Reds in 1902 and 1903. He finished his major league career 0–1 with a 3.48 ERA in two appearances and one start, and failed to strike anyone out. He was 0–4 as a hitter, too. Hooker played 13 years in the minor leagues, pitching in five of them, collecting a 22–14 record for five different teams. He spent most of his time in the Virginia League with the Lynchburg Shoemakers, as pictured on his T206 card. Hooker pitched exclusively until 1906, at which point he became an outfielder, pitching only in single appearances after that in 1906 and 1908. He also managed the Vicksburg Hill Billies in the Cotton States League in 1906, the Newport News Shipbuilders in the Virginia League in 1912, and the Clifton Forge Railroaders in the Virginia Mountain League in 1914. He retired after the 1915 season at the age of 34 as a .255 career hitter in the minors.

Born:
August 28, 1880
Richmond, VA

Died:
July 2, 1929
Richmond, VA

▷ Batted: N/A
▷ Threw: RH
▷ Position: P
▷ MLB Pitching Record: 0–1
▷ ERA: 3.48

Team:
Cincinnati Reds NL (1902–1903)

William Edward Hooker

Del Howard

Born:
December 24, 1877
Kenney, IL

Died:
December 24, 1956
Seattle, WA

▷ Batted: LH
▷ Threw: RH
▷ Position: OF/1B
▷ Career BA: .263

Teams:
Pittsburgh Pirates NL (1905)
Boston Beaneaters NL (1906–1907)
Chicago Cubs NL (1907–1909)

George "Del" Howard had played two-plus respectable seasons for the Pittsburgh Pirates and Boston Beaneaters when he was traded to the Cubs in June 1907 for Newt Randall and Bill Sweeney. He couldn't crack the strong Cubs lineup, but played a valuable role backing up at first base and in the outfield. A .263 career hitter, Howard hit just .243 for the Cubs in his three seasons in Chicago. He did, however, win two World Series with the Cubs in 1907 and 1908. After his MLB tour, Howard became player/manager of the Louisville Colonels in the American Association from 1910 to 1911, the San Francisco Seals in the Pacific Coast League from 1913 to 1914, and the Oakland Oaks in the Pacific Coast League from 1916 to 1922. After playing ten seasons in the minors, he retired with a .294 batting average.

George Elmer Howard

Harry Howell

Harry Taylor Howell

Born:
November 14, 1876
New Jersey

Died:
May 22, 1956
Spokane, WA

▷ Batted: RH
▷ Threw: RH
▷ Position: P
▷ MLB Pitching Record: 131–146
▷ ERA: 2.74

Teams:
Brooklyn Bridegrooms NL (1898)
Baltimore Orioles NL (1899)
Brooklyn Superbas NL (1900)
Baltimore Orioles/New York Highlanders AL (1901–1903)
St. Louis Browns AL (1904–1910)

Harry Howell was a hard-luck pitcher whose abilities were better than his record indicates. He just happened to play on some bad teams. Howell led the National League in games finished in 1900 and he led the American League in games finished in 1903. He did lose 20 or more games on three occasions, however (1901, 1904, 1905). He was a very durable pitcher, leading the American League in complete games in 1905. His 2.74 ERA is 83rd on the all-time list, and over his 13 MLB seasons, he pitched 244 complete games with 20 shutouts. Howell retired from the game after the 1910 season when he was 33 years old.

John Hummel

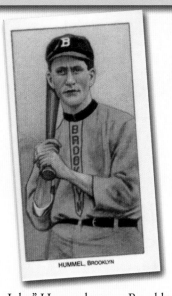

HUMMEL, BROOKLYN

"Silent John" Hummel wore a Brooklyn uniform for more than a decade, starting in 1905, when he hit .266 in 109 at bats as a 22-year-old rookie. He spent the next four seasons carving a reputation for being one of the most versatile players in the game, playing every non-pitching position except third base and catcher for the Superbas. In the last year before they became the Dodgers in 1911, he settled in at second base for 280 games over the next two seasons, leading the league in fielding at the position both years. After that, it was back to a utility role for the final 5 years of Hummel's 12-year career. After his tour with the Yankees, he was a player/manager in the minors for five different teams in five different leagues. He retired in 1926 at age 43 as a career .298 hitter in the minors.

Born:
April 4, 1883
Bloomsburg, PA
Died:
May 18, 1959
Springfield, MA

▷ Batted: RH
▷ Threw: RH
▷ Position: 2B/OF/1B/SS
▷ Career BA: .254

Teams:
Brooklyn Superbas/Dodgers/Robins NL (1905–1915)
New York Yankees AL (1918)

John Edwin Hummel

George Hunter

George Hunter played ten pro seasons starting in 1907, but only pitched in three of them. One of those was with the Brooklyn Superbas. He pitched well for them in 1909, posting a 2.46 ERA in 113.1 innings pitched, but he fell victim to the team behind him that lost 98 games that year. He went 4–10 in his 16 games and 13 starts. Hunter played 1 game for Brooklyn in the outfield in 1910 without getting an at bat, and then he played seven more seasons in the minors. After a brief stop with the Montreal Royals of the Eastern League, he moved on to the New York State League, where he played two seasons for the Wilkes-Barre Barons and five seasons for the Elmira Colonels. Hunter retired after the 1917 season with a minor league career .277 batting average.

HUNTER, BROOKLYN

Born:
July 8, 1887
Buffalo, NY
Died:
January 11, 1968
Harrisburg, PA

▷ Batted: Switch
▷ Threw: LH
▷ Position: OF/P
▷ MLB Pitching Record: 4–10
▷ ERA: 2.46
▷ Career BA: .228

Team:
Brooklyn Superbas NL (1909–1910)

George Henry Hunter

Frank Isbell

ISBELL, CHICAGO AMER.

Frank Isbell, nicknamed "Bald Eagle" due to his premature baldness, was a speedster with an average bat and decent glove. He was the starting first baseman for the White Sox teams that won the pennant in 1901 and won the World Series in 1906. Isbell was especially noted for his speed on the base paths. He led the league with 52 stolen bases in 1901, and ended up with 253 for his career. He also led the league in outs made in 1903 with 436. Isbell is one of the few major leaguers who actually played every position in his career. He even pitched, compiling a 4–7 record, and sometimes filled in as a catcher. After his MLB career, he managed and owned teams in the Western League. Isbell managed the Des Moines Boosters from 1912 through 1916, posting a 419–361 record and winning the league championship in 1915. He also served as president of the Wichita Witches from 1917 to 1926, and in 1931 he was president of the Topeka Senators.

Born:
August 21, 1875
Delevan, NY
Died:
July 15, 1941
Wichita, KS

▷ Batted: LH
▷ Threw: RH
▷ Position: 1B/2B
▷ Career BA: .250

Teams:
Chicago Orphans AL (1898)
Chicago White Sox AL (1901–1909)

William Frank Isbell

Fred Jacklitsch

JACKLITSCH, PHILA. NAT'L

Fred Jacklitsch carved out a 13-year major league career as a second-string catcher for the Phillies, the Superbas, the Highlanders, the Braves, and the Baltimore Terrapins of the Federal League. His best season was 1903, when he hit .267 in 176 at bats for the Superbas, with 8 doubles, 3 triples, a home run, and 21 RBI. In 1914 with Baltimore he collected 300-plus at bats for the first and only time in his career. He only had as many as 200 at bats in one other major league season. Jacklitsch played 397 of his 490 major league games as a catcher, but also played every other position except for pitcher during his career. He retired after his tour in Boston when he was 41 years old.

Teams:
Philadelphia Phillies NL (1900–1902, 1907–1910)
Brooklyn Superbas NL (1903–1904)
New York Highlanders AL (1905)
Baltimore Terrapins FL (1914–1915)
Boston Braves NL (1917)

Born:
May 24, 1876
Brooklyn, NY
Died:
July 18, 1937
Brooklyn, NY

▷ Batted: RH
▷ Threw: RH
▷ Position: C
▷ Career BA: .243

Frederick Lawrence Jacklitsch

Jim Jackson

JACKSON, BALTIMORE

Jim Jackson was one of the players who followed John McGraw from Baltimore to the Giants in 1902, but he was released after hitting just .182 in New York. Jackson went to St. Paul in the American Association and hit 21 home runs and stole 42 bases over two seasons in just 282 at bats. He returned to the majors in 1905 to play for Nap Lajoie in Cleveland, and hit .236 over two seasons in 800 at bats with 2 home runs and 40 stolen bases. Jackson was back in the minors in 1907 and finished out his pro career with ten seasons playing for the Columbus Senators in the American Association, the Baltimore Orioles in the Eastern League, and the Scranton Minors in the New York State League. He then was player/manager for the Wilmington Chicks in the Tri-State League. He retired in 1917 as a .284 career hitter in the minors.

Born:
November 28, 1877
Philadelphia, PA
Died:
October. 9, 1955
Philadelphia, PA

▷ Batted: RH
▷ Threw: RH
▷ Position: OF
▷ Career BA: .235

Teams:
Baltimore Orioles NL (1901)
New York Giants NL (1902)
Cleveland Naps AL (1905–1906)

James Benner Jackson

Davy Jones

JONES, DETROIT

David Jefferson Jones

Born:
June 30, 1880
Cambria, WI
Died:
March 30, 1972
Mankato, MN

▷ Batted: LH
▷ Threw: RH
▷ Position: OF
▷ Career BA: .270

Teams:
Milwaukee Brewers AL (1901)
St. Louis Browns AL (1902)
Chicago Orphans/Cubs NL (1902–1904)
Detroit Tigers AL (1906–1912, 1918)
Chicago White Sox AL (1913)
Pittsburgh Rebels FL (1914–1915)

Davy "Kangaroo" Jones played 15 seasons in the majors, mostly as a part-time outfielder for the Tigers, playing alongside Ty Cobb and Sam Crawford. In 1907, batting leadoff ahead of Cobb and Crawford, he finished seventh in the American League in on-base percentage at .357 and scored 101 runs, second only to Crawford himself. He also stole a career-high 30 bases that season, good for eighth in the American League. Jones played with the Tigers in their three consecutive trips to the World Series from 1907 to 1909; he hit .265 in 49 Series at bats with a .357 on-base percentage, scored 8 runs, and hit a home run against the Pirates in 1909. A trained pharmacist, Jones owned and operated a successful drug store in Detroit after he retired from baseball in 1915.

Tom Jones

Tom Jones played eight seasons at first base, six with the St. Louis Browns. His biggest contributions were in sacrifices; he led the American League with 40 in 1906 and finished in the top six in the league for the next four seasons. In August 1909, he was traded to the Tigers for Claude Rossman. Jones hit .262 for the Tigers in 179 games over the next two seasons, posted one of his 4 career homers, and drove in 63 runs. He played in the 1909 World Series against the Pirates, hitting .250 in 24 at bats with 1 double, 1 stolen base, and 2 RBI. After leaving Detroit, Jones played for the Milwaukee Brewers in the American Association for five seasons before managing the Johnsonburg Johnnies in the Interstate League in 1916. He then retired a with a .278 minor league batting average.

Born:
January 22, 1877
Honesdale, PA
Died:
June 21, 1923
Danville, PA

▷ Batted: RH
▷ Threw: RH
▷ Position: 1B
▷ Career BA: .251

Teams:
Baltimore Orioles AL (1902)
St. Louis Browns AL (1904–1909)
Detroit Tigers AL (1909–1910)

Thomas Jones

Dutch Jordan

Adolf "Dutch" Jordan came up to Brooklyn after two seasons with the Binghamton Bingoes in the New York State League. Jordan played two seasons for the Superbas in 1903 and 1904, hitting just .208 in 519 at bats and slugging just .260. Primarily a second baseman, he also played first and third base and the outfield for Brooklyn. That was the extent of his major league career, but Jordan went on to play ten more seasons in the minors, the first seven with the Atlanta Crackers in the Southern Association. A career .231 hitter in the minors, he hit .270 in 1905 for the Crackers, but hit less than .230 five times in the next 9 years. Jordan also played for the Chattanooga Lookouts and the Memphis Chickasaws in the Southern Association and the Dallas Giants in the Texas League. After his playing days, he managed off and on in the minors before retiring in 1921.

Born:
January 5, 1880
Pittsburgh, PA
Died:
December 23, 1972
West Allegheny, PA

▷ Batted: RH
▷ Threw: RH
▷ Position: 2B
▷ Career BA: .208

Team:
Brooklyn Superbas NL (1903–1904)

Adolf Otto Jordan

Ed Karger

Ed "Loose" Karger was a sub-.500 pitcher who played for several different teams in the majors. He won 15 games with the Cards in 1907 but he also lost 19 games that year. In 1910 he went 11–7 in his campaign with the Red Sox. His career 2.79 ERA was pretty good and he compiled 415 strikeouts over his 6-year career. Karger played four seasons for the St. Paul Saints of the American Association after his major league days. He was also player/manager for the Aberdeen Grays in the Dakota League in 1920 and 1921, after which he retired at age 38 with a 79–90 minor league pitching record.

Teams:
Pittsburgh Pirates NL (1906)
St. Louis Cardinals NL (1906–1908)
Cincinnati Reds NL (1909)
Boston Red Sox AL (1909–1911)

Born:
May 6, 1883
San Angelo, TX
Died:
September 9, 1957
Delta, CO

▷ Batted: RH
▷ Threw: LH
▷ Position: P
▷ MLB Pitching Record: 48–67
▷ ERA: 2.79

Edwin Karger

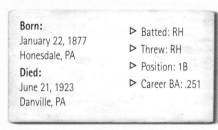

Rube Kisinger

Michigan native Charles "Rube" Kisinger got a chance to pitch for his local MLB team for a brief 2-year stint, winning a total of 9 games for the Tigers in 1902 and 1903. He was then traded to the Buffalo Bisons of the Eastern League and found success there, leading them to their first pennant in 1904 by winning 24 games. After 7 years in Buffalo, he pitched for the Jersey City Skeeters of the Eastern League before moving on to the Memphis Chickasaws, the New Orleans Pelicans, and the Nashville Volunteers of the Southern Association. Over the course of his minor league career, Kisinger went 205–160 before retiring in 1912 at age 39. He died in a train accident in 1941.

Team:
Detroit Tigers AL (1902–1903)

KISINGER, BUFFALO

Charles Samuel Kisinger

Born:
December 13, 1876
Adrian, MI
Died:
July 17, 1941
Huron, OH

▷ Batted: RH
▷ Threw: RH
▷ Position: P
▷ MLB Pitching Record: 9–12
▷ ERA: 3.00

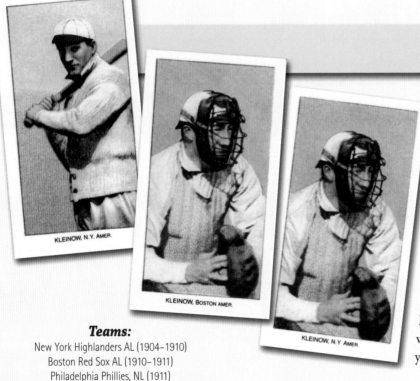

KLEINOW, N.Y. AMER.

KLEINOW, BOSTON AMER.

KLEINOW, N.Y. AMER.

Teams:
New York Highlanders AL (1904–1910)
Boston Red Sox AL (1910–1911)
Philadelphia Phillies, NL (1911)

John Peter Kleinow

Red Kleinow

John "Red" Kleinow was a backup catcher in the big leagues who was pretty good defensively but had a weak bat. He attended St. Edward's University before beginning his pro career in 1901 with the Minneapolis Millers in the Western League. After traveling around in the minors, he joined the Toledo Mud Hens of the American Association, where he hit his stride. Kleinow batted .294 for Toledo in 1902 and .320 in 1903, earning his ticket to the majors. His most productive year offensively was 1907, when he batted .264 with 71 hits. After his brief stint with the Phillies, Kleinow resurfaced in the minors to play 20 games in 1914 for the Montgomery Rebels in the Southern Association after which he retired from the game for good when he was 36 years old.

Born:
July 20, 1877
Milwaukee, WI
Died:
October 9, 1929
New York, NY

▷ Batted: RH
▷ Threw: RH
▷ Position: C
▷ Career BA: .213

Otto Knabe

Teams:
Pittsburgh Pirates NL (1905, 1916)
Philadelphia Phillies NL (1907–1913)
Baltimore Terrapins FL (player/manager: 1914–1915)
Chicago Cubs NL (1916)

A solid second baseman for four different teams, Otto "Dutch" Knabe is still the Phillies all-time leader in sacrifice hits with 216. Knabe also led the league in that category on four different occasions. He came up to the majors when he was 21 years old, where he put together a solid 11-season career between the National League and the Federal League. In 1912 he batted .282 but was less productive in most other categories. His best year was 1913, when he batted .263 and had 150 hits. As player/manager of the Baltimore Terrapins in the short-lived Federal League, he posted a 131–177 record. After his tour with the Cubs, Knabe played one season for the Richmond Virginians in the International League in 1917 before packing it in for good.

Franz Otto Knabe

Born:
June 12, 1884
Carrick, PA
Died:
May 17, 1961
Philadelphia, PA

▷ Batted: RH
▷ Threw: RH
▷ Position: 2B
▷ Career BA: .247
▷ Managerial Record: 131–177

Jack Knight

Jack "Schoolboy" Knight was signed out of the University of Pennsylvania as a 19-year-old shortstop, but he wound up playing all four infield positions during his career. His best year was 1910, when he batted .312 with 129 hits, good for fifth in the league. Knight's career pretty much went south after that, and after the 1913 season he traveled around the minors for 15 years. He played in the American Association for the Cleveland Spiders and the Minneapolis Millers, the Pacific Coast League for the Seattle Rainiers, the Oakland Oaks, and the Sacramento Senators, and the Western League for the Denver Bears. Knight finally called it a game after the 1928 season, retiring at age 42 with a .293 minor league batting average.

Teams:
Philadelphia Athletics AL (1905–1907)
Boston Americans AL (1907)
New York Highlanders/Yankees AL (1909–1911, 1913)
Washington Senators AL (1912)

John Wesley Knight

Born:
October 6, 1885
Philadelphia, PA
Died:
December 19, 1965
Walnut Creek, CA

▷ Batted: RH
▷ Threw: RH
▷ Position: SS/3B/1B/2B
▷ Career BA: .239

Harry Krause

Harry "Hal" Krause had a pretty good but short career in the major leagues. He led the American League with a 1.39 ERA in 1909 and went 18–8 that year. Overall, he had 298 K's over his five seasons. "Shoeless Joe" Jackson once said that Harry Krause was one of the toughest pitchers he ever faced. He went on to play in the Pacific Coast League for the Portland Beavers and then the Oakland Oaks, where he pitched for 12 seasons. Krause wrapped up his 20-year minor league career in 1929 at age 40 with a 300–249 record. He later managed the Tucson Cowboys in the Arizona-Texas League in 1937 and 1938. He is a member of the Pacific Coast League Hall of Fame.

Teams:
Philadelphia Athletics AL (1908–1912)
Cleveland Naps AL (1912)

Harry William Krause

Born:
July 12, 1888
San Francisco, CA
Died:
October 23, 1940
San Francisco, CA

▷ Batted: Switch
▷ Threw: LH
▷ Position: P
▷ MLB Pitching Record: 38–26
▷ ERA: 2.50

Art Kruger

Teams:
Cincinnati Reds NL (1907)
Cleveland Naps AL (1910)
Boston Doves NL (1910)
Kansas City Packers FL (1914–1915)

After 4 years with the Oakland Oaks in the Pacific Coast League, Art Kruger launched his MLB career with the Reds. In 1907 he batted a paltry .232 and was promptly sent back down to the minors. He played two seasons for the Columbus Senators in the American Association, batting .290 in 1909, and was again promoted to the big leagues. After playing only 16 games split between the Naps and the Doves, Kruger was sent back down to the Portland Beavers in the Pacific Coast League. He had several good seasons there, hitting as high as .299 in 1912. The 1914 season found Kruger back in the majors, playing for Kansas City in the Federal League, where he batted .259 with 114 hits, 47 RBI, and 11 stolen bases in 441 at bats, his best season by far. After the 1915 season, he finally called it quits when he was 34 years old.

Arthur Theodore Kruger

Born:
March 16, 1881
San Antonio, TX
Died:
November 28, 1949
Hondo, CA

▷ Batted: RH
▷ Threw: RH
▷ Position: OF
▷ Career BA: .232

Joe Lake

LAKE, ST. LOUIS AMER.

LAKE, N.Y. AMER.

LAKE, ST. LOUIS AMER.

Joe Lake came up to the Highlanders after going 25–14 for the Jersey City Skeeters of the Eastern League in 1907. He was a journeyman pitcher who had a relatively ineffective MLB career. He led the league with 22 losses in his rookie year, and did not fare much better than that later on. Lake did manage to go 14–11 in 1909, but then lost 17 games in 1910 and 15 games in 1911. He had a pretty good career 2.85 ERA, but never got a lot of support. Lake finished the 1913 season with the Minneapolis Millers in the American Association with a 5–3 record, and went 16–13 for them in 1914 before retiring from the game when he was 33 years old.

Teams:
New York Highlanders AL (1908–1909)
St. Louis Browns AL (1910–1912)
Detroit Tigers AL (1912–1913)

Born:
January 6, 1881
Brooklyn, NY

Died:
June 30, 1950
Brooklyn, NY

▷ Batted: RH
▷ Threw: RH
▷ Position: P
▷ MLB Pitching Record: 62–90
▷ ERA: 2.85

Joseph Henry Lake

Frank LaPorte

Frank LaPorte honed his skills with the Buffalo Bisons in the Eastern League, batting .291 over 3 years before joining the Highlanders late in the 1905 season. The 25-year-old rookie finished that season batting .400 in his first 40 major league at bats. A solid hitter and second baseman, LaPorte had some very good seasons in the American League and the Federal League. He batted .314 in 1911 for St. Louis, and in 1914, after moving to the Federal League, he batted .311 for the Hoosiers. Indianapolis won the pennant in 1914 behind LaPorte, who was the RBI champ that year with 107. As a second baseman, he was steady with good range. He also played some third base for several teams during his major league career.

Frank Breyfogle LaPorte

LA PORTE, N.Y. AMER.

Teams:
New York Highlanders AL (1905–1907, 1908–1910)
Boston Red Sox AL (1908)
St. Louis Browns AL (1911–1912)
Washington Senators AL (1912–1913)
Indianapolis Hoosiers FL (1914)
Newark Peppers FL (1915)

Born:
February 6, 1880
Uhrichsville, OH

Died:
September 25, 1939
Newcomerstown, OH

▷ Batted: RH
▷ Threw: RH
▷ Position: 2B/3B
▷ Career BA: .281

Bill Lattimore

LATTIMORE, TOLEDO

Texas native Bill Lattimore broke into the majors at 24 years old. Nicknamed "Slothful Bill" because of his slow playing style, Lattimore never made it past his rookie year, pitching just 4 games for the Cleveland Naps in 1908. He started in all four appearances, going 1–2 with a 4.50 ERA over 24 innings pitched. Those four starts were sandwiched among 5 years in the minors, mostly with the Toledo Mud Hens of the American Association, where he went 23–15 in 67 games over three seasons beginning in 1907. He finished up his playing days after going 13–10 in 1910 for the Fort Worth Panthers in the Texas League. Lattimore returned to manage the Topeka Savages in the Western League in 1916.

Born:
May 25, 1884
Roxton, TX
Died:
October 30, 1919
Colorado Springs, CO

▷ Batted: LH
▷ Threw: LH
▷ Position: P
▷ MLB Pitching Record: 1–2
▷ ERA: 4.50

Team:
Cleveland Naps AL (1908)

William Hershel Lattimore

Jimmy Lavender

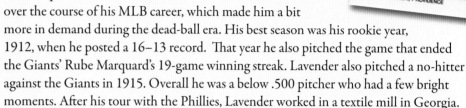

LAVENDER, PROVIDENCE

Jimmy Lavender was 28 years old when he finally got his shot in the majors. He had already spent 5 years in the minors, the last 3 in the Eastern League, where he put together a 48–61 record for the Providence Grays. A fairly inconsistent pitcher who used the spitball as his out pitch, he was usually among the National League leaders in wild pitches. Lavender was a versatile pitcher, who was used as both a starter and reliever over the course of his MLB career, which made him a bit more in demand during the dead-ball era. His best season was his rookie year, 1912, when he posted a 16–13 record. That year he also pitched the game that ended the Giants' Rube Marquard's 19-game winning streak. Lavender also pitched a no-hitter against the Giants in 1915. Overall he was a below .500 pitcher who had a few bright moments. After his tour with the Phillies, Lavender worked in a textile mill in Georgia.

Born:
May 26, 1884
Barnesville, GA
Died:
January 12, 1960
Cartersville, GA

▷ Batted: RH
▷ Threw: RH
▷ Position: P
▷ MLB Pitching Record: 63–76
▷ ERA: 3.09

Teams:
Chicago Cubs NL (1912–1916)
Philadelphia Phillies NL (1917)

James Sanford Lavender

Ed Lennox

LENNOX, BROOKLYN

Ed "Eggie" Lennox's biggest claim to major league fame may be that he spent 24 games as the third baseman to the famous "Tinker to Evers to Chance" double-play trio with the Cubs in 1912. He was spelling Heinie Zimmerman, even though it was Harry Steinfieldt who played third base for the Cubs in 1910 when "Baseball's Sad Lexicon" was written. After four nondescript seasons in the American League and National League, he returned to the minors for a year. Lennox then joined the Pittsburgh Rebels in the Federal League, where he found his groove. He hit .312 with 11 homers, 84 RBI, and 19 stolen bases, finished in the top five in the league in on-base percentage, slugging percentage, home runs, and walks, and finished eighth in RBI. Sandwiched between his MLB tours, he spent eight seasons in the minors, playing mostly for the Rochester Bronchos in the Eastern League and the Louisville Colonels in the American Association. Lennox retired from the game in 1916 as a .274 minor league career hitter.

Born:
November 3, 1883
Camden, NJ
Died:
October 26, 1939
Camden, NJ

▷ Batted: RH
▷ Threw: RH
▷ Position: 3B
▷ Career BA: .274

Teams:
Philadelphia Athletics AL (1906)
Brooklyn Superbas NL (1909–1910)
Chicago Cubs NL (1912)
Pittsburgh Rebels FL (1914–1915)

James Edgar Lennox

Glenn Liebhardt

Glenn Liebhardt had a fairly short career in the majors pitching for the Cleveland Naps for four seasons. He managed to go over the .500 mark by 1 game over the course of his major league career. His best year was 1907, when he went 18–14 with a 2.05 ERA. The next year he won 15 games, but he only won 1 game his last year. Liebhardt went on to pitch for the Columbus Senators and the Minneapolis Millers of the American Association and the Memphis Chickasaws of the Southern Association. He retired at age 31 in 1914 with a 123–112 minor league record. His son, Glenn Ignatius Liebhardt, who was born 1 year after his father left the majors, played for the Athletics and the Browns for three seasons in the 1930s.

Born:
March 10, 1883
Milton, IN
Died:
July 13, 1956,
Cleveland, OH

▷ Batted; RH
▷ Threw: RH
▷ Position: P
▷ MLB Pitching Record: 36–35
▷ ERA: 2.17

Team:
Cleveland Naps AL (1906–1909)

Glenn John Liebhardt

Vive Lindaman

Vive Lindaman showed promise in the minors, but was a relatively ineffective pitcher who had a short 4-year stint in the majors. He had a 24–7 record in 1905 with the Jersey City Skeeters of the Eastern League but he couldn't maintain his winning ways in the majors. When he got to Boston in 1906, he went 12–23, and followed that with 15-loss and 16-loss seasons. Lindaman really struggled for the Braves, and in 1909 he moved on to pitch for the Indianapolis Indians of the American Association. After a dismal 1910 season, he retired from the game when he was 32 years old.

Born:
October 28, 1877
Charles City, IA
Died:
February 13, 1927
Charles City, IA

▷ Batted: RH
▷ Threw: RH
▷ Position: P
▷ MLB Pitching Record: 36–60
▷ ERA: 2.92

Team:
Boston Braves NL (1906–1909)

Vivian Alexander Lindaman

Bill Malarkey

Bill Malarkey came up to the majors after one season with the Sharon Giants in the Ohio-Pennsylvania league. The 29-year-old rookie appeared in 15 games for the Giants in 1908, going 0–2. After his brief time in the majors, Malarkey played for the Buffalo Bisons in the Eastern League for three seasons, going 13–11 in 1909 and 10–6 in 1910. After moving to the Pacific Coast League's Oakland Oaks, he had some very good years. He went 20–12 in 1912 and 25–16 in 1913. It is surprising that he never got more of a chance in the majors. Malarkey retired after the 1915 season with a 107–97 record over his nine minor league seasons.

Team:
New York Giants NL (1908)

William John Malarkey

Born:
November 26, 1878
Port Byron, IL
Died:
December 12, 1956
Phoenix, AZ

▷ Batted: RH
▷ Threw: RH
▷ Position: P
▷ MLB Pitching Record: 0–2
▷ ERA: 2.57

Billy Maloney

Billy Maloney jumped directly from Georgetown University to the majors in 1901. He played 72 of his 86 games at catcher for the Brewers that year, hitting .293 in 290 at bats. Unfortunately, he wasn't a great catcher, and he caught for just 18 more games for the rest of his 6-year MLB career. After playing only 57 games between the Browns and the Reds in 1902, Maloney spent 2 years in the American Association with the Kansas City Cowboys and the Minneapolis Millers before the Cubs took him in the Rule V draft in 1905. That season, he played 145 games in the outfield, and led the National League with 59 stolen bases in 558 at bats while hitting .260. After hitting .229 or less in three seasons with Brooklyn, Maloney returned to the minors and played the 1909 season for the Rochester Bronchos in the Eastern League. After 3 more years playing for five teams in two leagues, he finished up with the San Antonio Bronchos of the Texas League in 1914. He retired at 36 years old as a .253 career hitter in the minors.

MALONEY, ROCHESTER

Born:
June 5, 1878
Lewiston, ME

Died:
September 2, 1960
Breckenridge, TX

▷ Batted: LH
▷ Threw: RH
▷ Position: OF/C
▷ Career BA: .236

Teams:
Milwaukee Brewers AL (1901)
St. Louis Browns AL (1902)
Cincinnati Reds NL (1902)
Chicago Cubs NL (1905)
Brooklyn Superbas NL (1906–1908)

William Alphonse Maloney

Rube Manning

MANNING, N.Y. AMER.

MANNING, N.Y. AMER.

Pitcher Walter "Rube" Manning came up to the majors after going 37–26 in two seasons for the Tri-State League's Williamsport Millionaires. He had a short stint with the Yanks, playing for 4 years, and did not have great success. His best year was 1908, when he went 13–16 with a 2.94 ERA. He managed to win another 7 games the following year but had 11 losses, and after his final campaign in 1910 he was out of the majors. Manning fared better after returning to the Tri-State League to play for the Reading Pretzels, Allentown, and Atlantic City. Over the course of four seasons from 1911 to 1914, he went 62–29. He continued on for three more seasons with the Toronto Maple Leafs in the International League and the Wilkes-Barre Barons in the New York State League. Manning retired from the game in 1917 when he was 34 years old with a 129–95 pitching record over nine seasons in the minors.

Team:
New York Yankees AL (1907–1910)

Born:
April 29, 1883
Chambersburg, PA

Died:
April 23, 1930
Williamsport, PA

▷ Batted: RH
▷ Threw: RH
▷ Position: P
▷ MLB Pitching Record: 22–32

Walter S. Manning

Doc Marshall

MARSHALL, BROOKLYN

William Riddle Marshall

Born
September 22, 1875
Butler, PA

Died
December 11, 1959
Clinton, IL

▷ Batted: RH
▷ Threw: RH
▷ Position: C
▷ Career BA: .210

Teams:
Philadelphia Phillies NL (1904)
New York Giants NL (1904 twice, 1906)
Boston Beaneaters NL (1904)
St. Louis Cardinals NL (1906–1908)
Chicago Cubs NL (1908)
Brooklyn Superbas NL (1909)

William "Doc" Marshall spent five seasons in the majors playing catcher with six different franchises. In 1907 he finally played an entire season with one team, hitting .201 in 268 at bats for the Cardinals and collecting the only 2 homers of his career. In 1909 Marshall got 149 at bats in a full season with Brooklyn, hitting .201 again. In 1906 and 1908, Doc played with two different teams, but in 1904, his rookie season, Marshall played with 4 different teams, including a one game, no at-bat, "cup of coffee" with the New York Giants. Apparently Doc always had trouble settling down. Before his playing days, he attended three different colleges. He hit .210 for his career in 756 at bats, with 2 home runs and 54 RBI. Marshall then played five seasons in the American Association for the Milwaukee Brewers and the St. Paul Saints, retiring in 1913 with a minor league career .258 batting average.

Al Mattern

MATTERN, BOSTON NAT'L

Pitcher Al Mattern had a 5-year stint with Boston after going 16–7 for the Holyoke Papermakers of the Connecticut State League in 1907 and 20–21 for the Tri-State League's Trenton Tigers in 1908. He went 15–21 in 1909 (with an ERA of 2.85) and 16–19 in 1910. Mattern was a real workhorse those 2 years, pitching 316 innings in 1909 and 305 in 1910. He led the league in batters faced (1,314) in 1909, but unfortunately he also led the league in earned runs (100), hits (322), and walks (108). In 1910 he led the league in games played (51) and shutouts (6). Mattern was probably a much better pitcher than his record indicates. He finished up playing in the minors in the International League for the Montreal Royals and the Newark Indians, retiring in 1914 with an 82–76 record.

Born:
June 16, 1883
West Rush, NY
Died:
November 6, 1958
West Rush, NY

▷ Batted: LH
▷ Threw: LH
▷ Position: P
▷ MLB Pitching Record: 36–58
▷ ERA: 3.37

Team:
Boston Doves/Rustlers/Braves NL (1908–1912)

Alonzo Albert Mattern

Jack McAleese

McALEESE, ST. LOUIS AMER.

Jack McAleese made his major league debut before playing in the minor leagues, pitching 1 game for the White Sox in 1901. He pitched three innings and gave up 3 runs on 7 hits with 1 walk and 1 strikeout. He then pitched in the Eastern League in 1902 and 1903, going 12–12 over the two seasons. In 1903 McAleese also played 56 games at first base. He then made the change from pitching to playing first base and the outfield. McAleese got a trip back to the majors in 1909 with the St. Louis Browns, where he hit .213 in 268 at bats with 7 doubles and 12 RBI. He retired after the 1910 season, but returned in 1912 to play for the Youngstown Steelmen in the Central League, hitting .213 in 80 at bats. Over his nine seasons in the minors, McAleese played for ten different teams in seven different leagues and batted .279.

Born:
August 22, 1878
Sharon, PA
Died:
November 15, 1950
New York, NY

▷ Batted: RH
▷ Threw: RH
▷ Position: OF
▷ Career BA: .213

Teams:
Chicago White Stockings AL (1901)
St. Louis Browns AL (1909)

John James McAleese

Pat McCauley

MCCAULEY, PORTSMOUTH

Pat McCauley made three catching cameos in the majors in 1893, 1896, and 1903, and only got more than 20 at bats with the Washington Senators in 1896. He hit .250 in 84 at bats that season, slugged 3 home runs, and drove in 11. Overall, he hit .193 for his major league career in 119 at bats with the St. Louis Browns, Washington Senators, and the New York Highlanders. Beginning in 1901, however, McCauley played nine seasons in the minors, six of them in the Eastern League with seven different teams. He hit .203 in the Eastern League and .205 over his minor league career. On his T206 card he is pictured in his uniform for the Portsmouth Truckers of the Virginia League, where he played for part of the 1909 season.

Born:
June 10, 1870
Ware, MA
Died:
January 17, 1917
Hoboken, NJ

▷ Batted: N/A
▷ Threw: RH
▷ Position: C
▷ Career BA: .193

Teams:
St. Louis Browns NL (1893)
Washington Senators NL (1896)
New York Highlanders AL (1903)

Patrick F. McCauley

Jim McGinley

McGINLEY, TORONTO

Jim McGinley was another player whose stint in the majors was just enough to tell his grandkids about. The Cardinals purchased him from the Haverhill Hustlers of the New England League in 1904. He made a total of four appearances over two seasons, winning 2 games. He pitched 30 innings with 6 career strikeouts, 8 walks, and gave up 33 hits. McGinley then returned to Haverhill and went 17–11 in 1905 before moving on to pitch six seasons for the Toronto Maple Leafs in the Eastern League. There he went 22–10 in 1907 and 22–13 in 1909. After a few years with the Binghamton Bingoes in the New York State League and the Worcester Busters in the Eastern League, he retired in 1918 with a 145–111 minor league record.

Team:
St. Louis Cardinals NL (1904–1905)

Born:
October 2, 1878
Groveland, MA
Died:
September 20, 1961
Haverhill, MA

▷ Batted: RH
▷ Threw: RH
▷ Position: P
▷ MLB Pitching Record: 2–2
▷ ERA: 3.30

James William McGinley

Pryor McElveen

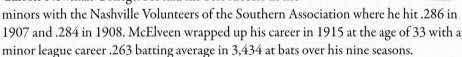

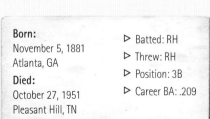

McELVEEN, BROOKLYN

Pryor "Humpty" McElveen played all over the Brooklyn Superbas' infield between 1909 and 1911, hitting .209 in 502 at bats with 4 home runs and 56 RBI. His best MLB season was 1910, when he hit .225 and posted a .305 slugging percentage. Primarily a third baseman, McElveen played every position in the majors except pitcher. Around those three seasons in the majors, he played nine seasons in the minors for eight different teams in six different leagues. McElveen started his baseball career in 1904 at age 22 after attending Carson-Newman College. He had his best success in the minors with the Nashville Volunteers of the Southern Association where he hit .286 in 1907 and .284 in 1908. McElveen wrapped up his career in 1915 at the age of 33 with a minor league career .263 batting average in 3,434 at bats over his nine seasons.

Team:
Brooklyn Superbas/Dodgers NL (1909–1911)

Born:
November 5, 1881
Atlanta, GA
Died:
October 27, 1951
Pleasant Hill, TN

▷ Batted: RH
▷ Threw: RH
▷ Position: 3B
▷ Career BA: .209

Pryor Mynatt McElveen

Stoney McGlynn

MCGLYNN, MILWAUKEE

Ulysses Simpson Grant "Stoney" McGlynn's name practically rivals his major league career in length. He debuted in 1906 at 34 years old and pitched 48 innings for the Cards. In 1907 he made 45 appearances and pitched 352.1 innings, going 14–25 with a 2.91 ERA over 39 starts, leading the league in starts and innings pitched. Unfortunately, he also led the league in walks, hits, and earned runs allowed. In 1908 he pitched 75 innings, going 1–6 with a 3.45 ERA. That was the last campaign of his major league career. McGlynn then pitched 5 more years in the minors, the first 3 with the Milwaukee Brewers in the American Association, where he went 65–57. He retired in 1915 with a 177–109 record from his eight minor league seasons.

Born:
May 26, 1872
Lancaster, PA
Died:
August 26, 1941
Manitowoc, WI

▷ Batted: RH
▷ Threw: RH
▷ Position: P
▷ MLB Pitching Record: 17–33
▷ ERA: 2.95

Team:
St. Louis Cardinals NL (1906–1908)

Ulysses Simpson Grant McGlynn

Harry McIntire

Harry "Rocks" McIntire went 71–117 over nine major league seasons. His winning percentage was mortally wounded, however, by his first five seasons with the very bad Brooklyn Superbas. His record in Brooklyn was 46–98 with a 3.11 ERA, including three seasons in which he lost 20 or more games. The highlight of his career also came during this period, however, when he threw a no-hitter through ten innings in August 1906 against the Pirates. Unfortunately, his team lost in the 13th inning due to a costly error. He also led the National League in hit batsmen in 1905, 1908, and 1909. In his next three seasons, with Chicago, he went 25–18 with a 3.56 ERA, and in 1910 he pitched five innings in the World Series. He retired after the 1913 season when he was 34 years old.

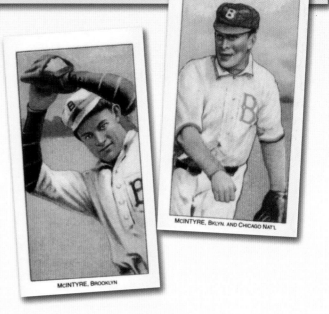

MCINTYRE, BROOKLYN

MCINTYRE, BKLYN. AND CHICAGO NAT'L

Born:
January 11, 1879
Dayton, OH
Died:
January 9, 1949
Daytona Beach, FL

▷ Batted: RH
▷ Threw: RH
▷ Position: P
▷ MLB Pitching Record: 71–117
▷ ERA: 3.22

Teams:
Brooklyn Superbas NL (1905–1909)
Chicago Cubs NL (1910–1912)
Cincinnati Reds NL (1913)

John Reid McIntire

George Merritt

MERRITT, JERSEY CITY

George Washington Merritt's major league career consisted of 47 at bats and 28 innings pitched with the Pirates between 1901 and 1903. He hit .213 with 5 RBI in his 47 at bats and went 3–0 in his 28 innings pitched with a 4.50 ERA, 7 strikeouts, and 6 walks. Merritt went on to play 12 more seasons in the minors in the Eastern League and the Southern Association. Seven of those years were with the Jersey City Skeeters, where he hit .301 in 1904. He finished up in the Southern Association, playing for the Memphis Chickasaws, the Little Rock Travelers, and the Chattanooga Lookouts. Merritt retired in 1915 at age 35 with minor league batting average of .249 and a pitching record of 57–57.

Born:
April 14, 1880
Paterson, NJ
Died:
February 21, 1938
Memphis, TN

▷ Batted: N/A
▷ Threw: RH
▷ Position: OF/P
▷ MLB Pitching Record: 3–0
▷ Career BA: .213
▷ ERA: 4.50

Team:
Pittsburgh Pirates NL (1901–1903)

George Washington Merritt

Billy Milligan

Billy Milligan didn't make it in the majors although he pitched and played the outfield rather well in the A-rated Eastern League. As an MLB rookie he went 0–3 for the A's in 1901. He then won 21 games for the Buffalo Bisons of the Eastern League in 1903, which earned him a shot with the Giants, where he went 0–1 in 1904. He finished 1904 in the Eastern League with the Providence Grays before returning to play four more seasons for Buffalo. In 1905 he batted .295 for the Bisons and won 19 games as a pitcher. He certainly was their MVP that year! He wrapped up his career with the Eastern League's Jersey City Skeeters. Milligan retired after the 1910 season at age 31 with a career .263 batting average and an 82–68 pitching record over his nine minor league seasons.

MILLIGAN, JERSEY CITY

Born:
August 19, 1878
Buffalo, NY
Died:
October 14, 1928
Buffalo, NY

▷ Batted: RH
▷ Threw: LH
▷ Position: OF/P
▷ MLB Pitching Record: 0–4
▷ Career BA: .250

Teams:
Philadelphia Athletics AL (1901)
New York Giants NL (1904)

William Joseph Milligan

Mike Mitchell

Mike Mitchell played 5 years in the minors, batting .339 in 1906 for the Portland Beavers in the Pacific Coast League to earn his shot in the big leagues at age 27. He was a consistent outfielder for four different teams during his 8-year MLB career. In 1909 and 1910 he led the National League in triples, and in 1909 he batted .310, good for second in the league. Mitchell then had several more solid seasons, batting in the 280s, and hit .291 in 1911. During his stint in the big leagues, he banged out 1,138 hits and 27 homers. He returned to the minors in 1916 to play for the Newark Indians in the International League for 1 year before retiring at age 36 as a minor league career .290 hitter.

MITCHELL, CINCINNATI

Teams:
Cincinnati Reds NL (1907–1912)
Chicago Cubs NL (1913)
Pittsburgh Pirates NL (1913–1914)
Washington Senators AL (1914)

Born:
December 12, 1879
Springfield, OH
Died:
July 16, 1961
Phoenix, AZ

▷ Batted: RH
▷ Threw: RH
▷ Position: OF
▷ Career BA: .278

Michael Francis Mitchell

MOELLER, JERSEY CITY

Danny Moeller

Starting in 1907, Danny Moeller carved out a 7-year career with Pittsburgh, Washington, and Cleveland. His best years were between 1912 and 1915, when he played regularly in the Senators' outfield. Dan actually got some MVP consideration in 1912 after hitting .276 with 6 home runs (fourth in the AL), 46 RBI, and 30 stolen bases. He stole 62 bases in 1913, a career high that was good for second in the league. In July 1915, Moeller stole second, third, and home against Cleveland as the Senators set the major league record for stolen bases in an inning with 8. Philadelphia tied that record in 1919, but the mark still stands today. Between his tours with the Pirates and the Senators, he played in the Eastern League for the Jersey City Skeeters and the Rochester Bronchos. After his stint with the Indians, he played for the Western League's Des Moines Boosters, retiring after the 1921 season with a .277 minor league career batting average. Moeller managed the Oklahoma City Indians of the Western League in 1920.

Born:
March 23, 1885
DeWitt, IA
Died:
April 14, 1951
Florence, AL

▷ Batted: Switch
▷ Throws: RH
▷ Position: OF
▷ Career BA: .243

Teams:
Pittsburgh Pirates NL (1907–1908)
Washington Senators AL (1912–1916)
Cleveland Indians AL (1916)

Daniel Edward Moeller

Herbie Moran

MORAN, PROVIDENCE

A mediocre outfielder for several teams, Herbie Moran did manage to start on the 1914 World Series championship Reds. He had a couple of decent seasons for the Dodgers batting .276 in 1912 and .266 in 1913. Moran batted a lowly .200 for the Braves in 1914, his last year in the majors. During his career, he jumped back to the minors several times, playing in the Eastern League for the Providence Grays in 1909 and the Rochester Bronchos in 1910 and 1911. After his MLB days, he played 3 more years in the minors for the Montreal Royals of the International League and the Little Rock Travelers of the Southern Association. He retired in 1918 after batting .278 over his ten minor league seasons. Moran managed in the minors for two seasons during the 1930s for the Williamsport Grays of the New York–Pennsylvania League and the New Waterford Dodgers in the Cape Breton Colliery League.

Born:
February 16, 1884
Costello, PA
Died:
September 21, 1954
Clarkson, NY

▷ Batted: LH
▷ Threw: RH
▷ Position: OF
▷ Career BA: .242

Teams:
Philadelphia Athletics AL (1908)
Boston Doves/Braves NL (1908–1910, 1914–1915)
Brooklyn Dodgers/Superbas NL (1912–1913)
Cincinnati Reds NL (1914)

John Herbert Moran

Mike Mowrey

MOWREY, CINCINNATI

Harry "Mike" Mowrey spent 13 years in the majors with stops of 5 years each in Cincinnati and St. Louis. Mowrey was known for two things. He was considered the best third baseman in baseball at handling bunts, a primary weapon of the era. He also had an odd technique of smothering hard grounders with his glove and then picking up the ball with his bare hand before throwing to first. Mowrey was only an average hitter, but finished tenth in the National League in 1910 with 70 RBI. In his one Federal League season with the Pittsburgh Rebels in 1915, he finished second in the league in stolen bases. Mowrey played on the Robins' pennant-winning team in 1916. He was a minor league player/manager from 1920 to 1926 for the Hagerstown Champs and the Chambersburg Maroons in the Blue Ridge League and the Scottsdale Scotties in the Middle Atlantic League.

Born:
April 20, 1884
Browns Mill, PA
Died:
March 20, 1947
Chambersburg, PA

▷ Batted: RH
▷ Threw: RH
▷ Position: 3B
▷ Career BA: .256

Teams:
Cincinnati Reds NL (1905–1909)
St. Louis Cardinals NL (1909–1913)
Pittsburgh Pirates NL (1914)
Pittsburgh Rebels FL (1915)
Brooklyn Robins NL (1916–1917)

Harry Harlan Mowrey

Tom Needham

NEEDHAM, CHICAGO NAT'L.

Tom "Deerfoot" Needham was the proverbial "no-bat, good-glove" ballplayer whose defensive abilities kept him in the majors. A weak hitter, Needham managed a .260 batting average his first year in the majors, but then plummeted after that with some seasons in the .180s range or below. His upside was his defensive versatility. Although primarily a catcher, he had a strong arm and good instincts and was a very good fielder. This allowed him to play the outfield and all infield positions except shortstop in addition to catching. He did not get many at bats during the second half of his career, but he managed to stay in the Bigs nevertheless. He wrapped up his career as manager of the Newark Bears in the International League for one season in 1917, finishing with an 86–68 record.

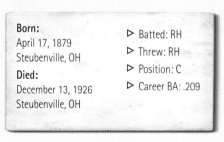

Born:
April 17, 1879
Steubenville, OH
Died:
December 13, 1926
Steubenville, OH

▷ Batted: RH
▷ Threw: RH
▷ Position: C
▷ Career BA: .209

Teams:
Boston Beaneaters/Doves NL (1904–1907)
New York Giants NL (1908)
Chicago Cubs NL (1909–1914)

Thomas Joseph Needham

Harry Niles

NILES, BOSTON AMER.

Harry Niles' claim to fame is that he broke up the perfect game being thrown by Hall of Famer Cy Young on June 30, 1908. Niles drew a walk, and was then thrown out trying to steal second base. Young had to settle for a no-hitter that day. Niles was a pretty good utility player who stole 30 bases in his rookie season and batted .289 in his second season. In his 5-year career, he played a variety of positions, including outfield, second and third base, and shortstop. After his MLB career, he played six seasons in the American Association for the Toledo Mud Hens, the Indianapolis Indians, the St. Paul Saints, and the Kansas City Blues. Niles retired in 1916 after hitting .273 in 4,499 at bats over nine minor league seasons.

Born:
September 10, 1880
Buchanan, MI
Died:
April 18, 1953
Sturgis, MI

▷ Batted: RH
▷ Threw: RH
▷ Position: OF/2B
▷ Career BA: .247

Teams:
St. Louis Browns AL (1906–1907)
New York Highlanders AL (1908)
Boston Red Sox AL (1908–1910)
Cleveland Naps AL (1910)

Herbert Clyde Niles

Rebel Oakes

A very dependable hitter and good, solid ballplayer, Ennis "Rebel" Oakes had a steady 7-year career in the majors. His best year was 1914, when he batted .312 for the Rebels in the new Federal League. The team was named after player/manager Oakes, who posted a 147–145 record in his two seasons at the helm. A very good outfielder, he had a total of 2,154 putouts in 2,366 chances. After the Federal League collapsed, Oakes was player/manager of the Denver Bears in the Western League from 1916 to 1917, where he excelled offensively and defensively. After a hiatus, Oakes returned to the game in 1921 at age 37 as player/manager in the Mississippi State League, batting .280 in 339 at bats for the Jackson Red Sox and the Greenwood Indians.

OAKES, CINCINNATI

Born:
December 17, 1883
Arizona, LA
Died:
February 29, 1948
Lisbon, LA

▷ Batted: LH
▷ Threw: RH
▷ Position: OF
▷ Career BA: .279
▷ Managerial Record: 147–145

Teams:
Cincinnati Reds NL (1909)
St. Louis Cardinals NL (1910–1913)
Pittsburgh Rebels FL (player/manager: 1914–1915)

Ennis Telfair Oakes

Frank Oberlin

OBERLIN, MINNEAPOLIS

Frank "Flossie" Oberlin was 30 years old when he came up to the majors after going 19–17 for the Springfield Senators of the Illinois-Indiana-Iowa League in 1905 and 18–16 for the Milwaukee Brewers of the American Association in 1906. He was an average pitcher who struggled in the big leagues. Oberlin did have a 3.18 ERA in 1906, but his stuff overall was not very good, and he wound up going 3–11 in 1907. Between his tours in Washington, Oberlin went back to the American Association to play for the Minneapolis Millers. Over his four major league seasons, he pitched 227 innings in 44 games and struck out 80 batters. Oberlin then played for the Utica Utes in the New York State League until he packed it in for good in 1916. He retired with an 81–85 minor league record.

Born:
March 29, 1876
Elsie, MI
Died:
January 6, 1952
Ashley, IN

▷ Batted: RH
▷ Threw: RH
▷ Position: P
▷ MLB Pitching Record: 5–24
▷ ERA: 3.77

Teams:
Boston Americans AL (1906–1907)
Washington Senators AL (1907, 1909–1910)

Frank Rufus Oberlin

Pete O'Brien

Pete O'Brien played most of his long career in the minors, around his major league tours. A weak hitter, his best year in the majors was 1906, when he batted .233 with 122 hits. He was an average fielder who usually played second base, but he also played third base and shortstop. After his MLB career, he played for eight different teams in three different leagues, including the St. Paul Saints of the American Association. He wrapped up his pro career in 1912 at age 35 after batting .254 over nine seasons in the minors.

O'BRIEN, ST. PAUL

Born:
June 17, 1877
Binghamton, NY
Died:
January 31, 1917
Jersey City, NJ

▷ Batted: LH
▷ Threw: RH
▷ Position: 2B
▷ Career BA: .223

Teams:
Cincinnati Reds NL (1901)
St. Louis Browns AL (1906)
Cleveland Naps AL (1907)
Washington Senators NL (1907)

Peter J. O'Brien

Bill O'Neill

O'NEIL, MINNEAPOLIS

Bill O'Neill was an outfielder who also played a little second base over two seasons for three teams. A utility player, he never managed to hit over .248 and was only a marginal fielder. Around his short time in the majors, he played five seasons in the minor leagues for the American Association. In 1905 he batted .322 for the Milwaukee Brewers and earned a second trip back to the majors. During his stint with the Sox, he got 1 at bat during their successful 1906 World Series bid. O'Neill then went back to play four seasons for the Minneapolis Millers in the American Association, where he batted .296 in 1909. He called it a game after the 1910 season, retiring at the age of 30 with a minor league career .278 batting average.

Born:
January 22, 1880
St. John, New Brunswick, Canada
Died:
July 20, 1920
Woodhaven, NY

▷ Batted: Switch
▷ Threw: RH
▷ Position: OF
▷ Career BA: .243

Teams:
Boston Americans AL (1904)
Washington Senators AL (1904)
Chicago White Sox AL (1906)

William John O'Neill

Bill Otey

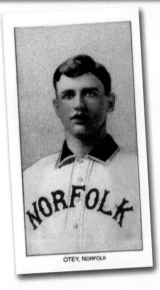

OTEY, NORFOLK

"Steamboat Bill" Otey had a short 3-year stint in the majors as a pitcher, and not a very successful one. After going 19–11 in 1906 and 22–10 in 1907 for the Norfolk Tars in the Virginia League, he earned a berth with the Pirates in 1907, where he pitched a grand total of 16.1 innings before returning to the minors. In 1909 Otey went 18–15 for Norfolk, earning him a trip back to the majors, this time with the Senators, where he went 0–1 in 1910 and 1–3 in 1911. In 100 innings pitched in the majors, he managed 33 K's but gave up 131 hits. His overall 5.01 ERA was extremely high for the time. Otey returned to the minors in 1911 and pitched for the Dayton Veterans in the Central League until he retired in 1914 with a minor league record of 96–79.

Born:
December 16, 1886
Dayton, OH
Died:
April 23, 1931
Dayton, OH

▷ Batted: LH
▷ Threw: LH
▷ Position: P
▷ MLB Pitching Record: 1–5
▷ ERA: 5.01

Teams:
Pittsburgh Pirates NL (1907)
Washington Senators AL (1910–1911)

William Tilford Otey

Pat Paige

PAIGE, CHARLESTON

As a minor leaguer, George "Pat" Paige, also known as "Piggy," mostly played at the A level and had some very good seasons and some very bad seasons. As a rookie in 1906, he lost 30 games for the Denver Grizzlies in the Western League. But he went 15–6 in 1907, 11–8 in 1908 for the Charleston Sea Gulls in the South Atlantic League, and 24–14 in 1910 for the New Orleans Pelicans of the Southern Association. He pitched in 2 games as a major leaguer, winning 1 of them. In 16 innings pitched, he gave up 21 hits and 8 earned runs, not very productive. After his tour with the Naps, he played four more seasons in the Southern Association for the Atlanta Crackers, the Montgomery Rebels, and the Chattanooga Lookouts. As a minor league pitcher he went 110–107, 3 games over .500.

Born:
May 5, 1882
Paw Paw, MI
Died:
June 8, 1939
Berlin, WI

▷ Batted: LH
▷ Threw: RH
▷ Position: P
▷ MLB Pitching Record: 1–0
▷ ERA: 4.50

Team:
Cleveland Naps AL (1911)

George Lynn Paige

Jim Pastorius

PASTORIUS, BROOKLYN

After playing in the minors for the Albany Senators in the New York State League for four seasons, "Sunny Jim" Pastorius stepped up to the Bigs at age 24. An ineffective pitcher who played on some pretty lousy teams, he had losing records for three of the four seasons that he played in the majors. His worst year was 1908, when he went a dismal 4–20, although he had a good 16–12 record in 1907 for a pretty bad Brooklyn team. Pastorius was probably a better pitcher than his major league record indicates, as was the case for many pitchers who hurled for the Superbas. Pastorius retired from the game after the 1909 season when he was 27 years old.

Born:
July 12, 1881
Pittsburgh, PA
Died:
May 10, 1941
Pittsburgh, PA

▷ Batted: LH
▷ Threw: LH
▷ Position: P
▷ MLB Pitching Record: 31–55
▷ ERA: 3.12

Team:
Brooklyn Superbas NL (1906–1909)

James Washington Pastorius

Harry Pattee

A shortstop for Brown University, Harry Pattee played his first season of professional baseball with the Jersey City Skeeters of the International League in the summer between his sophomore and junior years. His speed got him to the majors, after he stole 60 bases with Harrisburg in the International League in 1907. He played 80 games for Brooklyn in 1908, hitting .216 in 264 at bats with 9 RBI and 24 stolen bases. After his tour with Brooklyn, he returned to the International League to lead the Rochester Bronchos to pennants in 1909 and 1910. He then returned to Brown, where he coached from 1912 to 1921, compiling a 117–42–1 record (.736). He was inducted into the Brown Athletic Hall of Fame in 1971.

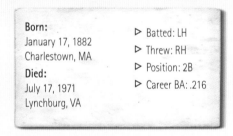

Born:
January 17, 1882
Charlestown, MA
Died:
July 17, 1971
Lynchburg, VA

▷ Batted: LH
▷ Threw: RH
▷ Position: 2B
▷ Career BA: .216

Team:
Brooklyn Superbas NL (1908)

Harry Ernest Pattee

Fred Payne

Frederick Thomas Payne

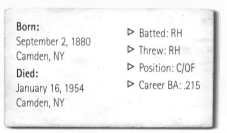

Born:
September 2, 1880
Camden, NY
Died:
January 16, 1954
Camden, NY

▷ Batted: RH
▷ Threw: RH
▷ Position: C/OF
▷ Career BA: .215

Teams:
Detroit Tigers AL (1906–1908)
Chicago White Sox AL (1909–1911)

Used as both an outfielder and a catcher, Fred Payne drifted between the minors and majors over his 16-year career. Starting with the Syracuse Stars in the New York State League, he was a decent hitter, always hovering around the .260 mark. Once he got to the big leagues, he did not fare as well, hitting as high as .270 and as low as .067. He did get 4 at bats in the 1907 World Series, and got his only major league homer in 1911, his final season in the big leagues. Payne then went back to play 6 years in the minors, and had some pretty good seasons for the Baltimore Orioles in the Eastern/International League and the Ottawa Senators in the Canadian League. He returned to the Syracuse Stars as manager and then managed the Newport News Shipbuilders in the Virginia League. He retired in 1917 at age 36 with a .251 minor league batting average.

Barney Pelty

Hub Perdue

Herbert Rodney Perdue

Barney Pelty's nickname, "The Yiddish Curver," reflected the two most notable aspects of Pelty's career. He was one of the first Jewish major leaguers, and he possessed a very impressive curveball, which helped him amass 92 big league wins over ten seasons. In 1906, he went 16–11 with a 1.59 ERA, good for second in the league. The following year, with just a 2.59 ERA, Pelty led the league in losses with 21. His career 2.63 ERA indicates that his .440 career-winning percentage is the result of his mound address. Of his 117 losses, the Browns were shut out in 32 of them, and Pelty won 22 of his 92 wins by shutout. After his playing career ended in 1912 he coached baseball and football and did some scouting. He was also a businessman and alderman in Farmington.

Born:
June 7, 1882
Bethpage, TN
Died:
October 31, 1968
Gallatin, TN

▷ Batted: RH
▷ Threw: RH
▷ Position: P
▷ MLB Pitching Record: 51–64
▷ ERA: 3.85

Teams:
Boston Rustlers/Braves NL (1911–1914)
St. Louis Cardinals NL (1914–1915)

Herbert "Hub" Perdue came up to the majors from the Nashville Volunteers of the Southern Association. He pitched four seasons in the National League, and went 37–44 in 108 appearances for Boston with a 4.03 ERA. After a 2–5, 5.82 start in 1914, the Braves traded Perdue to the Cardinals on June 28 for Ted Cather and George "Possum" Whitted. Perdue went 8–8, 2.82 for the Cards the rest of the way, but missed out on the Braves' great finish and World Series sweep over the A's in 1914. Legendary sportswriter Grantland Rice dubbed Perdue "The Gallatin Squash" for his hometown of Gallatin, Tennessee, and the vegetable called the Hubbard squash. After his MLB days, Perdue spent seven seasons in the minors, mostly playing in the Southern Association for the New Orleans Pelicans and the Nashville Volunteers, where he was player/manager in 1921. He retired at age 41 in 1923 with a 169–130 minor league pitching record.

Born:
September 10, 1880
Farmington, MO
Died:
May 24, 1939
Farmington, MO

▷ Batted: RH
▷ Threw: RH
▷ Position: P
▷ MLB Pitching Record: 92–117
▷ ERA: 2.63

Teams:
St. Louis Browns AL (1903–1912)
Washington Senators AL (1912)

Barney Pelty

George Perring

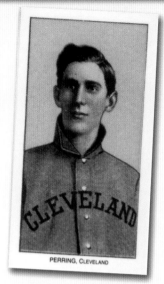

PERRING, CLEVELAND

George Perring's career is a good illustration of the relative talent level in the major leagues at the time of the Federal League's inception. Perring was a part-time utility infielder for the Cleveland Naps for 3 years from 1908 to 1910, hitting .220 with a .301 slugging percentage. After 4 years in the minors with the Columbus Senators of the American Association, he signed on with the Kansas City Packers in the Federal League at the age of 29. Over two seasons he hit .268 with 9 home runs and a .375 slugging percentage. Perring played one more full season for the Toledo Iron Men in the American Association in 1916. He gave baseball one last shot in 1919 in the Pacific Coast League with the Seattle Rainiers, hitting .167 in 30 at bats. After eight minor league seasons, he finished up with a .291 batting average.

Teams:
Cleveland Naps AL (1908–1910)
Kansas City Packers FL (1914–1915)

Born:
August 13, 1884
Sharon, WI
Died:
August 20, 1960
Beloit, WI

▷ Batted: RH
▷ Threw: RH
▷ Position: 3B
▷ Career BA: .248

George Wilson Perring

Francis Pfeffer

PFEFFER, CHICAGO NAT'L

Francis "Big Jeff" Pfeffer was the older brother of Edward Joseph "Jeff" Pfeffer, who also pitched in the major leagues. The younger Pfeffer won 25 games for Brooklyn in 1916, and led the Dodgers to the pennant that year. "Big Jeff," nicknamed for his resemblance to heavyweight champion James J. "Big Jeff" Jeffries, pitched six seasons in the majors, mostly with Boston. He went 31–39 in his career, losing 22 of those games in 1906, when he went 13–22. He had a shining moment in 1907, when he threw a no-hitter for Boston against Cincinnati. The two brothers pitched in the big leagues together in 1911 before "Big Jeff" retired at the end of the season.

Born:
March 31, 1882
Champaign, IL
Died:
December 19, 1954
Kankakee, IL

▷ Batted: RH
▷ Threw: RH
▷ Position: P
▷ MLB Pitching Record: 31–39
▷ ERA: 3.30

Teams:
Chicago Cubs NL (1905, 1910)
Boston Beaneaters/Doves/Rustlers NL (1906–1908, 1911)

Francis Xavier Pfeffer

Ed Phelps

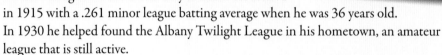

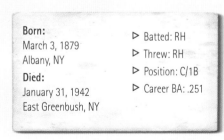

PHELPS, ST. LOUIS NAT'L

Ed "Yaller" Phelps was one of those players that teams love to have on their bench. He was a catcher and first baseman for 11 seasons in the National League. Phelps was very good defensively and had some good seasons behind the plate. A steady .251 lifetime hitter, he batted .282 in 1903 and always managed to get his bat on the ball. During his first stint with the Pirates, Phelps played in the 1903 World Series and batted .231 in 26 at bats. After his tour in Brooklyn he played in the New York State League for the Albany Senators and in the Western League for the Sioux City Indians. He retired in 1915 with a .261 minor league batting average when he was 36 years old. In 1930 he helped found the Albany Twilight League in his hometown, an amateur league that is still active.

Born:
March 3, 1879
Albany, NY
Died:
January 31, 1942
East Greenbush, NY

▷ Batted: RH
▷ Threw: RH
▷ Position: C/1B
▷ Career BA: .251

Teams:
Pittsburgh Pirates NL (1902–1904, 1906–1908)
Cincinnati Reds NL (1905–1906)
St. Louis Cardinals NL (1909–1910)
Brooklyn Dodgers/Superbas NL (1912–1913)

Edward Jaykill Phelps

Jack Powell

Although Jack "Red" Powell won 20 or more games four times, he was a hard-luck pitcher. He is 15th on the all-time list for pitching complete games, but he pitched for lousy teams and ended up eighth on the list for most career losses with 254. On four different occasions, Powell lost 19 games. His best year was 1898, when he went 23–15 for the Spiders. He had a lifetime 2.97 ERA, 1,621 strikeouts over 16 seasons, and lost 9 more games than he won. If Powell had pitched for better teams, he might have been one of the great ones. After St. Louis, he went 17–13 for the Louisville Colonels in the American Association in 1913. He retired in 1914 after playing one season for the Venice Tigers in the Pacific Coast League.

Born:
July 9, 1874
Bloomington, IL

Died:
October 17, 1944
Chicago, IL

▷ Batted: RH
▷ Threw: RH
▷ Position: P
▷ MLB Pitching Record: 245–254
▷ ERA: 2.97

Teams:
Cleveland Spiders NL (1897–1898)
St. Louis Perfectos/Cardinals NL (1899–1901)
St. Louis Browns AL (1902–1903, 1905–1912)
New York Highlanders AL (1904–1905)

John Joseph Powell

Billy Purtell

Billy Purtell's MLB career was brief and not that noteworthy. The 5-foot 9-inch, 170-pound infielder collected more than 201 at bats only twice during his 5 years in the majors. Purtell hit .258 for Chicago in 1909, but hit just .223 in 1910 and was traded to Boston in August. He was adept at the sacrifice bunt, however, and finished third in the AL in 1910 with 32 sacrifices. He hit just .227 in 1,124 at bats in the majors, but his minor league career was a different story. Purtell played 13 seasons in the minors over 23 years, hitting .273 for his career. He hit .311 as third baseman for the 1918 Toronto Maple Leafs, who went 88–39 in the International League that year. That team is considered one of the best minor league teams ever. Purtell retired as a player after the 1926 season at the age of 40, but returned to manage the Hagerstown Hubs in the Blue Ridge League in 1928.

Born:
January 6, 1886
Columbus, OH

Died:
March 17, 1962
Bradenton, FL

▷ Batted: RH
▷ Threw: RH
▷ Position: 3B
▷ Career BA: .227

Teams:
Chicago White Sox AL (1908–1910)
Boston Red Sox AL (1910–1911)
Detroit Tigers AL (1914)

William Patrick Purtell

Ambrose Puttmann

Ambrose "Putty" Puttmann pitched 33 games in the majors with the Highlanders and Cardinals over four seasons, starting in 1903. He compiled an 8–9 career record in 173.1 innings pitched with a 3.58 ERA. He hit well for a pitcher, with a .286 batting average in his 63 major league at bats. Puttmann's nine-season minor league career was a little more substantial and included four seasons with the Louisville Colonels of the American Association, as pictured on his T206 card. He only pitched for three seasons for the Colonels, compiling a 65–49 record in Louisville. He retired from the game in 1911 with an overall record of 91–78 in the minor leagues.

Born:
September 9, 1880
Cincinnati, OH

Died:
June. 21, 1936
Jamaica, NY

▷ Batted: N/A
▷ Threw: LH
▷ Position: P
▷ MLB Pitching Record: 8–9
▷ ERA: 3.58

Teams:
New York Highlanders AL (1903–1905)
St. Louis Cardinals NL (1906)

Ambrose Nicholas Puttmann

Lee Quillen

Newt Randall

QUILLEN, MINNEAPOLIS

RANDALL, MILWAUKEE

Lee Quillen batted .350 for the Lincoln Ducklings in the Western League in 1906, which punched his ticket to the majors, He was 24 years old and had already played five seasons in the minors. Quillen was a third baseman who came up for a "cup of coffee" with the White Sox in 1906 and 1907. In his rookie year he had only 9 at bats in 4 games. The following year he was up at the plate 151 times, but batted a dismal .192. After his disappointing stint in the majors, he played two seasons for the Minneapolis Millers of the American Association, but did not fare well. In 1910, Quillen returned to the Western League and had five good seasons. His best year was 1910, when he hit .316 for the Sioux City Packers. He retired from the game in 1914 as a .271 minor league hitter.

Team:
Chicago White Sox AL (1906–1907)

Born:
May 5, 1882
North Branch, MN
Died:
May 14, 1965
White Bear Lake, MN

▷ Batted: RH
▷ Threw: RH
▷ Position: 3B
▷ Career BA: .200

Leon Abner Quillen

Newton John Randall

Born:
February 3, 1880
New Lowell, Ontario,
Canada
Died:
May 3, 1955
Duluth, MN

▷ Batted: RH
▷ Threw: RH
▷ Position: OF
▷ Career BA: .211

Teams:
Chicago Cubs NL (1907)
Boston Doves NL (1907)

Newt Randall played one season in the majors, split between the Chicago Cubs and the Boston Doves. The year was 1907, and Randall hit .205 for the Cubs in 22 games in the outfield with 78 at bats before a June 24 trade sent him and Bill Sweeney to Boston for Del Howard. He hit .213 the rest of the way for Boston with a .260 slugging percentage and just 6 doubles in 258 at bats. Before 1907, and for nine seasons after, Randall carved out a pretty good minor league career, hitting .295 over 14 seasons, eight for the Milwaukee Brewers of the American Association. He hit 35 total home runs for the Brewers, and in 1911 slammed 42 doubles and 8 triples, good for a .432 slugging percentage.

Bob Rhoads

RHOADES, CLEVELAND

RHOADES, CLEVELAND

Bob "Dusty" Rhoads came up to the majors from the Memphis Egyptians of the Southern Association, where he went 22–12 in 1901 at age 21. He pitched eight seasons in the majors, going 97–82 with a career 2.61 ERA. His best season was 1906, when he went 22–10 with a 1.80 ERA for Cleveland. In September 1908, Rhoads threw a no-hitter for the Naps against the Boston Red Sox. However, he said his fondest memory was of a game against the Browns in which he gave up 23 hits but won 6–5 because Cleveland was more efficient with their 6 hits.

Teams:
Chicago Orphans NL (1902)
St. Louis Cardinals NL (1903)
Cleveland Naps AL (1903–1909)

Barton Emory Rhoads

Born:
October 4, 1879
Wooster, OH
Died:
February 12, 1967
San Bernardino, CA

▷ Batted: RH
▷ Threw: RH
▷ Position: P
▷ MLB Pitching Record: 97–82
▷ ERA: 2.61

Charlie Rhodes

Charlie "Dusty" Rhodes was a 21-year-old rookie when he broke in with the Cards in 1906. A fair pitcher, he had decent control but was not overly impressive with his stuff. As a rookie, he went 3–4 with a 3.40 ERA in 45 innings. Cincinnati claimed him off waivers from the Cards, but he returned to St. Louis and in 1909 he pitched the most innings of his career (61), going 3–5 with a 3.98 ERA. Rhodes then pitched five seasons in the minors. His best years were with the Omaha Rourkes of the Western League, where he went 17–5 in 1910 and 17–9 in 1911. Rhodes retired in 1914 with a 114–83 record over his ten minor league seasons. He died 4 years later at age 33.

Teams:
St. Louis Cardinals NL (1906, 1908–1909)
Cincinnati Reds NL (1908)

RHODES, ST. LOUIS NAT'L

Charles Anderson Rhodes

Born:
April 17, 1885
Caney, KS
Died:
October 26, 1918
Caney, KS

▷ Batted: RH
▷ Threw: RH
▷ Position: P
▷ MLB Pitching Record: 7–11
▷ ERA: 3.46

Lew Ritter

RITTER, KANSAS CITY

Lew Ritter hit only .219 over seven seasons in the majors, all with the Brooklyn Superbas. He had the good fortune of sharing the catching job with Bill Bergen, who was a .170 career hitter and still holds the record for the lowest career batting average for a player with 2,500 or more at bats. That allowed Ritter to collect 1,579 at bats for Brooklyn, hitting .219, driving in 120 runs, and even hitting a home run in 1905. He went on to play seven more seasons in the minors, mostly with the Kansas City Blues of the American Association and the Elmira Colonels of the New York State League. He managed the Colonels in 1913, and then served as a player only until he retired at age 39 after the 1915 season with a .244 minor league career batting average.

Born:
September 7, 1875
Liverpool, PA
Died:
May 27, 1952
Harrisburg, PA

▷ Batted: RH
▷ Threw: RH
▷ Position: C
▷ Career BA: .219

Team:
Brooklyn Superbas NL (1902–1908)

Lewis Elmer Ritter

Ike Rockenfield

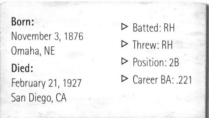

ROCKENFELD, MONTGOMERY

Ike Rockenfield is pictured in his Montgomery Climbers uniform on his T206 card. It was probably a bit challenging to capture him with any one team, as he played in 15 different uniforms over the course of his 11 years in professional baseball. He made it to the majors in 1905, and played one full season and part of the next for St. Louis, batting .221 in his 411 at bats. Back in the minor leagues, his 1909 season with Montgomery and his 1910 season with the Tacoma Tigers were the only 2 years he had 400 or more at bats and played for the same team for the entire season. Rockenfield collected 4,615 at bats, mostly as a second baseman, hitting .266 over his minor league career with 41 triples and 31 home runs. He retired from the game at age 35 after the 1912 season.

Born:
November 3, 1876
Omaha, NE
Died:
February 21, 1927
San Diego, CA

▷ Batted: RH
▷ Threw: RH
▷ Position: 2B
▷ Career BA: .221

Team:
St. Louis Browns AL (1905–1906)

Isaac Broc Rockenfield

Larry Schlafly

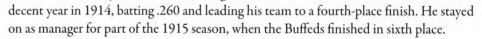

SCHLAFLY, NEWARK

Larry Schlafly surfaced from the minors in 1902 to play 10 games for Chicago in the National League. After that brief stint he went back to the minors, resurfacing in 1906 to play for the Senators. That was his best offensive year, when he batted .246 with 426 at bats. After the 1907 campaign, he went back to the minors to play for the Toronto Maple Leafs and the Newark Indians in the Eastern League. Schlafly then became player/manager for the Jersey City Skeeters in the International League. He went up to the majors one last time in 1914 as player/manager of the Buffalo Buffeds in the newly formed Federal League. He had a decent year in 1914, batting .260 and leading his team to a fourth-place finish. He stayed on as manager for part of the 1915 season, when the Buffeds finished in sixth place.

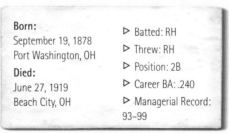

Born:
September 19, 1878
Port Washington, OH
Died:
June 27, 1919
Beach City, OH

▷ Batted: RH
▷ Threw: RH
▷ Position: 2B
▷ Career BA: .240
▷ Managerial Record: 93–99

Teams:
Chicago Orphans NL (1902)
Washington Senators AL (1906–1907)
Buffalo Buffeds FL (player/manager: 1914; manager: 1915)

Harry Fenton Schlafly

Admiral Schlei

Teams:
Cincinnati Reds NL (1904–1908)
New York Giants NL (1909–1911)

Born:
January 12, 1878
Cincinnati, OH

Died:
January 24, 1958
Huntington, WV

▷ Batted: RH
▷ Threw: RH
▷ Position: C
▷ Career BA: .237

George "Admiral" Schlei got his chance in the majors with his hometown team, the Cincinnati Reds, in 1904. Nicknamed for Admiral Schley, a hero of the Spanish-American War, Schlei played eight seasons in the National League for the Reds and the Giants. A starting catcher from 1904 to 1908 for the Reds, he was considered a solid defensive catcher during the dead-ball era. His best offensive season was 1906, when he hit .245 with 4 homers and 54 RBI in 388 at bats. His home run total was good for eighth in the league that season. Schlei finished up with 3 years in the minors, playing for the Louisville Colonels in the American Association and the Memphis Chickasaws in the Southern Association before retiring in 1915 at age 37.

George Henry Schlei

Jim Scott

Deadwood native, "Death Valley Jim" Scott arrived in the majors after attending Nebraska Wesleyan University. A pretty good pitcher on some mediocre teams, he ranks 17th on the all-time ERA list (2.30). In 1910 he led the American League in games finished with 17. He won 20 games in 1913 for the pale hose, but unfortunately he also lost 20. In 1915 he pitched 7 shutouts, good for first in the league. On the whole, "Death Valley Jim" was one of those number-four or number-five starters who keep their teams in the game and hope for the best. After his tour with the Sox, Scott had some very good seasons pitching for the San Francisco Seals in the Pacific Coast League, going 23–14 in 1920, 18–15 in 1921, and 25–9 in 1922. In 1926, when he was 38, he went 15–13 for the New Orleans Pelicans in the Southern Association. He retired in 1927 with a 175–119 minor league record, but came back in 1946 to manage the Watertown Athletics in the Border League.

Team:
Chicago White Sox AL (1909–1917)

Born:
April 23, 1888
Deadwood, SD

Died:
April 7, 1957
Jacumba, CA

▷ Batted: RH
▷ Threw: RH
▷ Position: P
▷ MLB Pitching Record: 107–113
▷ ERA: 2.30

James Scott

Spike Shannon

SHANNON, KANSAS CITY

William "Spike" Shannon was a fleet-footed outfielder who had a couple of good seasons with St. Louis and New York. Primarily a leadoff hitter with good speed, Shannon led the league in plate appearances in 1906 and 1907. He also led the National League in runs scored in 1907. During his relatively short five-season career, Spike swiped 145 bases. When his bat abandoned him, he played three seasons for the Kansas City Blues in the American Association. After managing the Virginia Ore Diggers in the Northern League in 1913, Shannon became an umpire in the minors. He then resurfaced in the Federal League as an umpire and an arbiter.

Born:
February 7, 1878
Pittsburgh, PA
Died:
May 16, 1940
Minneapolis, MN

▷ Batted: Switch
▷ Threw: RH
▷ Position: OF
▷ Career BA: .259

Teams:
St. Louis Cardinals NL (1904–1906)
New York Giants NL (1906–1908)
Pittsburgh Pirates NL (1908)

William Porter Shannon

Bud Sharpe

Bayard "Bud" Sharpe had two tours with Boston's National League franchise. The first was his rookie season in 1905, when he hit .182 for the Beaneaters in 170 at bats. He then returned to the minors, and played mostly for the Newark Indians of the Eastern League until the Pirates signed him in 1910. Pittsburgh traded him to the NL Boston Doves after just 4 games. Sharpe hit .239 for Boston with 14 doubles and 29 RBI in 439 at bats that year before returning to the minors as team captain of the Eastern League's Buffalo Bisons. He then went on to manage the Oakland Oaks of the Pacific League, leading them to their first pennant. In his 6-year minor league career, Sharpe played 761 games, won two pennants, and was considered a fielding leader at first base. Plagued by ill heath throughout his career, Sharpe died of tuberculosis in 1916 at age 34.

SHARPE, NEWARK

Born:
August 6, 1881
West Chester, PA
Died:
May 31, 1916
Haddock, GA

▷ Batted: LH
▷ Threw: RH
▷ Position: 1B
▷ Career BA: .222

Teams:
Boston Beaneaters/Doves NL (1905, 1910)
Pittsburgh Pirates NL (1910)

Bayard Heston Sharpe

Al Shaw

SHAW, ST. LOUIS NAT'L

Al Shaw had a relatively short stint in the big leagues, playing for two seasons in the National League and resurfacing later in the Federal League. A mediocre hitter for St. Louis, his best year for them was 1908, when he batted .264. After his tour with the Cards, Shaw went back to the minors and played three seasons for the Toronto Maple Leafs in the Eastern League and two seasons for the Jersey City Skeeters in the International League. In 1914, he came back to the major leagues with a vengeance, and batted .324 with 376 at bats for the Brooklyn Tip-Tops in the renegade Federal League. After hitting a respectable .281 for Kansas City in 1915, Shaw returned to the minors for one final season, playing for the Toledo Iron Men in the American Association. He retired at age 35 with a .272 batting average in 3,004 at bats over his nine minor league seasons.

Born:
March 1, 1881
Toledo, IL
Died:
December 30, 1974
Danville, IL

▷ Batted: LH
▷ Threw: RH
▷ Position: OF
▷ Career BA: .281

Teams:
St. Louis Cardinals NL (1907–1909)
Brooklyn Tip-Tops FL (1914)
Kansas City Packers FL (1915)

Albert Simpson Shaw

Hunky Shaw

Royal "Hunky" Shaw had one pinch-hit appearance in the major leagues, going 0 for 1 for the Pirates in 1908. That was the payoff for three pretty good minor league seasons in which Shaw hit .276 in 1906 and .278 in 1907 for the Tacoma Tigers in the Northwest League. He also hit 7 home runs for Tacoma in 1907. Back in the minors after his brief stint in the majors, Shaw hit .236 for the Eastern League's Jersey City Skeeters in 225 at bats in 1908. He split 1909 between the Worcester Busters in the New England League and the Providence Grays in the Eastern League. The third baseman and outfielder then played seven more seasons in the minors on the West Coast, including two seasons with the San Francisco Seals in the Pacific Coast League. In a minor league career that spanned 12 seasons and 5,300 at bats, Shaw hit 269 points higher than he did in the majors, finishing at .269.

Born:
September 29, 1884
Yakima, WA
Died:
July 3, 1969
Yakima, WA

▷ Batted: Switch
▷ Threw: RH
▷ Position: 3B/OF
▷ MLB BA: .000

Team:
Pittsburgh Pirates NL (1908)

Royal N. Shaw

Bill Shipke

"Skipper Bill" Shipke showed promise when he led the Western League in homers in 1905, drawing the attention of the Cleveland Naps. He signed with the Naps, but only had 6 at bats in the majors (without a hit) in 1906 before going back to the Western League to hit .260 and steal 35 bases. Washington bought him from the Des Moines Champs for the 1907 season, and although he finished second in fielding at third base, he hit just .196 and posted his only MLB home run. He only hit .208 in 1908 and was replaced in the starting lineup by Bob Unglaub, who was purchased from the Red Sox midseason. In 1909, Shipke went 2 for 16 (.199) for Washington in his final big league season. Shipke returned to the Western League to play for the Omaha Rourkes until 1914. He managed the Huron Packers of the South Dakota League in 1920 and the Aberdeen Grays of the Dakota League in 1922, and then scouted in the minors until he died in 1940.

Born:
November 18, 1882
St. Louis, MO
Died:
September 10, 1940
Omaha, NE

▷ Batted: RH
▷ Threw: RH
▷ Position: 3B
▷ Career BA: .199

Teams:
Cleveland Naps AL (1906)
Washington Senators AL (1907–1909)

William Martin Shipke

Happy Smith

Henry "Happy" Smith played three minor league seasons for the San Jose Prune Pickers and the Oakland Commuters of the California League before he got a shot to play for one season in the majors in 1910. He came to the Superbas in an April 13 trade that sent three players to Brooklyn in exchange for Harry McIntire. Smith played in 35 games in the outfield and hit .237 in 76 at bats, scoring 6, driving in 5, and stealing 4 bases. After his MLB stint he played two seasons for the Montgomery Billikens/Rebels in the Southern Association, hitting .331 over 1,037 minor league at bats. With stats like that, it's surprising he didn't get another shot in the big leagues.

Henry Joseph Smith

Team:
Brooklyn Superbas NL (1910)

Born:
July 14, 1883
Coquille, OR
Died:
February 26, 1961
San Jose, CA

▷ Batted: LH
▷ Threw: RH
▷ Position: OF
▷ MLB BA: .237

Heinie Smith

SMITH, BUFFALO

Basically a part-time second baseman, George "Heinie" Smith had 1 decent year as a starter, batting .252 for the Giants in 1902. He also managed the Giants for part of that year, without success, going 5–27, before he was replaced by John McGraw. After his MLB days, Smith went to the Eastern League for 10 more years as both a player and manager for the likes of the Rochester Bronchos and the Buffalo Bisons. He had some moderate success as manager of the Bronchos in 1903 and 1904 and the Bisons from 1907 to 1909. Smith retired at age 42 after a brief stint as manager of the Erie Yankees in the Canadian League. He was a career .255 hitter in the minors.

Born:
October 24, 1871
Pittsburgh, PA
Died:
June 25, 1939
Buffalo, NY

▷ Batted: RH
▷ Threw: RH
▷ Position: 2B
▷ Career BA: .238
▷ Managerial Record: 5–27

Teams:
Louisville Colonels NL (1897–1898)
Pittsburgh Pirates NL (1899)
New York Giants NL (1901; player/manager: 1902)
Detroit Tigers AL (1903)

George Henry Smith

Syd Smith

Around his time in the majors, University of South Carolina alumnus Syd Smith put together a respectable 12-year career in the minors. The catcher had his best MLB year in 1911, when he batted .299 as a part-time player for the Naps. Smith was not very successful in the majors, but was quite a hitter in the minors, batting as high as .326 for the Atlanta Crackers in the Southern Association and .284 over his minor league career. Between his tours with the Naps and the Pirates, he played for the Columbus Senators in the American Association. After his MLB days he went back to the minors as player/manager of the Shreveport Gassers in the Texas League from 1915 to 1917. After a hiatus, Smith returned to manage Shreveport again in 1925 before retiring at age 41.

SID SMITH, ATLANTA

Born:
August 31, 1883
Smithville, SC
Died:
June 5, 1961
Orangeburg, SC

▷ Batted: RH
▷ Threw: RH
▷ Position: C
▷ Career BA: .247

Teams:
Philadelphia Athletics AL (1908)
St. Louis Browns AL (1908)
Cleveland Naps AL (1910–1911)
Pittsburgh Pirates NL (1914–1915)

Sydney A. Smith

Bob Spade

Bob Spade had a successful minor league career before his time in the majors, winning 25 games in 1905 for the Macon Brigands in the South Atlantic League, 20 games in 1906, and posting a 64–33 minor league career record. He was 30 years old when he came up to the majors. Basically a .500 pitcher, in 1907 he had an excellent 1.00 ERA in 27 innings pitched, but his best year was 1908, when he went 17–12. Spade had a pretty good bat for a pitcher, hitting .294 in 1909. He went to Cuba along with his Reds teammates in 1908 for a series of exhibition games. He later managed in the Blue Grass League for 1 year in 1912. Reportedly, Spade was penniless when he died and his fans raised the funds to pay for his funeral expenses.

SPADE, CINCINNATI

Robert Spade

Teams:
Cincinnati Reds NL (1907–1910)
St. Louis Browns AL (1910)

Born:
January 4, 1877
Akron, OH
Died:
September 7, 1924
Cincinnati, OH

▷ Batted: RH
▷ Threw: RH
▷ Position: P
▷ MLB Pitching Record: 25–24
▷ ERA: 2.96

Tubby Spencer

SPENCER, BOSTON AMER.

Ed "Tubby" Spencer played nine seasons in the majors, interrupted by time in the minors. A good defensive catcher, he did not have much of a bat at the major league level and was used primarily as a backup. In 1907 he batted .265 with 230 at bats for St. Louis, his best year. In 1917 he led the American League hit-by-pitch list with 9. In between his major league years, the burly 5-foot 10-inch, 215-pound catcher spent time in the minors playing for the likes of the St. Paul Saints and Louisville Colonels in the American Association. Spencer finished up in the Pacific Coast League playing for the Salt Lake City Bees, the Seattle Indians, and the Los Angeles Angels. He retired in 1925 at age 41 with a .271 minor league batting average.

Teams:
St. Louis Browns AL (1905–1908)
Boston Red Sox AL (1909)
Philadelphia Phillies NL (1911)
Detroit Tigers AL (1916–1918)

Born:
January 26, 1884
Oil City, PA
Died:
February 1, 1945
San Francisco, CA

▷ Batted: RH
▷ Threw: RH
▷ Position: C
▷ Career BA: .225

Edward Russell Spencer

Charlie Starr

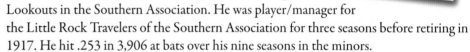

STARR, BOSTON NAT'L

A journeyman second baseman, Charlie Starr played for four teams in three seasons. He never batted over .222, and his on-base percentage was an anemic .315. He was also considered a mediocre infielder who didn't have a lot of tools, but he was one of the fortunate ones that made it to the big leagues. After his three seasons in the majors, Starr moved on to play in the minors, first as shortstop for two seasons for the Buffalo Bisons of the Eastern League and then as second baseman for the Mobile Sea Gulls, the New Orleans Pelicans, and the Chattanooga Lookouts in the Southern Association. He was player/manager for the Little Rock Travelers of the Southern Association for three seasons before retiring in 1917. He hit .253 in 3,906 at bats over his nine seasons in the minors.

Born:
August 30, 1878
Pike County, OH
Died:
October 18, 1937
Pasadena, CA

▷ Batted: N/A
▷ Threw: RH
▷ Position: 2B
▷ Career BA: .211

Teams:
St. Louis Browns AL (1905)
Pittsburgh Pirates NL (1908)
Boston Doves NL (1909)
Philadelphia Phillies NL (1909)

Charles Watkin Starr

Jim Stephens

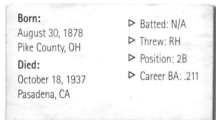

STEPHENS, ST. LOUIS AMER.

After studying at Villanova University, 22-year-old Jim Stephens came up to St. Louis from the Texas League. Also known as "Little Nemo," Stephens was a weak-hitting catcher who shared catching duties for the Browns. He never hit better than .249 in his career and was only a marginal defensive player. In 1911, while playing against the New York Highlanders, Browns' catchers Stephens and Nig Clarke allowed 15 stolen bases in one game. Stephens allowed 7 of the 15...a bad day at the office. After his tour with the Browns, he caught for the Buffalo Bisons in the International League, the Dallas Giants in the Texas League, and the Springfield Green Sox in the Eastern League. He retired after the 1917 season at age 33.

Team:
St. Louis Browns NL (1907–1912)

James Walter Stephens

Born:
December 10, 1883
Salineville, OH
Died:
January 2, 1965
Oxford, AL

▷ Batted: RH
▷ Threw: RH
▷ Position: C
▷ Career BA: .220

Ed Sweeney

Edward "Jeff" Sweeney played nine seasons in the majors, eight of them with the Highlanders/Yankees. His best season was 1913, when he hit .265 with 2 home runs and 40 RBI in 351 at bats. It is said that Sweeney got the infamous Hal Chase out of New York in 1913 by telling manager Frank Chance that Chase was undermining Chance in the clubhouse. Chase was immediately traded to the White Sox, where he lasted less than a year before jumping to the Federal League. A notorious but popular player, Chase met his pro baseball demise when he was implicated in the 1919 Black Sox scandal. Sweeney finished up in the majors with a .232 career average, 3 homers and 151 RBI. He stole 63 bases in his career, and his 19 stolen bases in 1914 are still a Yankees' record for stolen bases by a catcher. Between and after his MLB tours, Sweeney played five seasons in the minors, mostly in the American Association and the Pacific Coast League. He later worked as an electrical switchman in Chicago.

Born:
July 19, 1888
Chicago, IL
Died:
July 4, 1947
Chicago, IL

▷ Batted: RH
▷ Threw: RH
▷ Position: C
▷ Career BA: .232

Teams:
New York Highlanders/Yankees AL (1908–1915)
Pittsburgh Pirates NL (1919)

Edward Francis Sweeney

Bob Unglaub

Bob Unglaub broke into the majors at age 22 after attending Maryland Agricultural College. He was the prototypical utility man who had a decent bat and a pretty good glove. He batted a commendable .286 in 1908, splitting the season between Boston and Washington. Unglaub had a short managerial stint with the Red Sox in 1907, going 9–20. After his MLB days, he went back to the minors for 6 years. He was player/manager of the Fargo-Moorhead Graingrowers in the Northern League from 1913 to 1916. Over a minor league career that spanned 10 years, he played for eight teams in six leagues and hit .286 in 4,136 at bats. He was killed at the young age of 35 in an accident that occurred while he was supervising locomotive repair work in Baltimore in 1916.

Born:
July 31, 1881
Baltimore, MD
Died:
November 29, 1916
Baltimore, MD

▷ Batted: RH
▷ Threw: RH
▷ Position: 1B/3B/2B/O
▷ Career BA: .258
▷ Managerial Record: 9–20

Teams:
New York Highlanders AL (1904)
Boston Americans/Red Sox AL (1904–1905, 1908; player/manager: 1907)
Washington Senators AL (1908–1910)

Robert Alexander Unglaub

Jake Thielman

Jake Thielman had a promising rookie season with the Cardinals in 1905, leading the team in wins with 15. However, he also lost 16 games, with a 3.50 ERA, and from there he bounced between the major and minor leagues. Those 15 wins in his rookie season proved to be half of his career total, but due in part to a nifty 11–8, 2.33 campaign in 1907 with the Naps, Jake finished above .500 with a 30–28 career mark. Thielman completed all 18 of his starts in the 1907 season, and 49 of his 56 career starts. His last season in the majors was 1908, when he went 4–3 with a 4.04 ERA. He returned to the minors to pitch for the Louisville Colonels in the American Association in 1909, going 10–7 and batting .262. Thielman wrapped up his pro career by playing outfield for the Oklahoma City Indians in the Texas League in 1910.

Teams:
St. Louis Cardinals NL (1905–1906)
Cleveland Naps AL (1907–1908)
Boston Red Sox AL (1908)

Born:
May 20, 1879
St. Cloud, MN
Died:
January 28, 1928
Minneapolis, MN

▷ Batted: RH
▷ Threw: RH
▷ Position: P
▷ MLB Pitching Record: 30–28
▷ ERA: 3.16

John Peter Thielman

Heinie Wagner

WAGNER, BOSTON AMER.

WAGNER, BOSTON AMER.

Charles "Heinie" Wagner's career as a shortstop was mostly undistinguished, especially in the field, where he committed 218 errors between 1907 and 1910. He was known for his exceptionally large feet, which he used to block base runners from second base. After playing his rookie year with the Giants and then four seasons with the Newark Sailors in the Eastern League, Wagner played 11 seasons with the Red Sox, winning two World Series. He finished tenth in MVP voting in 1912, hitting .274 with 68 RBI and 21 swipes. After his MLB playing days, he managed the Portland Blue Sox of the New England League in 1919 and the Norfolk Mary Janes of the Virginia League in 1920. He then coached for Boston and was hired to manage the Sox in 1930. After three straight seasons in last place, Wagner led the Red Sox to their fourth-straight last-place finish with a 52–102 record (.338). That was the only season he ever managed in the major leagues.

Teams:
New York Giants NL (1902)
Boston Americans/Red Sox AL (1906–1918; manager: 1930)

Charles F. Wagner

Born:
September 23, 1880
New York, NY
Died:
March 20, 1943
New Rochelle, NY

▷ Batted: RH
▷ Threw: RH
▷ Position: SS
▷ Career BA: .250
▷ Managerial Record: 52–102

Jack White

WHITE, BUFFALO

Team:
Boston Beaneaters NL (1904)

Jack White played most of his pro career in the Eastern League, starting out in 1901 with the Syracuse Stars and playing two seasons for the Toronto Maple Leafs of the Eastern League. He then had the distinction of playing for the Boston Beaneaters for exactly 1 day—June 26, 1904. He had 5 at bats, 1 run, no hits, and his BA was .000. He had three chances in the outfield and made 2 putouts. White then returned to the Maple Leafs for two seasons, played 6 years for the Buffalo Bisons, and finished up in the New York State League with the Syracuse Stars in 1912 and 1913. As a minor league outfielder, White posted a .281 average over his 13 seasons.

John Wallace White

Born:
January 19, 1878
Traders Point, IN
Died:
September 30, 1963
Indianapolis, IN

▷ Batted: RH
▷ Threw: RH
▷ Position: OF
▷ MLB BA: .000

WILHELM, BROOKLYN

WILHELM, BROOKLYN

Kaiser Wilhelm

Teams:
Pittsburgh Pirates NL (1903)
Boston Beaneaters NL (1904–1905)
Brooklyn Superbas NL (1908–1910)
Baltimore Terrapins FL (1914–1915)
Philadelphia Phillies NL (player/manager: 1921; manager: 1922)

As a major league pitcher, Irvin "Kaiser" Wilhelm was not very effective. After two 20-loss seasons with Boston, Kaiser moved to Brooklyn where he lost 22 games in 1908 and had a dismal 3–13 season in 1909. After going 12–17 in the Federal League, Wilhelm managed the Phillies for 2 years, again with no success, compiling an 83–137 record. In between his MLB tours, Kaiser played 11 seasons in the minors, mostly for the Birmingham Barons of the Southern Association, the Rochester Hustlers of the International League, and the Elmira Colonels of the New York State League, compiling a 165–125 record. After the Phillies, Wilhelm managed the Bridgeport Bears of the Eastern League and the Syracuse Stars/Hazleton Mountaineers of the New York–Pennsylvania League before retiring in 1929 at age 55.

Born:
January 26, 1874
Wooster, OH
Died:
May 22, 1936
Rochester, NY

▷ Batted: RH
▷ Threw: RH
▷ Position: P
▷ MLB Pitching Record: 56–105
▷ ERA: 3.44
▷ Managerial Record: 83–137

Irvin Key Wilhelm

Lucky Wright

William Wright was nicknamed "Lucky" Wright early in his career in the minor leagues, but by the time he reached the majors, pitching in 5 games for Cleveland in 1909, Wright was better known as "The Deacon." After 4 fairly notable years in the minors with the Decatur Commodores of the Illinois-Indiana-Iowa League and the Oakland Oaks of the Pacific Coast League, Wright finally got his chance in the majors with the Naps, and in three of his four starts the local scribes professed he was quite unlucky in suffering losses. In his first game, a Tigers steal of home and a great catch by Ty Cobb that prevented Wright from doubling in a key situation were the game-breaking plays in a 3–2 loss. Wright was sent down to the American Association's Toledo Mud Hens in May 1909 and never returned to the majors. After injuring his arm, "The Deacon" was out of baseball in 1910.

WRIGHT, TOLEDO

Team:
Cleveland Naps AL (1909)

Born:
February 21, 1880
Waterville, OH
Died:
July 7, 1941
Tontogany, OH

▷ Batted: RH
▷ Threw: RH
▷ Position: P
▷ MLB Pitching Record: 0–4
▷ ERA: 3.21

William Simmons Wright

Irv Young

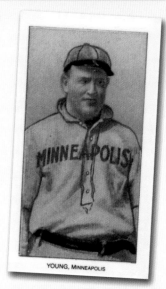

YOUNG, MINNEAPOLIS

Nicknamed "Young Cy" and "Cy the Second," Irv Young was kind of a hard-luck pitcher. He started for the Beaneaters and then worked as a reliever for the Pirates and White Sox. In 1905 and 1906, he led the National League in games started, complete games, innings pitched, and batters faced. He went 20–21 in 1905, 16–25 in 1906, and 10–23 in 1907. Young struck out 560 batters over his major league career and his 3.11 ERA was pretty good. Around his MLB tours, he pitched in the minors for seven seasons, mostly for the Minneapolis Millers and the Milwaukee Brewers in the American Association. He retired after the 1916 season at age 38 with a 98–85 minor league record.

Born:
July 21, 1877
Columbia Falls, ME
Died:
January 14, 1935
Brewer, ME

▷ Batted: LH
▷ Threw: LH
▷ Position: P
▷ MLB Pitching Record: 63–95
▷ ERA: 3.11

Teams:
Boston Beaneaters/Doves NL (1905–1908)
Pittsburgh Pirates NL (1908)
Chicago White Sox AL (1910–1911)

Irving Melrose Young

7

UNDERSTANDING THE VALUE WITHIN THE T206 SET

Some T206 cards are literally worth a fortune,

and others are still fairly affordable for the average collector.

The following pages, penned by Joe Orlando, president of Professional Sports Authenticator (PSA) and editor of *Sports Market Report*, discuss all aspects and components that have made the T206 collection one of the most desirable in the world. Most of the images in this chapter are from the magnificent "Twinight Collection" of Richard and Adam Cohen.

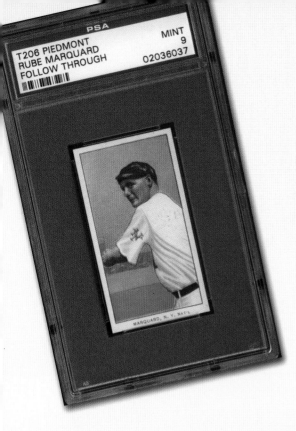

We can analyze the history of a collectible and its scarcity,

but at the end of the day most people want to talk about its value. Of course, there are many factors that can impact the value of a collectible, and there are plenty of reasons why the T206 set receives so much attention from collectors. In this chapter, we take a look at the composition of the set, different aspects of its appeal, and how condition can have a major impact on the value of the cards.

I n the hobby, the ultimate question is...

W hat is it worth?

The Wagner and the Rarities

We lead off with the power cards inside the T206 set,

the major rarities that can frustrate even the most seasoned collector and the cards that can break most bank accounts. Most classic trading card sets are anchored by key cards that grab headlines and draw attention to the set. For example, the 1952 Topps set has the iconic Mickey Mantle card and the 1933 Goudey set has the coveted quartet of Babe Ruth. While it's true that some hobbyists do not consider these T206 power cards to be requirements for set builders due to their extreme scarcity, the set can never be entirely complete without them. There are other variations and rarities within this vast set but the following four are the headliners.

At the top of this tough list is *the* card of all cards—the T206 Honus Wagner. This card is now a symbol of the entire card-collecting hobby, and has taken on a life of its own over the years. It has become a legend and, of course, there is a hefty price to pay to own a piece of history. In 2009, 100 years after the set first hit the streets, a PSA Poor 1 sold for $400,000 at auction, and that is the lowest grade possible on the PSA scale (for more on the PSA scale, see the table on page 199). As you can clearly see, this card is highly desirable in any grade.

While the reason behind the rarity of this card has been subject to debate over the years, no one disputes its importance. Of the 50 or so copies known at this time, the vast majority of them have Sweet Caporal backs, with a few Piedmont backs discovered as well (for more on card backs, see page 195), including the finest example of them all, the PSA NM-MT 8 copy that sold for nearly $3,000,000 in 2007.

When it comes to the T206 rarities, it doesn't end with Wagner.

A card that is nearly as difficult to acquire is the only T206 card to feature future Hall of Fame pitcher Eddie Plank. To this day, there is still no clear explanation for the rarity of Plank card. The most prevalent theory is that a poor printing plate caused many of the Plank cards to be destroyed since they could not pass quality control. Whatever the reason, the Plank card remains the second-most valuable card in the set due to its relatively small surviving numbers.

In recent years, a fourth major rarity has risen to prominence.

Joe Doyle, a pitcher with a modest track record, is on one of the most valuable error cards in the entire hobby. The Magie/Magee error card is more famous and the Wagner rarity is more valuable, but this card is clearly the toughest to find. The error occurred when the manufacturer put "NAT'L" next to Doyle's name instead of "AMER" to denote the league he played in. Larry Doyle, a second baseman, played for the New York Giants of the National League, while Joe Doyle played for the New York Highlanders of the American League – causing the mix-up. This card has sold for well over $100,000 since only a handful of copies are known to exist.

The third major rarity of note is the T206 Sherry Magee error card.

Magee was a fine major leaguer, although he is not a Hall of Famer. On his T206 card Magee's name was initially, and accidentally, spelled "Magie," but the error was quickly corrected by the manufacturer. As a result, the error card was produced in much fewer numbers than the corrected version, leaving collectors with a tough-to-find and desirable rarity.

A Showcase of Hall of Famers

When collectors evaluate the overall appeal

of a set, one of the aspects they focus on is the balance between stars and commons throughout. One of the most appealing parts of the T206 issue is the plethora of not just stars, but Hall of Famers, it contains. There are 76 different cards featuring Hall of Famers within the set, if you include the Plank and Wagner rarities, a tremendous number compared to most other sets produced throughout history, and especially compared to those issued during the era.

Some Hall of Fame players are on just one card while others are on multiple cards with different backgrounds or poses. For example, Tris Speaker has only one card (shown batting) while Ty Cobb has a total of four cards: two portraits (red and green) and two different poses with bats (on and off the shoulder). Most of the Hall of Famers have more than one pose, and thus, more than one card, in the legendary set.

It is not uncommon for some baseball card sets to have only a couple of dozen cards or fewer featuring players who ended up enshrined in Cooperstown.

In fact, that is part of what makes the T206 issue so different from the rest and thus, so attractive to so many hobbyists.

The Poses and Variations

As just mentioned, a fascinating feature of the T206 set is the fact that a healthy portion of the players depicted can be found on more than one card. There are action shots, various poses, and, of course, the ultra-popular portraits. Of all the different poses, the portraits garner the most interest and generally carry the most value.

In addition to the different poses, there are variations of the same poses. For example, Christy Mathewson has one portrait and two pitching poses that are virtually identical in overall design. The subtle detail distinguishes the two pitching cards. In one pitching pose, Mathewson is shown wearing a white cap while the other card shows him wearing a dark cap. There are also some subtle differences in his face and jersey design that differentiate the two cards.

There are also slight variations within the portrait cards. The most popular portrait variations belong to Ty Cobb, but Frank Chance, a fellow Hall of Famer, is another example. One of Chance's portraits has a red background while the other has a yellow background. Like the Mathewson pitching cards, there are some other subtle differences on each Chance portrait, but the pose is the same.

The portraits are so popular that collectors who cannot afford to buy the entire T206 set sometimes choose to collect the portraits alone. From the beautiful array of colors to the vintage uniforms to the period hairstyles, these portraits capture each ballplayer in a simple yet distinguished format.

The Backs

These cards were all produced by the American Tobacco Company

(ATC), but they were packaged with various brands to promote sales. The two most common backs feature ads for Sweet Caporal and Piedmont cigarettes. The less common backs include Polar Bear, Sovereign, Old Mill, Cycle, American Beauty, El Principe de Gales, Tolstoi, Hindu, Carolina Brights, Broad Leaf, Lenox, Uzit, and the very rare Drum. The tougher the back is to find, the higher the price of the card, and major premiums have been paid for the rarest backs.

As a collector, you need 524 cards to complete the basic set, regardless of backs.

There are some collectors, however, who take it a step further by collecting the back variations. If you decided to collect *every* possible player and back variation, the set would number in the thousands. Incredible patience, deep pockets, and a lot of luck are needed to do it, but there are those who have accepted the challenge. It is, however, not for the faint of heart.

You will also notice that there are even card variations within the same brand. In addition to the brand, the backs contain information about the factory, series, district, and state. The Sweet Caporal backs have the largest number of factory/series/district/state combinations of all the different brands, with several possible variations. Collecting by back brand is tough enough, but adding these variations to the master checklist is bordering on the insane! Most of the advanced hobbyists who collect different back brands choose to avoid this complication, but these variations do exist.

The Ty Cobb Back

Most people do not consider the Ty Cobb Red Portrait with Ty Cobb Back part of the T206 set, but it would be ludicrous not to discuss such an important card. With less than 15 examples known at this time, it remains one of Cobb's most desirable issues. The cards were inserted into Ty Cobb tobacco tins, which have become very desirable items in their own right over the years. These colorful tins are a nice companion piece to the T206 set and can make a wonderful display.

The Ty Cobb Back card looks virtually identical to the regular T206 Red Portrait Cobb with two major exceptions. First, instead of having the brand on the reverse, it simply reads " 'TY COBB' KING OF THE SMOKING TOBACCO WORLD" in all capital letters. Second, and less noticeable, is the slightly glossier coating that was added to this particular card to help protect it from staining since it was distributed inside tobacco tins. Most of the surviving copies are low-grade examples, and some are stained despite the manufacturer's efforts.

Condition and Grading

Since the hobby explosion of the 1980s, a lot has changed as the industry has evolved. Of course, the Internet has had a huge impact on the way people buy, sell, and trade sports collectibles. Thanks to the Internet, collectors have access to more items than they ever dreamed of 20 or 30 years ago. Even when it comes to the hobby, there is no doubt we live in a Web world, dominated by online auctions.

In addition to the transformation of how transactions take place, third-party authentication and grading services have helped improve collectibles commerce. When the hobby quickly turned into a nationwide phenomenon, it became plagued by conflicts of interest and questionable material. Sellers, who had a financial interest in the collectibles they were offering, also acted as the authenticators and graders, determining if items were genuine and identifying the grades of the items (if applicable) prior to their sale.

Conflicts of interest in such a system were unavoidable, even for sellers who were trying their best to accurately describe the items they were offering. At the time, there was no universally accepted standard, so items were being sold based on honest—and sometimes not-so-honest—interpretations of general guidelines. Consumers had to rely on the mere word of sellers and often nothing more. When collectors tried to sell or trade such items, they could not use the prior seller's word since it did not attach to the items. Thus, while not necessarily at fault, sellers had an unfair advantage.

Today, the playing field has been leveled, and both buyers and sellers have benefited from the advent of third-party authentication and grading services. Buyers have been given peace of mind, knowing that a third party—one that has zero financial interest in the collectible—has rendered an unbiased opinion about the authenticity or grade of an item on a scale of 1 to 10, with 10 being the best. In addition, sellers of certified collectibles have more liquid products that they can often sell for a major premium because of increased interest from the buyers.

This all started in the early 1990s. For years, the concept of third-party authentication and grading was perceived as radical. But, by the end of the decade, the hobby embraced it for all the benefits such services offer. Professional Sports Authenticator (PSA), the leading third-party service in the hobby, receives over a million items per year from people around the globe and has certified over a billion dollars' worth of collectibles in its history, including many of the most valuable items ever discovered.

In the current market, it is virtually impossible to sell a high-end collectible for anywhere near its true value if it has not been properly authenticated or graded

by a reputable third-party service. In fact, in many cases, you can't sell the item at all. Consumers have learned from their past experiences. Before most of them spend their hard-earned money, they demand assurance from someone qualified and someone other than the seller. This has forever changed the way collectibles are bought and sold.

So how does third-party grading affect the T206 set?

All other things being equal, condition is the ultimate factor in determining value when it comes to cards. In other words, if you have ten T206 Ty Cobb Red Portraits and each of them has the same back, the only thing that differentiates them in terms of value is condition. Widely accepted standards are now a part of the hobby, so collectors can purchase cards that are already certified and they will know exactly what they are buying at the point of sale.

Since the T206 set is such an important issue and the cards, in many cases, can sell for large sums of money, most collectors require certification by a reputable third-party company before they will buy them. If you decide to collect individual cards from this classic series or take on the entire set, you should follow the same procedure. Buying certified cards will enhance your overall collecting experience and help protect your investment.

Keep in mind that the vast majority of existing T206 cards are found in low to mid-grade condition. These tiny pieces of cardboard can exhibit a lot of wear and tear after 100 years of traveling, which is what makes high-grade copies so scarce and desirable. Thanks to great discoveries over the years, like the *Southern Find*, where several hundred T206s were found together, some well-preserved copies have made their way into the hobby in remarkable condition.

As is the case in other collectible fields, variations in grade can result in huge differences in value. It is just like the world of collectible coins, currency, stamps, or even the world of diamonds. Several individual stones may be all the same cut and size but the slightest variation in quality will alter the price dramatically.

As an example, the following table shows the approximate current market value of various grades of the T206 Ty Cobb Red Portrait:

PSA GRADE	ESTIMATED VALUE
PSA PR 1 (Poor)	$ 265 – $ 300
PSA FR 1.5 (Fair)	$ 300 – $ 350
PSA Good 2	$ 500 – $ 550
PSA VG 3 (Very Good)	$ 700 – $ 800
PSA VG–EX 4 (Very Good to Excellent)	$ 1,000 – $ 1,250
PSA EX 5 (Excellent)	$ 1,750 – $ 2,000
PSA EX–MT 6 (Excellent to Mint)	$ 2,650 – $ 3,000
PSA NM 7 (Near Mint)	$ 4,750 – $ 5,000
PSA NM–MT 8 (Near Mint to Mint)	$15,000 – $20,000
PSA Mint 9 (Mint)	$75,000+

For those of you not familiar with the PSA grading scale, a PSA EX 5 (Excellent) is a relatively attractive card. It usually exhibits general wear along the edges or corners but otherwise has no major condition defects. As you climb up the scale, the cards become more pristine and the differences become harder to see for the average person.

Just like the examples mentioned earlier, a subtle variation in condition can be the difference between a $5,000 T206 Cobb and a $20,000 T206 Cobb, a difference in value that is not subtle at all. Defects may be hard to see with the naked eye, but professional graders are trained to spot such hard-to-see defects and render an overall grade on the card.

If you decide to collect this fascinating issue, or start a collection of any trading cards, it is extremely important to research the collectibles as well as the services that certify them. Not all third-party services carry the same level of respect and brand strength. Get advice from other experienced hobbyists and investigate as best you can. An informed collector is more likely to be a happy one.

In the end, we hope this book helps you assemble your own collection of T206 cards. This classic set has captivated hobbyists for decades and, after 100 years, its legend just continues to grow.

INDEX

MILLER, PITTSBURG

MCBRIDE, WASHINGTON

SCHULTE, CHICAGO NAT'L.

ABOUT THE AUTHORS

TOM ZAPPALA IS A BUSINESSMAN IN the Greater Boston area who has a passion for anything related to baseball history. He has had a particular interest in the T206 collection for about 20 years, focusing on player profiles and backgrounds, and enjoys the hunt for new and exciting information on the lesser-known players. He is also the cohost of a popular talk radio show broadcast in northern Massachusetts and southern New Hampshire. He loves his wife, his four great kids, and his Red Sox. Those things, along with a Grey Goose martini and two baseball-size olives, make life great.

ELLEN ZAPPALA IS PRESIDENT OF ATS Communications, a multimedia marketing and consulting company. She was publisher of a group of six newspapers in Massachusetts and New Hampshire for many years, and also served as president of the New England Press Association. She has developed a fond affection for the players that are featured in this wonderful collection, especially for those that overcame great odds to make it to the big leagues.

JOE ORLANDO IS PRESIDENT OF Professional Sports Authenticator and PSA/DNA Authentication Services and editor of *Sports Market Report*. An advanced collector of sportscards and memorabilia, Orlando is the author of *The Top 200 Sportscards in the Hobby* and *Collecting Sports Legends*. He has appeared on several radio and television programs as a hobby expert, including ESPN's *Outside the Lines* and HBO's *Real Sports*.

LOU BLASI HAS BEEN A TALK RADIO host in the Greater Boston area for the last 12 years, and is the senior analyst for Insiderbaseball.com with credits on MLB.com, ESPN Radio, and the Chicago Sports Review. Blasi was program director for an all sports radio station in southern Florida broadcasting the Florida Marlins, Miami Dolphins, and Orlando Magic. He is also a minor league talent evaluator.